D0151413

Library

Fairy Lore

**Recent Titles in
Greenwood Folklore Handbooks**

Folk and Fairy Tales: A Handbook
D.L. Ashliman

Campus Legends: A Handbook
Elizabeth Tucker

Proverbs: A Handbook
Wolfgang Mieder

Myth: A Handbook
William G. Doty

GR
549
.A85
2006

Fairy Lore

A Handbook

D. L. Ashliman

Greenwood Folklore Handbooks

GREENWOOD PRESS

Westport, Connecticut • London

OCM 61513014

Santiago Canyon College
Library

Library of Congress Cataloging-in-Publication Data

Ashliman, D. L.
  Fairy lore : a handbook / D.L. Ashliman.
    p. cm.—(Greenwood folklore handbooks, ISSN 1549–733X)
    Includes bibliographical references and index.
    ISBN 0–313–33349–1 (alk. paper)
    1. Fairies. 2. Fairy tales—Classification. I. Title. II. Series.
  GR549.A85   2006
  398′.45—dc22   2005025972

British Library Cataloguing in Publication Data is available.

Copyright © 2006 by D. L. Ashliman

All rights reserved. No portion of this book may be
reproduced, by any process or technique, without the
express written consent of the publisher.

Library of Congress Catalog Card Number: 2005025972
ISBN: 0–313–33349–1
ISSN: 1549–733X

First published in 2006

Greenwood Press, 88 Post Road West, Westport, CT 06881
An imprint of Greenwood Publishing Group, Inc.
www.greenwood.com

Printed in the United States of America

The paper used in this book complies with the
Permanent Paper Standard issued by the National
Information Standards Organization (Z39.48–1984).

10   9   8   7   6   5   4   3   2   1

Contents

Preface

The student of fairy lore faces the same dilemma as the first-person narrator in Hughes Mearns's famous poem: "As I was going up the stair, I met a man who wasn't there." Why study something that isn't there? However, even if that man wasn't there, Mearns's narrator responded as though he were. Similarly, for all of recorded history many of our forebears have behaved as though they were surrounded by unseen sprites called variously fairies, elves, trolls, mermaids, and such.

The study of these beings, like the scholarly examination of religion or psychology or politics, is laden with preconceived notions. The primary sources I refer to in the following pages typically cite individuals who assert first-hand experience with fairies, although most educated observers dismiss such claims as fantasy, self deception, or outright fraud. And theologians—at least in times past—have identified these creatures as satanic demons, to be avoided at any cost. The study of fairy lore is an exercise in evaluating contradictory opinions.

"The science of fairy tales," to use a phrase coined by Edwin Sidney Hartland in 1891, is—in part—a psychological and sociological investigation into the roots of faith. Who believes in fairies, and why? But it is also an inquiry into emotion and esthetics. Why have these unseen beings played such an important role in the belief systems of countless people? And why does their magic continue both to haunt us and to delight us through the fiction that we now label *fairy tales?* The answers to these questions lie not only in legends inherited from the past, but also in our own psyches. The goal of this handbook is to present a sampling of these legends and to examine them—if this is possible—both sympathetically and objectively.

One
Introduction

CELTIC AND GERMANIC TRADITIONS

The term *fairies,* as used in this handbook, is collective and generic, designating supernatural entities of many types. Customs and beliefs concerning elves, dwarfs, gnomes, trolls, mermaids, brownies, pixies, leprechauns, and many more, all belong to fairy lore. Stories about such beings are found in traditional cultures around the world and in all periods of recorded history.

This handbook concentrates on northwestern Europe, not because the region presents richer or more diverse case studies than other areas, but rather because the fairy beliefs of Celtic and Germanic cultures demonstrate substantial unity, exhibiting similarities in content, structure, and function. Thus my primary focus is on the German-speaking countries (Germany, Austria, and Switzerland); Scandinavia (Sweden, Denmark, Norway, and Iceland); Britain (Scotland, Wales, and England); and Ireland—as well as their immediate neighbors.

The cultural and linguistic borders of these nations have always been in flux, and the migration of people and ideas has enriched belief systems throughout time. Celtic and Germanic fairy lore owes much to adjacent cultures. In fact, the word *fairy* comes to English from the French *fée,* with its connection to the Fates of Greek and Roman mythology, goddesses who determined the course of individual human lives. The word *fay* (an archaic synonym for *fairy*) shows this connection.

The original form of the English word *fairy* was *fay-ery* (with various spellings), signifying the condition or quality of a *fay.* It parallels such constructions

Fairies dancing on a mushroom. Woodcut after a drawing by W. H. Brooke, from Thomas Crofton Croker, *Fairy Legends and Traditions* (1826).

as *devilry* from *devil*, *sorcery* from *sorcerer*, and *witchery* from *witch*. With time the word (here usually spelled *faerie*) came to designate the location or state of a fairy realm, then finally the supernatural beings themselves (now usually spelled *fairy* and *fairies*).

SOURCES

Popular Culture and Folklore

Images of various fairy types abound, even in today's rational world. We all have a perception of Cinderella's fairy godmother, Snow White's seven dwarfs, Pinocchio's fairy conscience, Hans Christian Andersen's little mermaid, the elves who bake Keebler cookies, Peter Pan's companion Tinker Bell, that jolly old elf Santa Claus, the tooth fairy, Germany's garden gnomes, Norway's trolls, and Ireland's leprechauns. To this list one also must add the term *fairy*, designating—usually disparagingly—a male homosexual, probably because of its effeminate overtones.

These images, while based on traditional concepts, derive from recent popular culture. Other remnants of fairy lore survive as well, although their origins are often obscure. The metal *cobalt* was named after *kobolds*, German goblins believed to have placed it in silver ore, where it was commonly found. Nightmares have nothing to do with female horses, but rather were the names of fairy-like spirits that plagued sleeping humans. The term *mare's nest* (a place of confusion and disorder) has a similar derivation. The expression *to cry like a banshee* exists long after we have forgotten that the banshees were Irish fairies who with their wailing predicted someone's imminent death. *Glamour,* now a designation for beauty, once defined a spell of deception exercised by fairies. The word *oaf* now applies to any clumsy or awkward individual, but once referred to a deficient fairy child left as a substitute for an abducted human baby. Similarly, *urchins* were once mischievous shape-shifting fairies who often assumed the form of hedgehogs, but now are rascally human children. These terms, plus many more—including countless place names—reflect an ancient belief system now only dimly and imperfectly remembered.

Superstitions

Nonverbal customs deriving from ancient fairy belief survive as well. Our forebears once nailed horseshoes above their doorways to keep them safe from fairies, a good-luck practice still widely observed. We encapsulate four-leaf clovers into keychain ornaments to carry as good-luck charms, but have forgotten that our ancestors used them to see through fairy deceptions. Into the twentieth century in many remote areas of Europe, housewives would shout a warning before throwing out wash water, lest they should hit any invisible people. The once widespread practice of spilling small amounts of food or drink onto the ground as an offering to the fairies finds a playful parallel in the cookies and milk left for Santa Claus on Christmas Eve (Lady Wilde, pp. 50, 81).

DEPICTIONS

How Large Are Fairies?

Fairies come in different sizes. Gervase of Tilbury, writing in 1211, described the *portune,* an English household sprite, as "very small in stature, measuring less than half a thumb" (p. 677). Similarly, Shakespeare's Mercutio said that the fairy queen Mab was "no bigger than an agate-stone on the forefinger of an alderman" (*Romeo and Juliet,* act 1, scene 4). Following this tradition, visual artists typically have portrayed fairies thumb-sized and often fitted with butterfly-like wings, although most folk narratives do not support their having wings.

The word *dwarf* derives from the Old Norse *dvergr.* It is nowhere stated in earlier sources that such beings were small in stature, although in recent centuries this quality has evolved into such an important characteristic that the word *dwarf* has come to be a synonym for *small.* In Germany diminutive constructions such as *Männlein* (manikin) are often used to designate dwarfs and other underground people. In Cornwall the term *small people* applies to an important branch of fairies.

On the other hand, concurrent with the many legends depicting fairies as very small are numerous accounts giving them ordinary human size. A first-hand account from Wales dated March 24, 1772, describes a company of dancing fairies as "a little bigger than we, but of a dwarfish appearance" (Croker, vol. 3, p. 249). Some of the best-known fairy encounters deal with seductions and marriages between mortals and fairies, and in such pairings the fairies are virtually always of normal human stature.

Giant-sized fairies also exist. The German-Swiss alchemist and medical researcher Theophrastus von Hohenheim (1493–1541), better known as Paracelsus, theorized that the giants of ancient myths were the progeny of forest or air sprites (sylphs). He explained that just as humans and beasts sometimes give birth to abnormal offspring, so do the various elemental beings; the malformed offspring of sylphs are the giants (Paracelsus, pp. 247–50).

Apart from this theoretical connection between giants and fairies, reports of fairy sightings across many centuries often describe beings of superhuman size. For example, the medieval English hero Wild Edric encountered fairy women who were "taller and larger than women of the human race" (Burne, p. 59), and in the early twentieth century W. Y. Evans-Wentz recorded the testimony of an Irish mystic who claimed to have seen the sidhe folk many times, describing them as "opalescent beings ... about fourteen feet in stature" (p. 62). A Welsh water fairy was described as "a figure of gigantic stature" (Croker, vol. 3, p. 254).

The inconsistencies about size in traditional fairy descriptions have been addressed by folklore collectors. "Everything is capricious about them, even

Tiny fairies riding on a stalk of grain and a cattail. Woodcut after a drawing by W. H. Brooke, from Thomas Crofton Croker, *Fairy Legends and Traditions* (1826).

their size. They seem to take what size or shape pleases them," explained W. B. Yeats (*Fairy and Folk Tales of Ireland,* pp. 11–12), then adding, in another book, "it is something in our eyes that makes them seem big or little" (*Celtic Twilight,* p. 49). This last claim is an example of *glamour,* a magic spell cast by fairies making things appear quite different from normal reality.

Fairy Bodies

The nature of fairies' physical makeup has engaged the common folk and sophisticated commentators alike. If, as is commonly believed, fairies do not have bodies of flesh and bone, then they are not subject to ordinary physical limitations. Many accounts support this view. For example, the Icelandic legend "The Genesis of the Hidden People" (printed in chapter three) tells of a human who attempts to embrace a young woman, but his hand passes through her, as though she were nothing but air. She explains that she is one of the hidden people and thus consists only of spirit. On the other hand, countless legends depict sexual relations between fairies and mortals, often producing offspring. Representative examples of such stories are included in chapter three under the headings "Seduced by a Fairy," "Fairy Taboos," and "Fairy Brides."

Many serious thinkers have assigned fairy bodies a position between spirit and substance. Foremost among these is Paracelsus, who posited four basic types of elemental beings similar to the nymphs of Greece: gnomes inhabiting rocks and soil, salamanders fire, sylphs air, and undines water. With reference to physical makeup, he assigned them an intermediate place between the flesh from Adam and spirits, which have no bodies. These elemental beings possess bodies of "a subtle flesh and cannot be bound nor grasped." Like spirits, they can pass through solid objects; but unlike spirits, "they bear children, talk and eat, drink and walk." And finally, these beings are mortal; but not having descended from Adam, they are ineligible for eternal life. Upon death they simply cease to exist (pp. 227–28).

Robert Kirk, a Scottish minister and a true believer in fairies, writing in 1691, came to similar conclusions:

> These *siths* or fairies ... are said to be of a middle nature betwixt man and angel, as were demons thought to be of old; of intelligent fluidious spirits, and light changeable bodies, (like those called astral), somewhat of the nature of a condensed cloud, and best seen in twilight. These bodies be so pliable through the subtlety of the spirits that agitate them, that they can make them appear or disappear at pleasure. (p. 5)

Jacob and Wilhelm Grimm, probably influenced by Paracelsus, describe "the quiet folk" living within the cliffs near Plesse Castle in central Germany as being mortal creatures of flesh and blood, like humans, but with the ability to make themselves invisible and to walk through cliffs and walls as easily as we pass through air (*German Legends,* no. 30).

Legends from around the world reinforce views that fairies possess "astral" bodies with fewer physical limitations than those of humans. However, as is always the case in fairy lore, there are contradictions and exceptions. Fairies reportedly have been captured in ordinary cloth bags ("Krachöhrle, Where Are You?") or simply by seizing them ("The Kildare Lurikeen"); they have had their skulls crushed with a threshing flail ("Riechert the Smith"); and they have been detained when a hole in the wall is stopped up ("The Alp"). Full texts of these legends are reproduced in chapter three.

Physical Appearance

The question "What do fairies look like?" is not easily answered, for here as elsewhere in fairy lore contradictions abound. Even within a narrowly defined area—say western Ireland in the nineteenth century—descriptions from reputed first-hand observers substantially disagree with one another.

These apparent contradictions are often attributed to fairies' capriciousness and their abilities as shape changers. Lady Gregory said of one such family: "The sidhe ... are shape changers; they can grow small or grow large, they can take what shape they choose" (p. iii). Also in Ireland, Thomas Crofton Croker offered the following conclusion to his discussion of another family of fairies: "The reader, it is to be hoped, will not be able to form a perfect notion of the pooka; for indistinctness, like that of an imperfectly remembered dream, seems to constitute its character, and yet Irish superstition makes the pooka palpable to the touch. Its appearance is variously described as a horse, a goat, a bird, and a bat" (vol. 1, p. 283). W. B. Yeats adds: "The pooka ... has many shapes—is now a horse, now an ass, now a bull, now a goat, now an eagle. Like all spirits, he is only half in the world of form" (*Fairy and Folk Tales of Ireland,* p. 87).

Possibly the most famous of shape-changing fairies is the Hedley Kow. Not to be confused with the common *cow,* this fairy creature from the village of Hedley in northern England was a master shape shifter and unrelenting trickster, sharing many traits with his kinsman Robin Goodfellow. In an account recorded by Joseph Jacobs (*More English Fairy Tales,* pp. 55–59), a woman found a large pot filled with gold pieces lying by the roadside. Because it was too heavy to carry she tied her shawl to it and dragged it along behind her.

As she made her way homeward she saw the treasure successively transform itself to silver, then to iron, and then to stone. Reaching her gate, she turned to untie her shawl from the stone, when "it seemed to give a jump and a squeal, and grew in a moment as big as a great horse; then it threw down four lanky legs, and shook out two long ears, flourished a tail, and went off kicking its feet into the air and laughing like a naughty mocking boy." Two additional adventures with the Hedley Kow are reprinted in chapter three.

Whether by actual shape shifting or by magically distorting human perception, fairies do assume many forms, ranging from "clouds of dust, but with all sorts of colors" (Gregory, p. 14), to giant water bulls (Campbell, vol. 4, p. 300). Shape changing is an ability shared by supernatural beings in many cultures. In an account from the German island of Rügen, a dwarf takes the shape of "a pretty bright insect," then later reveals himself in the form of "a little ugly black chap, about six inches long." Another story from the same island describes one of the underground people who "turned himself into every form of birds, beasts, and men" (Keightley, pp. 197–201). There is scarcely any fairy type that has not, in one account or another, assumed a variety of shapes: human, animal, or inanimate. Even a simple straw can be a fairy in disguise, as learned by a German shepherd boy who naively took one into his room one evening. Pushing one end inside the other, he hung it on a nail. The next morning he discovered an ugly woman hanging there, twisted into a grotesque circle (Knoop, p. 83).

Pooka as a bat. Woodcut after a drawing by W. H. Brooke, from Thomas Crofton Croker, *Fairy Legends and Traditions* (1826).

Hedley Kow. Illustration by John D.
Batten, from Joseph Jacobs, *More
English Fairy Tales* (1894).

Shape shifting notwithstanding, certain aspects of fairy appearance have
established themselves. The stereotypical mermaid, with the upper torso of a
beautiful woman and the tail of a fish, and combing her long hair, is too well
known to require documentation. But even here there are contradictions.
Lady Gregory, reporting from Ireland in 1916 claimed: "The mara-warra
(mermaid) was seen on the shore not long ago, combing out her hair. She
had no fish's tail, but was like another woman" (p. 10). First-hand observers
in nineteenth-century North Germany stated: "Mermaids have totally the
appearance of ordinary humans, but can be recognized because the bottoms
of their dresses are wet" (Kuhn and Schwartz, p. 175).

Dwarfs, leprechauns, brownies, and pixies are known as small people with
leathern faces; while other fairy types are airy, dainty, and beautiful. But contradictions can be found to all these stereotypes. While trolls are famously
ugly and grotesque, accounts of beautiful troll women do exist (Keightley,
pp. 108–109). Swiss and Swabian underground people sometimes have goose
feet, or no feet at all (Baader, p. 18; Rochholz, p. 273). A Welsh peasant
sketched from memory a pooka without arms (Sikes, p. 21). Scandinavian
elves, especially females, are attractive and alluring from the front, but from
behind they are "as hollow as a dough trough" (Thorpe, p. 309); or when
disrobed they reveal an animal's tail (Hofberg, p. 148) or a body covered with
hair (Christiansen, p. 124), or a back that looks like the bark on a fir tree
(Kvideland and Sehmsdorf, p. 217).

Pooka, as drawn by a Welsh peasant with a
bit of coal. From Wirt Sikes, *British Goblins*
(1881).

Taking all available reports into account, essentially the only conclusion that one can reach concerning the appearance of fairies is that they look like what they want to look like, or perhaps, they look like what we want them to look like.

Glamour

Another aspect of fairy shape shifting is *glamour,* not in the word's modern definition, *attractiveness,* but rather in its original sense, designating a magic and deceptive charm cast over something to give it an appearance that differs from this-worldly reality. Fairies were masters of such illusory transformations. In most traditional accounts they used such powers to make the ordinary and ugly appear elegant and beautiful, although their visual deceptions take other forms as well.

Humans would not know that such magic illusions occur, if it were never possible to see through the glamour. As the following legends illustrate, the most common way of exposing this deception was by using an ointment regularly applied to the eyes of newborn fairies, but occasionally—always by mistake—made available to humans.

In the English tale "The Fairy's Midwife" (Hartland, *English Fairy and Other Folk Tales,* pp. 91–94), one night a midwife was called to "a neat cottage," where she helped a "decent-looking woman" give birth. Also present were "a couple of tidy children"—all in all a normal family. As usually happens in tales of this kind (Christiansen type 5070), the midwife was asked to apply a certain ointment to the newborn's eyes. Having finished this task, she rubbed one of her own eyes with the same salve. The anointed eye saw everything differently. The mother now appeared as "a beautiful lady attired in white." The infant "was now seen wrapped in swaddling clothes of a silvery gauze ... , [and] looked much prettier than before." But the other children had degenerated into "little flat-nosed imps, who ... with many a grimace and grin were busied to no end in scratching their own polls [heads], or in pulling the fairy lady's ears with their long and hairy paws."

Sometimes a fairies' house disappears altogether. Another tale of the same type concludes when a midwife, again after touching one of her eyes with ointment, sees that instead of sitting in a neat and comfortable cottage, she is actually beneath "the large overhanging branches of an ancient oak, whose hollow and moss-grown trunk she had before mistaken for the fireplace" (Keightley, pp. 311–12).

In a similar legend (Kennedy, pp. 96–99), "a fine-looking dark man mounted on a black horse" took a midwife to attend to his expectant wife. Following a ghostly ride, during which the midwife did not know whether they were going forward or backward, they arrived at a magnificent castle. Passing through "a big hall and great rooms all painted in fine green colors, with red and gold bands and ornaments, and the finest carpets and chairs and tables and window curtains, and fine ladies and gentlemen walking about," they came to a chamber "with a beautiful lady in bed." After delivering the lady of a healthy child, the midwife was given ointment to rub all over the newborn. While so doing her eye began to itch, and she rubbed it with an ointment-covered finger. Suddenly she saw things quite differently: "The beautiful room was a big rough cave, with water oozing over the edges of the stones, and through the clay; and the lady, and the lord, and the child, weazened [wizened], poverty-bitten crathurs [creatures]—nothing but skin and bone, and the rich dresses were old rags." Her services now finished, she let herself be conducted back home, without letting the fairies know what she now could see. Upon leaving, she observed that the once magnificent castle was now nothing more than an earthen dike, and that the horse that had brought her here was only a stalk of ragweed. Upon reaching her home, the new father slipped five guineas into her hand as payment, but when she looked at them the next morning, they were but five withered oak leaves.

This last episode with so-called "fairy gold" works both ways. Sometimes fairies pay their debts with worthless items that at first appear to be valuable, as in the above instance; but in other cases they offer apparently worthless tokens that later prove to be valuable. The only sure thing about fairies is that experiences with them are seldom what they seem to be.

In addition to fairy ointment, another help in penetrating fairy glamour is the four-leaf clover (or shamrock), whose good-luck reputation continues to our own time. An Irish legend illustrates its power: A showman had convinced a crowd of villagers that he could make a rooster carry a great log of Norway timber in his bill, but his deception was revealed when a young girl who was carrying an armful of fresh grass for her cow observed that the rooster had only a piece of straw in his beak. Her load of grass included a four-leaf clover, which enabled her to see things as they actually were (Kennedy, pp. 102–103).

Clothing

In most accounts fairies' clothing is described as old-fashioned, but of a style familiar to that worn by nearby humans. Depending upon circumstances, it is either luxurious and elegant, or tattered and torn. In some instances fairies wear no clothes at all.

A fairy's midwife. Illustration by John D. Batten, from Joseph Jacobs, *English Fairy Tales* (1898).

The most famous legends dealing with fairies' clothing are those known generically as "The New Suit" (Christiansen type 7015). In these stories well-meaning humans reward a helpful household spirit with a new set of clothes, which then causes him to abandon their house. Sometimes the sprite's departure is brought about by his pride in the new clothes; he now considers himself too good to work at his former tasks.

In other instances the explanation is more mystical. Somehow a household spirit will remain with a family only if the reward is exactly right—neither too little nor too much. The new costume represents a too generous payment, so the sprite must leave. Examples of legends featuring new clothes for household spirits include "The Shoemaker and the Elves," with a complete text reproduced in chapter three; and "The Cauld Lad of Hilton" and "The Kildare Pooka," both discussed in a different context in chapter four.

Green is the color most often mentioned for fairies' clothing, especially for those fairy types associated with the earth. In some accounts, not only do the fairies wear green clothing, but their skin is green as well.

The most famous of these legends is "The Green Children," recorded in Latin by the medieval chronicler Ralph of Coggeshall, with an English translation published by Thomas Keightley (pp. 281–83). As reported, in the twelfth century harvesters working near the Suffolk village of Wulfpit (now called Woolpit) discovered two lost children, a boy and a girl, clothed in green and with green skin. The frightened pair, unable to speak English, at first refused to eat anything but green beans. With time they learned to speak English and became accustomed to the local food, and their skin gradually took on a more normal color. Soon afterward the boy took ill and died, but the girl lived to maturity, with time marrying a man from King's Lynn. Tradition explains that the green children were fairies who had accidentally wandered away from their underground realm. A children's book based on this incident is *Maudie and the Green Children* by Adrian Mitchell and Sigune Hamann (1996). The village sign of Woolpit still features a boy and girl in silhouette.

Another legendary being identified by color is the Green Man, also known as Jack-in-the-Green. Characterized by a mask and clothing of foliage, this enigmatic figure played a role in ancient festivals and rituals, and his carved image is often found in medieval churches, especially in England. His name and dress suggest that he was a nature deity or spirit, which would give him an affinity with woodland fairies.

Not all fairies wear green. In some instances fairy tribes distinguish themselves by the different colors of their costumes. "The trooping fairies wear green jackets, the solitary ones red," reported Yeats in his *Fairy and Folk Tales of Ireland* (p. 289). Shakespeare drew on this tradition when he had his

Mrs. Page disguise a band of children as "fairies, black, grey, green, and white" in order to torment Falstaff in *The Merry Wives of Windsor* (act 5, scene 5). Similarly, a family of Welsh sprites were known as "elves of the blue petticoat" (Jacobs, *Celtic Fairy Tales,* p. 224).

Male fairies nearly always wear caps, which are most often red. In Germany the caps (called *Nebelkappen*—fog caps) have the magical ability to make their wearers invisible. Water fairies use a magic cap, known in Irish as a *cohuleen druith,* to enable them to travel between underwater realms and the earth. Sealskins play the same role for the water fairies known as selkies, and certain air-borne fairies rely on feathery robes for their magic transportation. Stories featuring these various magic garments include "Riechert the Smith," "The Lady of Gollerus," and "The Swan Maiden," all reprinted in chapter three.

Language

Fairies, in most accounts, are readily understood when they speak to their human neighbors. Consequently their language is rarely an issue, and commentators seldom mention it. There are exceptions. One of Europe's earliest fairy legends is contained in the *Itinerarium Cambriae,* the description of a journey through Wales in 1188 by Giraldus Cambrensis (Keightley, pp. 404–406). Here we read that a twelve-year-old boy named Elidurus (also spelled Elidor) ran away from a strict teacher, then spent two days cowering beneath an overhanging river bank. Finally he was approached by two little men who led him into a subterranean realm, "a country full of delights." He lived in this fairyland for some time. Moreover, he enjoyed the freedom of coming and going between there and his own homeland. However, tempted by his mother, he violated the fairies' trust and stole a golden ball from them. The fairies recovered the ball, and from that time forward Elidurus was unable to find the way back to their underground country. During his sojourn with the fairies he learned their language, which, according to Giraldus, was similar to Greek. He recorded two phrases: *Udor udorum* (bring water) and *Halgein udorum* (bring salt).

Other accounts of fairy language (when it differs from the local vernacular) are less specific, typically stating only that it could not be understood by humans. An important exception to this general rule is found in the stories of J.R.R. Tolkien. A professor of Anglo Saxon at Oxford University, Tolkien invented "Elvish" languages for personal diversion, then wrote fantasy fiction to provide a setting in which such languages could exist. His major works—*The Hobbit* (1937) and the trilogy *The Lord of the Rings* (1954–55)—are embellished with Elvish runes, letters, names, words, and phrases. Of special interest in this regard are appendices E and F to the third part of *The Lord of the Rings,* which comprise detailed studies of various Elvish languages. *The Silmarillion* (published posthumously in 1977) also contains informative linguistic commentary, as do the twelve volumes of the series *The History of Middle-earth,* with various individual titles, compiled from J.R.R. Tolkien's literary remains by his son Christopher and published between the years 1986 and 1996.

Tolkien never claimed to have discovered languages actually spoken in Middle-earth, but his unchallenged expertise in philology plus his fertile imagination gave him the tools he needed to come up with self-consistent and convincing linguistic details.

DESIGNATIONS

Circumlocutions

Questions of language lead quite naturally to those of nomenclature. What do fairies call themselves, both collectively and individually, and how should humans refer to them? The organization of fairy folk into named families, tribes, and types will be treated in chapter two. However, one important naming issue should be addressed early on. According to longstanding and widespread tradition, fairies of all types take offense when humans refer to them directly. Thus circumlocutions and euphemisms abound. The Scots talk of the *good* neighbors, even when warning about these neighbors' propensity to abduct children, cripple livestock, and steal crops. Similarly, the Irish, using the least specific terms possible, often call fairies simply *they, them, themselves,* or *the others.*

The following list of fairy designations, gleaned from various nineteenth-century sources, illustrates our European ancestors' fear of offending their invisible neighbors by referring to them directly: boys, children of the twilight, fair folk, forest folk, forgetful people, gentry, good children, good neighbors, good people, hidden people, invisible people, little people, the others, people of the hills, quiet folk, their mother's blessing (offspring of a pleased mother), they, them, themselves, twilight beings, *tylwyth teg* (Welsh for *fair folk*), underground people, unseen people, and untiring ones.

Names of Individuals

In many accounts the fairies' dislike of hearing humans use their family or tribal names is surpassed by an individual fairy's fear that his or her personal name will be disclosed. The most famous such tale is the Grimm brothers' "Rumpelstiltskin," in which a dwarf loses power over a young mother when she discovers his name. Variants of this story (Aarne-Thompson type 500) are told throughout Europe, always featuring different—and by human standards comically grotesque—names. An English version is titled "Tom Tit Tot" (Jacobs, *English Fairy Tales,* pp. 1–8).

Many other stories demonstrate how humans can gain power over supernatural beings of various types by discovering their personal names. Fairies, mermaids, demons, trolls, and werewolves, are all subject to a loss of control when thus confronted. These accounts clearly reflect ancient widespread beliefs about the sancity of names.

One fairy's reluctance to reveal her name leads to humorous consequences in the tale called "Ainsel" (Own Self) in Northumberland, with different titles in other dialect regions. Told throughout Europe, the story relates how a fairy child flew down the chimney, paying a surprise visit to a boy. As they played together, the boy asked the fairy what she was called, to which she replied, "My Own Self," then asked the boy for his name. He responded cautiously, "It's My Own Self too." With time the fire grew dim, so the boy stirred the coals with a poker. A spark fell on the fairy's foot, and she cried out with pain. Her mother shouted down the chimney, "Who hurt you?" "My Own Self," answered the fairy child, referring to the boy. The mother replied, "Then you have no one to blame but your own self," upon which she jerked her little one up the chimney, and they disappeared (Keightley, p. 313).

FAIRYLAND

Avalon

Some of our oldest legends depict fairies as visitors from a distant island, a realm beneath the sea, or a subterranean domain. Generically called *faerie,* this land is a place of splendor and luxury, a social utopia, and a refuge from hardship and illness. In the English-speaking world the most famous such paradise is Avalon (the Island of Apples), the home of King Arthur's fairy sister Morgan le Fay. *The Life of Merlin* (ca. 1150) by Geoffrey of Monmouth contains the following description:

The Island of Apples, which is called the Fortunate Island, has its name because it produces all things for itself. There is no work for the farmers in plowing the fields. All cultivation is absent except for what nature manages by herself. On its own the island produces fertile crops and grapes and native apples by means of its own trees in the cropped pastures. On its own the overflowing soil puts forth all things in addition to the grass, and in that place one lives for one hundred years or more. (http://www.lib.rochester.edu/camelot/GMAvalon.htm)

Today Avalon is associated with Glastonbury Tor, a prominent hill rising above its namesake city in Somerset, England. Once nearly surrounded by water, the hill has been identified with the fairy island of Avalon since 1191, when monks at the nearby Benedictine Abbey of St. Mary discovered the supposed grave of King Arthur and Queen Guinevere in their local cemetery. Although skeptics may charge that this "discovery" was little more than a medieval marketing scheme to enhance the abbey's reputation as a sacred site, Glastonbury Tor is even today reputed to be the home of the fairy king Gwyn ap Nudd, the site of a secret entry into an underground fairyland, and a center for paranormal phenomena of many types. Fairy lore, still alive in the region, now shares the stage with Wicca adherents, Ley-line researchers, mystics, psychics, UFO seekers, and neo pagans of many different persuasions.

Tir na n'Og

Another legendary fairyland of great antiquity is Tir na n'Og (Land of Youth), usually perceived as an island west of Ireland, but also identified as an underground realm or a land beneath the sea. True to its name, the most prominent quality of Tir na n'Og is the suspension of the aging process for all who dwell there. The most famous human visitor to Tir na n'Og was the legendary Celtic poet and hero Ossian (also spelled Oisin), who went there with a fairy lover and spent 300 (or 150, according to some accounts) years there. Upon his return to earth his aging process accelerated, and he suddenly became a grizzled old man.

The suspension of time is a common motif in legends about visits to fairyland, wherever the location, and whatever the purpose of the visit. Washington Irving's Rip Van Winkle was patterned after any number of European visitors to fairyland. Irving's character fell asleep after accepting a drink from some dwarf-like characters in New York's Catskill Mountains, then awoke after what he perceived to be an hour or two, only to discover that twenty years had lapsed. European legends featuring this motif include "The Old Age of Oisin" and "Touching the Elements," both included in chapter three.

Fairyland in Our Midst

The unrelenting advance of geographic exploration from the time of Christopher Columbus onward steadily reduced the number of areas remote enough to accommodate a fairyland. With the passing of centuries, fairyland became more and more a place or a condition very close to home. Writing in 1916, Lady Gregory said of Tir na n'Og: "It is under the ground or under the sea, or it may not be far from any of us" (p. iii).

This, of course, is not an altogether new view. Many traditional accounts of fairyland place it in a nearby grave mound, earthen fort, natural hill, or simply beneath the ground. Reflecting this, a common Gaelic name for fairies is *sidhe* (pronounced *shee*), a word that originally designated mounds thought to house fairies, then later evolved into a name for the mound dwellers themselves. Similarly, one of the most common terms for dwarfs and elves in Scandinavia is *hill folk,* and in Germany they are often called *underground people.*

If we have fairies literally beneath our feet, does that mean that we are competing with them for room? Numerous legends address this question, often attributing bad fortune to the violation of fairy space. Special precaution was called for in the construction of new buildings. An Irish legend (Gregory, p. 25) tells how a man, planning to build a new house, first consulted a wise woman for advice on its placement. She made five heaps of stones at different places on his property, then told him to build on the location where the stones were not disturbed that night. The next morning, only one pile of stones remained standing, and so he built his house there.

Fairies were particularly sensitive to the location of church construction. Croker (vol. 3, pp. viii–x) tells about a church atop Gads Hill near Newport

Silbury Hill in Wiltshire, England, is the largest prehistoric man-made mound in Europe, and said to be a fairy hill. Photograph by the author.

on the Isle of Wight. It was to have been built at the foot of the hill, but during construction one night the half-finished walls were moved mysteriously to a new site at the hill's summit. The workmen pulled down the walls and rebuilt them on the original site, only to have the structure moved once again. They again dismantled the half-built church and moved it to the foot of the hill. This time they kept watch during the night and observed a band of little people demolishing their work and moving the bricks to the hilltop, after which they danced in a circle at the original building site. Recognizing the futility of attempting to construct a church on an active fairy ring, the workmen completed the church at the hill's summit with no further mishaps. Similar tales are told about church construction at many other locations as well (Christiansen type 7060).

The story "Paddy Corcoran's Wife," as recorded in Yeats's *Fairy and Folk Tales of Ireland* (pp. 35–37), illustrates a common housekeeping fear: Do not splash the fairies when you dispose of your wastewater. Kitty Corcoran suffered from ill health for several years, not understanding the cause until one day a little woman dressed in red came into her sickroom. Introducing herself as one of the good people, the stranger told Kitty that for as long as she had been ill, she had been throwing out her dirty water between dusk and sunrise, the very time when the good people were passing her door. "If you throw it out in a different place and at a different time," concluded the fairy, "the complaint you have will leave you." Kitty complied with the request and was quickly restored to good health.

In other legends the fairies' victims are cattle or horses which befoul fairy space beneath their stalls. The situation is remedied when the animal owner moves the stall to a different site. For examples of these situations see the stories "Raginal" and "Why Deunant Has the Front Door in the Back" in chapter three of this handbook.

HUMAN QUALITIES

Through the process called anthropomorphism, all cultures interpret their deities and other supernatural entities in human and personal terms. Nowhere is this more obvious than in fairy lore. Whatever their origin, in most accounts fairies are very human in their appearance, habits, and emotions. Furthermore, their human (sometimes all-too-human) qualities strongly resemble the characteristics of their closest neighbors.

Fairies reputedly are excellent musicians, but they always favor the instruments used by their immediate human neighbors. Frequently mentioned are fiddles, harps, and bagpipes, with flutes, trumpets, and horns playing a role in some locales. Their great skill notwithstanding, fairies often abduct human musicians to perform at special events, as exemplified in the legends "Fiddler Lux from Buttwil" and "Touching the Elements," both reproduced in chapter three.

Apart from music and dancing, fairy diversions include games and sports, and those specifically mentioned—say parading, hurling, racing horses, or playing nine-pins—are always familiar to the human storytellers. When circumstances dictate, fairies conduct feasts, celebrations, rituals, coronations, baptisms, weddings, and funerals—all resembling human events—although as a rule they are more elaborate and sumptuous.

Most fairy lore extant today stems from agricultural communities. The following comment about Welsh fairies has counterparts in many other rural areas: "In the agricultural districts of Wales, the fairies are accredited with a very complete variety of useful animals; and Welsh folklore, both modern and medieval, abounds with tales regarding cattle, sheep, horses, poultry, goats, and other features of rural life" (Sikes, p. 108). Even the diminutive fairy tribes can practice animal husbandry, their cattle, horses, and dogs being appropriately scaled to the size of the owners (Evans-Wentz, pp. 53, 203).

Fairies engage in other human occupations as well. They make and repair shoes, and work as miners, smiths, and pewterers. They peddle and trade goods, holding their own human-like markets and fairs (Keightley, pp. 294–95).

A water fairy with her harp. Woodcut after a drawing by W. H. Brooke, from Thomas Crofton Croker, *Fairy Legends and Traditions* (1826).

Their social structure resembles that of neighboring humans, featuring kings, queens, soldiers, and workers. They engage in rivalries and warfare with other fairy groups, normally using weapons familiar to their human neighbors. For example, an early twentieth-century account from Ireland describes a band of fairies armed with "guns and cutlasses" (Gregory, p. 27), whereas fairies of earlier centuries favored flint darts as weapons.

Fairies' emotional and physical needs are human-like. They become angry if lied to or cheated and are especially sensitive toward insults and broken promises. They display envy and jealousy. They love and defend their children and other family members. Although they are said to possess "astral" bodies, they require sleep, food, and drink. Indeed, they readily accept gifts of food from humans and are often accused of stealing food from farms, marketplaces, and dairies.

THE RELIGION OF FAIRIES

The humanization of fairies has led quite naturally to the assumption that they too practice religion. Curiously, although fairies are often depicted as natural enemies of Christianity, their own religion often closely parallels that of their Christian neighbors. Visitors to underground and underwater fairy kingdoms often describe cities that include churches not unlike those built on earth.

One legend, the account of an earthling's marriage to a nixie and their life in a village beneath the waters of Lake Mansfeld in southeastern Germany, includes the revealing sentence: "It goes without saying that there was a church in the village" (Woeller, p. 246). Such fairy structures are normally described as being much more splendid than their earthly counterparts, but fairy folk nonetheless sometimes find it more convenient to borrow their human neighbors' buildings than to use their own. For example, dwarfs who guard treasures in Mount Untersberg near Salzburg reputedly go into the city at midnight where they hold religious services in the cathedral (Grimm, *German Legends,* no. 27). Similarly, fairies have been seen conducting a funeral at a church near St. Ives in Cornwall (Hunt, p. 102).

Many legends depict fairies conducting baptisms for their own offspring, and they often recruit humans to help with the services (Kuhn and Schwartz, pp. 261–62). In such cases it is not the male-dominated priesthood that they require, but rather some unspecified female quality. The human helpers are nearly always women, who serve as godmothers. Their precise duties, beyond lifting the infant from the baptism, are seldom described.

"The Convent Nixie at Guben" (Haupt, vol. 2, pp. 232–33) from eastern Germany gives an interesting account of one sprite's encounter with Christianity. The nixie, described as a heathen, fell in love with a human man, and they had a number of secret trysts. However, his conscience intervened, and he broke off their relationship, pledging himself instead to the Virgin Mary. The nixie responded by joining a convent as a novice. Her service was marked by sincerity and humility, and with time she became a nun, ultimately advancing to the office of abbess. However, she could not hide her watery origins. Nixies' clothing, according to widespread belief, is always wet at the bottom hem, and when one of the nuns noticed and revealed the abbess's damp clothing, the entire convent turned against her. Her response was to abandon the Christian world and return to her original home beneath the water.

For all their interest in human religion, fairies were given little chance of salvation by Christian theologians. The view that they were demons unworthy of redemption prevailed from the earliest times into the Renaissance. Following a somewhat different path, Paracelsus (pp. 226–28) wrote in the early sixteenth century that "the four kinds of spirit-men, namely the water people, the mountain people, the fire people, and the wind people," not being from Adam, have no souls, and thus cease to exist at death.

A widespread migratory legend (type 5050) shows that Paracelsus' view was popularly believed throughout Europe. A Scottish variant (Campbell, vol. 2, p. 75) is concise and uncompromising. It relates how "a beautiful green lady" approached a man reading the Bible and asked him if his scripture gave individuals such as her any hope for salvation. Upon hearing his answer that only the offspring of Adam had this opportunity, she screamed in despair and jumped into the sea.

Scandinavian versions of this legend usually end more optimistically, with the sprite being offered at least some hope for salvation. A very positive version is the Swedish tale "The Näck [a water spirit] Longs for Salvation" (Lindow, p. 123). It begins when a boy shouts to a näck "You'll never get God's grace. You're too ugly for that!" After reporting this incident to his father, the boy was told to return to the river and say "My father has read more than I have, and he says you will get the grace of God." The boy followed his father's orders, and when the näck heard the good news he played his fiddle ever so beautifully, then sank down into the water.

Additional examples of these legends are reproduced in the section "The Fairies' Prospect of Salvation" in chapter three.

SEDUCTION

Fairies are sexual beings and often initiate relationships with humans. Although some intimate affairs between humans and fairies develop into long-lasting and mutually satisfying relationships, most end tragically. Folklore is replete with warnings about dangerous liaisons between mortals and super-natural beings. Many of these stories can be interpreted as cautionary tales showing the unhappy consequences of sexual encounters (or even seemingly innocent flirtations) with forbidden partners.

Entire classes of fairies are cast as tempters and seductresses. For example, in Brittany the morgan, a water fairy, is described as a seductress whose passion is never satisfied, and whose embrace kills any man who touches her (Evans-Wentz, pp. 200–201).

In most cases the human's death comes only if he or she tries to break off the relationship. A Swedish legend "The Sea Nymph" (Hofberg, pp. 75–76) offers an example: One night a number of fishermen saw a woman's hand reach in through the door of their hut. One of them, a newly-married man, took hold of the hand, only to be pulled into an underwater realm where he lived with his abuctress, a sea nymph. Three years later he learned that his wife was about to remarry. He asked for permission to see the bridal procession, and the nymph agreed, but only under the stipulation that he not enter the house. Back on earth, he could not resist and went inside. Straight away a tempest came up, blowing half the roof off the house. The man immediately fell ill and died three days later.

A seductive nixie. Illustration by Ludwig Richter, from Ludwig Bechstein, *Deutsches Märchenbuch* (1857).

For the full text of a legend from the Isle of Man about a liaison between a man and a mermaid with similarly tragic consequences see "A Fatal Encounter" in chapter three.

The seduction does not have to be overtly sexual. The sirens of ancient Greece lured sailors to their deaths by singing, a trait that they seem to have bequeathed to their northern European cousins, the mermaids and nixies. One of the most famous of these is Lorelei, immortalized in poems by Clemens von Brentano, Joseph von Eichendorff, and Heinrich Heine. This nixie, once a beautiful woman who threw herself into the Rhine River because of a faithless lover, now sits on a rock in the river near St. Goarshausen, combing her hair and singing an irresistible song that lures boatmen to their deaths. Heine's version of this story, especially as set to music by Friedrich Silcher in 1836, is known to every German schoolchild. As a curious political aside, during Adolf Hitler's Third Reich, school anthologies presented Heine's poem as a "German

Lorelei. Woodcut after a drawing by A. Ehrhardt, from Ludwig Bechstein, *Deutsches Sagenbuch* (1852).

folksong—author unknown." Heine was Jewish, and the Nazi regime could not admit that this ikon of their culture had anything but "Aryan" roots.

Not all supernatural temptation comes from females. Mermaids and nixies have their male counterparts, called variously mermen, water men, or nixes, and these too can lead members of the opposite sex astray. For example, in the German folk ballad "Es freit' ein wilder Wassermann" (A Wild Water Man Went Courting) a merman wins the love of Dorothee, the queen of England, then takes her to an underwater realm where they live together for seven years and produce seven sons. Homesickness strikes her when she hears the sound of English church bells, and she gains permission to attend church in her native land. Once there, she resists returning beneath the sea with her husband, whereupon he kills her with a sword (Fromm, pp. 27–29).

Most tales of seduction and abduction are told from the human partner's point of view, be it a man or a woman. An important exception is the Scottish folk ballad "Tam Lin," a narrative told from the perspective of the girl left behind, the jilted lover. This story further distinguishes itself by depicting a successful rescue of a human victim from the clutches of a demonic lover. Robert Burns crafted a very readable version. (pp. 364–69). Francis James Child's collection *English and Scottish Popular Ballads* (no. 39) includes nine versions, with no fewer than eight different spellings for the rescued man's name: Tam Lane, Tam Lin, Tam-a-Line, Tamlane, Tamlene, Thomas, Tom Line, and Tomlin. In retelling this story, I follow Joseph Jacobs' narrative (*More English Fairy Tales,* pp. 172–76), which he takes primarily from Sir Walter Scott's *Minstrelsy of the Scottish Border.*

Tam Lin was engaged to marry Janet, the daughter of a Scottish earl, but shortly before their wedding the fiancé disappeared. Days afterward she was wandering in the Carterhaugh Wood, when Tam Lin suddenly appeared at her side. Asked about his mysterious absence, he explained, "I grew drowsy while hunting and fell asleep. When I awoke I was in Elfland, companion to the queen of the elves. It is a beautiful place, but I am afraid. Once each seven years the elves must sacrifice someone to hell, and in spite of the queen's favor, I fear that I will be the one." He then told her how she could rescue him from the elves' power. The next night, Halloween, the elves would ride out in procession. He would be astride a white horse. Having protected herself with holy water, she should pull him from the horse. The elves would attempt to keep him with their magic powers, but with courage and faith Janet could prevail. He then told her exactly what to expect, and how she could counter each of the elves' moves.

Janet came to the appointed place the next night, and everything proceeded as Tam Lin had predicted. She identified him in the troop, then pulled him from his horse, taking him into her arms. In quick succession the elves transformed Tam Lin into an adder, a snake, a dove, and a swan. Janet kept hold of each creature. Finally they turned him into a bar of red-hot iron, which—acting on Tam Lin's previous instructions—she cast into a well. Finally, also as predicted, Janet found herself holding the naked Tam Lin. She covered him with her mantle, and the troop of elves rode away. The couple, now safe, rode homeward, and soon afterward they were married.

Another famous Scottish ballad describing a man's abduction by a fairy queen is "True Thomas," reproduced in chapter three. Additional related stories are included in the sections "Seduced by a Fairy" and "Fairy Brides," also in chapter three.

CHANGELINGS

Abductions of individuals targeted to become fairies' lovers and spouses are told throughout Europe, but even more common are accounts of stolen infants. The folkloric record makes it clear that pre-industrial Europeans' greatest fear concerning fairies was that the latter would steal a newborn baby, leaving in its place a misshapen fairy child known as a changeling. Accounts of such abductions are found throughout Europe, and beyond, stretching from the pre-Christian era into the twentieth century. My own folktale archive contains nearly 200 such legends.

As late as 1924 it was reported that in sections of rural Germany many people were still taking traditional precautions against the supernatural exchange of infants (Ranke, p. 138). Outside of Europe the opinion survived even longer. Writing in 1980, Hasan M. El-Shamy reports: "The belief that the jinn may steal a human infant and put their own infant in its place is widespread in numerous parts of Egypt" (p. 179).

This superstition's longevity and widespread distribution is easily explained. We all want reasons for events that fall outside of our control, especially those that have a direct bearing on our welfare. The changeling belief explained why some children fail to develop normally and justified the withdrawal of family support for such handicapped individuals.

Descriptions of fairy changelings gleaned from a sampling of legends suggest that the stories ultimately stemmed from actual experiences with children suffering from such ailments as autism, Down syndrome, hydrocephalus, or any other condition that resulted in a child's failure to thrive and develop properly. Symptoms specifically described in the legends include a swollen head, strangely staring eyes, a flat nose, incessant crying, misbehavior, failure to learn to talk or walk, and a voracious appetite.

Elves abduct a human baby. Illustration by Walter Crane, from Jacob and Wilhelm Grimm, *Household Stories* (1886).

Infants were deemed vulnerable to fairy exchange above all during their first six weeks of life, and during that period special precautions were called for. Foremost among these was Christian piety. One woman lost her baby to the fairies on "one unlucky day, when she happened to sleep too long in the morning, and, consequently, had not time to say her prayers" (Kennedy, p. 85). Another child was stolen by the fairies because a mother, who had given birth during the absence of her sailor husband, had put off the child's baptism, wanting the father to be present at the ceremony. The story ends happily with the child's safe recovery, punctuated by a reminder about "the wickedness of neglecting to get young babies baptized as soon as possible after they're born" (Kennedy, pp. 76–80).

Additionally, there were special rituals and charms. In northeastern Scotland, after first dressing a newborn child, "it was turned three times heels over head in the nurse's arms, and blessed, and then shaken three times with the head downward. These ceremonies kept the fairies at a distance" (Gregor, p. 7). General-purpose protective measures also were applied: lighted candles, salt, iron, special herbs, and other materials and methods reputed to guard against fairies. Finally, constant supervision was prescribed. Many legends describe how an infant was stolen while its mother was absent with other duties.

A noteworthy aspect of most changeling legends is that the parents whose child was misbehaving or failing to properly develop were not the ones who first suggested that the infant was a changeling. This diagnosis typically was made by someone outside the family: a priest, neighbor, landlord, fairy doctor,

A mother fights with the fairies to prevent
them from abducting her child. Illustration
by T. H. Thomas, From Wirt Sikes, *British
Goblins* (1881).

or even a perfect stranger. There was thus a shared responsibility for any actions
that followed, and these were often very drastic. A standard approach was to
torture the suspected changeling, thus forcing its fairy parents to rescue it. The
abuses inflicted on these babies were unspeakably cruel, and if actually carried
out would have been fatal.

The Irish story "The Brewery of Eggshells" illustrates the situation, describing a distraught mother's reluctance to apply the prescribed methods of revers-
ing a fairy exchange: "Although its face was so withered, and its body wasted
away to a mere skeleton, it had still a strong resemblance to her own boy. She
therefore could not find it in her heart to roast it alive on the griddle, or to
burn its nose off with the red hot tongs, or to throw it out in the snow on the
roadside, notwithstanding these, and several like proceedings, were strongly
recommended to her for the recovery of her child" (Croker, vol. 1, p. 55).

It is impossible to determine how often these extreme punishments were
actually inflicted on malformed or mentally retarded children. In 1826 in
Tralee, Ireland, a grandmother drowned her four-year-old grandson, who
could neither stand, walk, nor speak. Brought to trial, she testified that she
had not intended to kill the child, but rather "to put the fairy out of it." She

was found not guilty (Croker, vol. 2, pp. vi–vii). Writing in 1849, W. R. Wilde stated: "About a year ago a man in the county of Kerry [Ireland] roasted his child to death, under the impression that it was a fairy. He was not brought to trial, as the crown prosecutor mercifully looked upon him as insane" (p. 28). Court records between about 1850 and 1900 in Germany, Scandinavia, Great Britain, and Ireland reveal numerous proceedings against defendants accused of torturing and murdering suspected changelings, but even where guilty verdicts are reached the penalties are seldom as severe as in comparable cases not involving changeling beliefs (Hartland, *Science of Fairy Tales,* pp. 121–22; Piaschewski, pp. 141–46).

Undoubtedly, similar incidents were even more common in earlier centuries, but prior to the mid nineteenth century, the public acceptance of this superstition and a general lack of children's rights made it unlikely that such cases would be prosecuted. For example, in the medieval epic *Njal's Saga,* we read that when Iceland formally adopted Christianity in the year 1000 openly killing unwanted children was made illegal, although—its anonymous author claims—infanticide committed secretly was officially allowed for a number of years afterward (Hreinsson, vol. 3, ch. 105).

The mistreatment of changelings in folklore accounts often (although not always) leads to a happy outcome for the human parents and their rightful child. To halt the abuse of their offspring, the otherworldly parents frequently rescue the changeling and return the stolen mortal child. Stories with these fantasy endings provided hope, wish fulfillment, and escape to an era that was plagued with birth defects and debilitating infant diseases.

Not all changeling accounts have happy endings. Often the child thought to be a changeling is driven away or killed, but the healthy original child is not returned. The tales that omit the safe recovery of the rightful child illustrate a painful aspect of family survival in pre-industrial Europe. A peasant family's very subsistence frequently depended upon the productive labor of each member, and it was enormously difficult to provide for a person who was a permanent drain on the family's scarce resources. The fact that a changeling's ravenous appetite is so frequently mentioned indicates that the parents of these unfortunate children saw in their continuing presence a threat to the sustenance of an entire family.

Cruel abuse was not the only way to force demonic parents to reclaim their misshapen children, although this was the most frequently described method. A more humane approach was to force the changeling to laugh or to make him utter an expression of surprise, which—according to popular belief—would expose his true identity and force his supernatural parents to take him away. A common trick was to make preparations in the presence of the changeling to brew beer or to cook stew in eggshells. Typically the changeling responds with surprise, claiming that he is as old as a nearby forest, but has never before witnessed such a sight. (I use masculine pronouns here advisedly, because in nearly all changeling legends both the abducted child and his replacement are males.)

Although children, especially those not yet baptized, were most vulnerable to fairy abduction, adults were at risk as well. Recently delivered mothers were often taken, ostensibly to serve as wet nurses for fairy infants. Similarly, for some inexplicable reason expectant fairy mothers often needed the help of human midwives, who were abducted for this purpose, although these were nearly always safely returned once their services were no longer needed, and they were often very generously paid for their work.

Unexplained disappearances and premature deaths, especially in Ireland and Scotland, were often attributed to fairy abduction. In such cases the corpse was said to be a mere image, typically made of wood and sometimes called a *stock,* created by the fairies to mislead the mourners. Following the burial the "glamour" would leave this image, and only a few withered leaves or other such refuse would remain in the coffin. The ostensibly deceased individual would be "away" with the fairies.

MISFORTUNE

Accidents, Illness, and Premature Death

Collective memory has been kind to fairies. Today they mostly are perceived as benevolent and helpful, if sometimes mischievous, sprites. This positive recollection is an authentic inheritance from the past, but only part of the story. Good fortune did attend many encounters between fairies and humans. Household and farm spirits helped with menial tasks and often blessed their hosts with prosperity and good health. Mine spirits showed their mortal counterparts where to dig. And in those instances where fairies required human help, for example in midwifery or migration, the payment was often so generous that many succeeding generations benefited from it (Haupt, p. 36).

These good acts notwithstanding, traditional fairy lore is replete with accounts of acts harmful to humans, warnings of behavior that might make one vulnerable to fairy attack, and recommendations of proactive steps to guard against fairy harm. Belief in fairies and other supernatural powers enabled our ancestors to individualize misfortunes of every kind. These were not random, impersonal events, but rather intentional acts by willful beings, against whom protective measures could be taken. Crop failures were attributed to pilfering by fairies (Grimm, *German Legends,* no. 156). Violent storms were caused by vindictive mermaids (Gregory, pp. 10–11). Even normally harmless (although potentially dangerous) annoyances such as losing one's way while returning home after dark were blamed on fairies (Sikes, pp. 22–24).

"The devil made me do it" is a much-used excuse, even by those who may not believe in a personal Satan. In previous generations fairies often played this same role. Pookas caused accidental falls in old Ireland (Croker, vol. 1, p. 283). Kobolds set houses and barns afire in Germany (Knoop, p. 79). Accidental drownings did not just happen, but rather were willful acts by water spirits demanding their yearly human sacrifices (Christiansen type 4050). Sudden illness was caused by "fairy stroke," a blow inflicted by one of the invisible people.

Fairy lore reflects the harshness of life in pre-industrial Europe. Many legends depict competition for food, mates, and living space between humans and their supernatural neighbors. Somehow the premature death of a loved one was easier to bear if it could be interpreted as an abduction by the fairies. The victim was not dead, but "away," to use a common euphemism, and there was always hope that he or she might return. Lady Gregory dedicates an entire chapter to events of this kind in Ireland, many of which allegedly occurred in the twentieth century (pp. 169–244).

Theft of Food

For individuals living on the edge of survival—and that includes a great many people in traditional cultures—a constant concern is maintaining an adequate food supply. The loss of a cow, the failure of a crop, or the spoilage of stored food could threaten not only a family's well-being, but its very survival. It should thus come as no surprise that folktales of all kinds deal with food. The universally known, but obviously fictitious "Hansel and Gretel" states the problem succinctly: A family of four has food enough for only two. The children must be sacrificed, or everyone will starve. Fairy legends go one step further. They account for food shortages by blaming fairies for crop failures, sick cattle, and other inexplicable losses.

Robert Kirk, writing in the seventeenth century, articulated the belief that fairies often feed "on the foison [nourishment] or substance of corns and liquors, or corn itself that grows on the surface of the earth, which these fairies steal away, partly invisible, partly preying on the grain, as do crows and mice" (p. 5). Expressed in more modern terms: Food that fails to nourish as expected has had its essence sucked out by fairies, leaving it devoid of nutritional value;

and a field that yields a smaller harvest than anticipated likely has been raided by pilfering fairies.

These beliefs are documented well into the twentieth century. Commenting on Irish fairies, Lady Gregory recorded in 1916: "For their feasts they choose the best of all sorts, taking it from the solid world, leaving some worthless likeness in its place; when they rob the potatoes from the ridges, the diggers find but rottenness and decay; they take the strength from the meat in the pot, so that when put on the plates it does not nourish" (pp. iii–iv).

Similar examples present themselves in legends told throughout Europe. If butter fails to "come" in the churn, fairies—possibly in the form of butterflies—have stolen the butterfat from the milk, a crime also commonly attributed to witches. If a cow goes dry, or gives less milk than expected, the fairies (or witches) are to blame. If cattle fail to thrive, the fairies literally have eaten the meat off their bones, leaving behind nothing but skeletons covered with skin. The section "Thieving Fairies" in chapter three includes two legends further illustrating these problems.

PROTECTION

Christian Piety

If, in one's mind, a misfortune has an identifiable cause, then preventative measures must also exist. Reflecting the view that fairy mythology and Christianity were in essence two competing and mutually antagonistic belief systems, Christian piety is by a very wide margin the most frequently mentioned guarantee against fairy attacks. In popular lore the church is the first line of defense against not only werewolves, vampires, and demons; but also fairies, elves, and trolls.

The horror-movie image of a priest armed with a crucifix and facing down a vampire is familiar to everyone. However, for the most part it has been forgotten that the cross on hot cross buns was originally cut into the unbaked dough to prevent theft by elves. The same sign was carved into tools and utensils as protection against "sprites of doubtful character" (Croker, vol. 3, p. 38; Henderson, pp. 220–21; Keightley, pp. 304–5; Kuhn and Schwartz, pp. 163–64).

Fairy folk were left powerless in the presence of sign of the cross, even if made accidentally, as illustrated by the following Danish legend: A smith came upon a troll unsuccessfully trying to remove two crossed straws from a heap of coal. Wise to such matters, the smith picked up the coal, leaving the cross intact. Upon arriving home he discovered that the pieces of coal were a

great treasure. The troll had lost control over it because of the cross accidentally formed by two straws (Thiele, vol. 2, pp. 194–95).

Laxity in religious devotion could put anyone at risk. Kennedy tells of an
Irishwoman who put herself under the power of the fairies when she "made a
bad confession." As a result she was abducted on her wedding night. She later
communicated to her husband: "The fairies got power over me because I was
only thinking of you, and did not prepare myself as I ought for the sacrament"
(Kennedy, p. 101). There are counterparts to this cautionary tale in many
countries.

Non-Christian Methods

Fairy lore is an inheritance from the pre-Christian past, and as such it
encompasses numerous protective measures that have no apparent connection to Christian beliefs or rituals. First among these is the use of iron as a
guard against supernatural powers. It is widely theorized that this belief stems
from prehistoric conflicts between Neolithic cultures and more advanced
groups possessing iron tools and weapons. The Celtic tribes, among the first
Europeans to develop an Iron Age culture, offer a reasonable example. Their
prehistoric expansion from the Danube River basin in all directions, including to the British Isles, brought them into contact with indigenous peoples
(for example, the Picts in Britain) with only Stone Age technology. The Celts'
iron tools and weapons were indeed magical, in comparison to their competi-
tors' primitive stone axes and flint arrowheads.

Legends from all parts of Europe document iron being used to incapacitate
witches, werewolves, and fairies of all types. The form of the iron seems to
matter but little: a horseshoe, a door lock, a knife, or a simple bar. "Any old
iron will do, the older the better," reported Lady Wilde (p. 104).

An untitled Welsh legend recorded by John Rhys (pp. 86–89) illustrates
iron's magical power against fairies in two different episodes. The story takes
place in the parish of Beddgelert and begins with a young man secretly watching fairies dance. He was romantically stricken by one of the females, who
was more beautiful than any human he had ever seen. Driven by passion, he
rushed into the crowd of fairies, seized the woman, and carried her home,
with her family in hot pursuit. However, he bolted the door with iron, so
"they could not get near her or touch her in any way." He asked the captive
fairy repeatedly to marry him, which she finally agreed to do, but only if he
would promise never to touch her with iron. He accepted this condition,
and they married. After several years of happy marriage, one morning the
two of them tried to catch a frisky horse. In attempting to bridle the horse,

Horseshoe hung in a doorway to bring good luck. Photographed by the author at the Highland Folk Museum, Newtonmore, Scotland.

the man accidentally hit his wife with the iron bit, and she immediately vanished from sight.

Fairies' reputed fear of iron leads to a major discrepancy in folk belief. In spite of iron's reputed magic powers against them, many fairy types—especially elves, dwarfs, and trolls—are known to be skillful blacksmiths. A legend from Shetland offers a dramatic example of this inconsistency: A blacksmith's teen-aged son was abducted and carried into a hill by the trows. Armed with a Bible and a knife, the boy's father approached the trows' hill. Finding it open, he shoved the knife above the entrance, which then "could not close because of the presence of steel." The Bible caused the trows to flee, and their prisoner was able to escape. Back at home, he was of even greater help to his father than before, because during his captivity he had learned from the trows a special art of tempering scythes (Nicolson, pp. 21–22).

Salt is another magical substance, one of great antiquity and used around the world as a prophylactic against evil spirits. This reputation probably derives from salt's proven effectiveness as a food preservative. European fairy accounts contain many references to salt's protective qualities (Lady Wilde, pp. 44, 106–107; Hunt, pp. 108–109).

The natural world produced many plants and herbs helpful against fairies. In Germany caraway seeds were used not only as a spice, but also to prevent dwarfs from stealing bread (Kuhn and Schwartz, pp. 165, 224). *Dorant* is an untranslatable German word designating a variety of magical plants, with the specific plant differing from region to region. Plants so designated include gentian, toadflax, and yarrow (Kuhn, vol. 1, pp. 279–80). In Ireland garlands of primroses or marsh marigolds protected cows from the theft of milk by witches and fairies (Lady Wilde, pp. 104, 106).

The most frequently mentioned protective plant in Britain is the rowan tree, also called mountain ash. The rowan is possibly connected with Yggdrasil, the world tree of Norse mythology, depicted as an ash tree, and called in the *Prose Edda* "the best and greatest of all trees" (Snorri, p. 42). Saint-John's-wort is used as a protective herb throughout Europe (Kuhn, vol. 2, p. 29). Another plant with widespread magical reputation is the four-leaf clover, which enables a person to see fairies who would otherwise be invisible, and also to see through the deceptive illusions of sorcerers (Hunt, pp. 107–109; Kennedy, pp. 102–103).

Running water, in some contexts, is considered to be an effective barrier against supernatural powers of many kinds, as noted by Robert Burns at the conclusion of his famous ballad "Tam o' Shanter": "It is a well-known fact that witches, or any evil spirits, have no power to follow a poor wight [fellow] any farther than the middle of the next running stream" (p. 295). Confirming this belief for Ireland, Evans-Wentz reports: "When out on a dark night,

Leaves from the rowan tree, traditionally used for protection against fairies. Photographed by the author at the Botanic Gardens, Glasgow, Scotland.

if pursued by fairies or ghosts one is considered quite safe if one can get over some stream" (p. 38).

Others are more skeptical. In the words of another observer of the Irish situation: "Fairies don't cross streams, you say! How then could the Leinster fairies cross over the Suir and Barrow [rivers] to have a hurling match with the Munster fairies, or the fairies of Ireland have a battle with the Scotch fairies?" (Kennedy, p. 104).

Many legends describe the protective power of a lighted candle or a blazing fire on the hearth. Fire's nearly universal function as a guard against evil spirits is summarized by Lady Wilde: "Fire is a great preventative against fairy magic, for fire is the most sacred of all created things, and man alone has power over it. If a ring of fire is made round cattle or a child's cradle, or if fire is placed under the churn, the fairies have no power to harm. And the spirit of the fire is certain to destroy all fairy magic, if it exist" (p. 39).

DEPARTURE OF FAIRIES

A common theme in the legends of many regions is the disappearance of fairies. Storytellers of all generations agree on one particular: There are not as many fairies now as there used to be. A string of creative writers have bemoaned this loss, ironically or otherwise. In the fourteenth century Chaucer's wife of Bath complained that "no one sees elves any more" (*Canterbury Tales*, line 864). Some three hundred years later the poet Richard Corbet, in his poem "The Fairies' Farewell," lamented, "But now, alas, they all are dead, or gone beyond the seas" (Gardner, pp. 218–20). In the early years of the twentieth century, if we can believe Rudyard Kipling, there was still one fairy left in England—Puck, of Shakespearian fame, who, as we read in the novel *Puck of Pook's Hill* (1906), was unwittingly conjured up by two children playing in a meadow. He introduced himself to the children, while bemoaning his fate:

I'm the only one left. I'm Puck, the oldest old thing in England.... There's no good beating about the bush: it's true. The people of the hills have all left. I saw them come into Old England and I saw them go. Giants, trolls, kelpies, brownies, goblins, imps; wood, tree, mound, and water spirits; heath-people, hill-watchers, treasure-guards, good people, little people, pishogues, leprechauns, night-riders, pixies, nixies, gnomes, and the rest—gone, all gone! (pp. 8–10)

Others saw them leaving as well, singly from individual locations, and entire communities in mass exoduses.

Individuals

Many legends address the departure of one individual fairy, usually a household spirit. In a large family of stories (Aarne-Thompson type 113A) a fairy assumes the form of a cat and then establishes itself as a family pet in a human household, where it remains until one day it hears that someone with an unusual name has died. The deceased may be a competitor who had sent the fairy-cat into exile and whose death makes a return home possible; or he may be a king, leaving the household spirit as successor to the throne. In any event, upon hearing the news, the fairy-cat rushes away, never to be seen again by its human hosts.

Similar events are related in migratory legends of type 6060B. Here a peasant at work hears a voice announcing that someone, again with a strange name, has died. When he returns home he reports the experience, only to be interrupted by wailing from another part of the house, usually the cellar. Investigating, the family discovers evidence of a mysterious guest, obviously a household spirit, but one who has now left. Examples of these two tale types, "The Troll Turned Cat" and "Prilling and Pralling Is Dead," are included in chapter three.

In the above stories the household spirits abandon their adopted households for external reasons. In other cases the human hosts commit some infraction that effects the departure. A frequent cause, and one discussed above in the section titled "Clothing," is the gift of a new suit. Ironically, in such tales it is the host's generosity that drives the elf away. In other instances it is stinginess or thoughtlessness.

As is well documented, brownies, pixies, kobolds, and other such household spirits normally serve their masters well, expecting only some small reward in return, typically a simple meal. In one famous case, a brownie-like elf established himself at a Welsh farm, where he was of great service to the maidservant, expecting in return only a bowl of bread and milk each night. However, one night, "by way of cursedness," she filled the elf's bowl with urine. The next morning he seized her by the neck, then beat her and kicked her from one end of the house to the other, after which he left the farm, never to be seen there again (Rhys, pp. 593–94).

A legend from Pomerania (a historic region now divided between Germany and Poland) follows a similar pattern, although in this case the offering of food was not spoiled maliciously. The story relates how a traveling journeyman found shelter for the night in a peasant's barn. He saw a plate of food sitting on a beam. The uninvited wanderer should have known that the food was an offering for a kobold, but he was hungry, so he ate it. Shortly afterward a gigantic fellow carrying a huge load of straw on his back came into the barn. Without noticing the journeyman, he unloaded the straw, then went to the plate. Finding it empty he cried out angrily, "Sixty miles on foot, sixty shocks of straw carried on my back, and no breakfast yet!" With that he set the barn afire and disappeared. Thus the thoughtless act of a stranger deprived a peasant of supernatural help from that time forward (Knoop, p. 79).

The catalog of infractions that drive helpful spirits away, usually forever, includes a host of human weaknesses, foremost being ridicule, failure to keep secrets, breaking promises, and violation of privacy. A legend from Germany's Black Forest provides an example of this last category:

One winter evening two earth people came to a peasant's house and asked for food. He complied, and in return they presented him with a small bar of gold. This arrangement continued for some time, with the peasant exchanging food for gold every evening. The earth people always wore long robes that completely covered their feet. Curious to know what they were hiding, the peasant scattered ashes in front of his doorway in order to see what kind of tracks his underground guests left. After their last visit, he ascertained from the tracks that their feet resembled those of geese. However, his benefactors noticed what he had done, and they never again returned. Moreover, the peasant's health soon failed, his accumulated wealth disappeared, and he died a miserable death (Baader, pp. 18–19). This story, like many others, suggests that the principle reason for the departure of helpful elves is quite simply that we humans no longer deserve them.

Mass Migration

The situation with the exodus of entire communities is more complicated. Here too, in some instances, human shortcomings are responsible for the fairies' departure. For example, the underground people left the town of Hasel in southwestern Germany because of the sinfulness of its inhabitants (Baader, p. 18), and dwarfs abandoned a cave near the town of Naila in Bavaria because of their human neighbors' cursing, swearing, and desecration of Sundays (Grimm, *German Legends,* no. 34).

However, in most recorded instances it is human piety, not human sinfulness, that drives away the fairies. The single most frequently mentioned cause of the fairies' departure is their abhorrence of church bells. This aversion, documented in countless legends throughout Europe, is based both on the traditional conflict between fairies and the ever-advancing Christianity, as well as their mistrust of sounds foreign to their natural world. Their dislike of the noise of industrialization—steam engines and the like—is also frequently mentioned (Grimm, *German Legends,* nos. 34, 36).

Fairies show more antipathy toward some branches of Christianity than others. It was widely believed in protestant Europe that Roman Catholicism was inherently more amenable toward fairies than were the Protestant faiths, leading to the opinion that the Reformation was the leading force in exiling the fairies (Hunt, p. 98). Even among Protestants not all denominations were deemed equally responsible. Thus, in nineteenth-century Wales it could be noted: "It is a common remark that the Methodists drove them away" (Sikes, p. 6).

In at least one instance, the fervor of a single minister caused them to leave. According to a Shetland legend the trows abandoned these islands, fleeing northward to Faroe, because of the prayers of James Ingram, who served as a minister at North Yell and Fetlar from 1803 to 1821 (Nicolson, p. 17). Political leaders, too, were credited with (or blamed for) the fairies' departure. In the words of one observer: "When Old Fritz [Frederick the Great] came to power, he no longer wanted to put up with them [the dwarfs] in his land, so he exiled them across the Black Sea" (Kuhn and Schwartz, p. 163).

Whatever the cause, the fairies left in great masses. In most instances their route took them at first across a named river or lake, but their final destination is seldom given. Ironically, for all their supernatural power, the fairies often called upon humans for help in starting their exodus, hiring them as ferrymen or wagon drivers. Two legends depicting such withdrawals are reproduced in chapter three under the heading "Departure."

WORKS CITED

Baader, Bernhard. *Volkssagen aus dem Lande Baden.* Karlsruhe: Herder, 1851.
Bechstein, Ludwig. *Deutsches Märchenbuch.* Leipzig: Wigand, 1857.
———. *Deutsches Sagenbuch.* Leipzig: Wigand, 1852.
Burne, Charlotte Sophia. *Shropshire Folk-Lore.* London: Trübner, 1883.
Burns, Robert. *Complete Poems and Songs.* New Lanark, Scotland: Geddes and Grosset, 2003.
Campbell, J. F. *Popular Tales of the West Highlands.* 4 vols. Paisley and London: Gardner, 1890.
Child, Francis James. *The English and Scottish Popular Ballads.* 5 vols. Boston: Houghton, Mifflin, 1882–98.
Christiansen, Reidar T. *The Migratory Legends.* Helsinki: Suomalainen Tiedeakatemia, 1958.
Croker, Thomas Crofton. *Fairy Legends and Traditions of the South of Ireland.* 3 vols. London: Murray, 1825–28.

El-Shamy, Hasan M. *Folktales of Egypt*. Chicago: U of Chicago P, 1980.

Evans-Wentz, W. Y. *The Fairy-Faith in Celtic Countries*. London: Frowde, 1911.

Fromm, Hans, ed. *Deutsche Balladen*. Munich: Hanser, 1968.

Gardner, Helen. *The New Oxford Book of English Verse*. Oxford: Oxford UP, 1972.

Geoffrey of Monmouth. *The Life of Merlin,* http://lib.rochester.edu/camelot/ GMAvalon.htm.

Gervase of Tilbury. *Otia Imperialia: Recreation for an Emperor*. Trans. S. E. Banks and J. W. Binns. Oxford: Clarendon, 2002. Manuscript completed in 1211.

Gregor, Walter. *Notes on the Folk-Lore of the North-East of Scotland*. London: Folk-Lore Society, 1881.

Gregory, Lady Isabelle Augusta. *Visions and Beliefs in the West of Ireland*. New York and London: Putnam, 1920.

Grimm, Jacob and Wilhelm. *The German Legends of the Brothers Grimm*. Trans. Donald Ward. 2 vols. Philadelphia: Institute for the Study of Human Issues, 1981.

———. *Household Stories*. Trans. Lucy Crane. London: Macmillan, 1886.

Hartland, Edwin Sidney. *English Fairy and Folk Tales*. London: Scott, 1890.

———. *The Science of Fairy Tales: An Inquiry into Fairy Mythology*. London: Scott, 1891.

Haupt, Karl. *Sagenbuch der Lausitz*. 2 vols. Leipzig: Engelmann, 1862–63.

Henderson, William. *Notes on the Folk-Lore of the Northern Counties of England and the Borders*. London: Longmans, Green, 1866.

Hofberg, Herman. *Swedish Fairy Tales*. Trans. W. H. Myers. Chicago: Conkey, 1893.

Hreinsson, Vidar, ed. *The Complete Sagas of Icelanders,* 5 vols. Reykjavik: Leifur Eiriksson, 1997.

Hunt, Robert. *Popular Romances of the West of England*. London: Hotten, 1871.

Jacobs, Joseph. *Celtic Fairy Tales*. London: Nutt, 1892.

———. *English Fairy Tales*. London: Nutt, 1898. First published 1890.

———. *More English Fairy Tales*. New York and London: Putnam, n.d. First published 1894.

Keightley, Thomas. *The Fairy Mythology*. London: Bohn, 1850.

Kennedy, Patrick. *Legendary Fictions of the Irish Celts,* 2nd ed. London: Macmillan, 1891. First published 1866.

Kipling, Rudyard. *Puck of Pook's Hill*. Garden City, NY: Doubleday, n.d. First published 1906.

Kirk, Robert. *The Secret Commonwealth of Elves, Fauns, and Fairies*. London: David Nutt, 1893. Based on a manuscript of 1691.

Knoop, Otto. *Volkssagen, Erzählungen, Aberglauben, Gebräuche und Märchen aus dem östlichen Hinterpommern*. Poznan, Poland: Jolowicz, 1885.

Kuhn, Adalbert, and Wilhelm Schwartz. *Norddeutsche Sagen, Märchen und Gebräuche*. Leipzig: Brockhaus, 1848.

Kuhn, Adalbert. *Sagen, Gebräuche und Märchen aus Westfalen*. 2 vols. Leipzig: Brockhaus, 1859.

Kvideland, Reimund, and Henning K. Sehmsdorf. *Scandinavian Folk Belief and Legend.* Minneapolis, U of Minnesota P, 1988.

Lindow, John. *Swedish Legends and Folktales.* Berkeley: U of California P, 1978.

Luther, Martin. *Werke, kritische Gesamtausgabe: Tischreden.* Weimar: Böhlau, 1912–21.

Nicolson, John. *Some Folk-Tales and Legends of Shetland.* Edinburgh: Allan, 1920.

Paracelsus [Theophrastus von Hohenheim]. *Four Treatises.* Ed. Henry E. Sigerist. Baltimore: Johns Hopkins U P, 1996.

Piaschewski, Gisela. *Der Wechselbalg: Ein Beitrag zum Aberglauben der nordeuropäischen Völker.* Breslau: Maruschke & Berendt, 1935.

Ranke, Friedrich. *Die deutschen Volkssagen* Munich: Beck, 1924.

Rhys, John. *Celtic Folklore: Welsh and Manx.* Oxford: Oxford UP, 1901.

Rochholz, Ernst Ludwig. *Schweizersagen aus dem Aargau.* Aarau, Switzerland: Sauerländer, 1856.

Sikes, Wirt. *British Goblins: Welsh Folk-Lore, Fairy Mythology, Legends, and Traditions.* Boston: Osgood, 1881.

Snorri Sturluson. *The Prose Edda.* Trans. Jean I. Young. Berkeley: U of California P, 1954.

Thiele, J. M. *Danmarks Folkesagn.* 3 vols. Copenhagen: Rosenkilde og Bagger, 1968.

Thomas, W. Jenkyn. *The Welsh Fairy Book.* London: Unwin, [1908].

Thorpe, Benjamin. *Northern Mythology.* Ware, Hertfordshire: Wordsworth, 2001. First published 1851.

Wilde, Lady Francesca. *Ancient Legends, Mystic Charms, and Superstitions of Ireland.* London: Chatto and Windus, 1919. First published 1887.

Wilde, W. R. *Irish Popular Superstitions.* Dublin: McGlashan, 1852.

Woeller, Waltraud. *Deutsche Volksmärchen.* Frankfurt am Main: Insel, 1985. Woeller's Source: Emil Sommer, *Sagen, Märchen und Gebräuche aus Sachsen und Thüringen.* Halle: Anton, 1846.

Yeats, William Butler. *Fairy and Folk Tales of Ireland.* New York: Macmillan, 1983. Contains *Fairy and Folk Tales of the Irish Peasantry,* first published 1888, and *Irish Fairy Tales,* first published 1892.

———. *The Celtic Twilight.* Bridport, Dorset: Prism, 1990. First published 1893.

Two
Definitions and Classifications

TAXONOMY

The classification of living things (taxonomy) has occupied scientists from Aristotle onward. From the very beginning, their observations presented problems not easily solved. For example, should the starfish be grouped together with other fish, in recognition of their shared aquatic environment? One pathway led to an affirmative answer, as evidenced by the creature's name *starfish,* although few scientists today would agree with that decision.

The difficulties faced by biologists seeking to categorize visible (if sometimes only through a microscope) life forms are slight in comparison to those confronting a folklorist trying to create a self-consistent catalog of the living things reported from the invisible realm of faerie. The observations of science, by definition, are replicable. On the other hand, experiences with the "unseen people" (a common circumlocution for *fairy folk*) are idiosyncratic and highly personal. Although such encounters frequently have been reported, they often contradict each other, and can rarely—if ever—be repeated on demand. Furthermore, there is no governing body of fairy belief, no authoritative council or "peer review" to separate authentic sightings from counterfeit ones. Thus the principal actors in fairy mythology are ill defined. Famed as magical shape shifters, they make their appearances in different forms and wearing different costumes. Moreover, they often play contradictory and overlapping roles.

No self-consistent system of categorizing and defining fairy folk has yet evolved, but a few divisions do present themselves. I offer them here with the disclaimer that their boundaries are inexact and fluid, and that exceptions can always be found.

1. Abode. Where do fairies live, work, and play?
2. Appearance. Are they large or small; beautiful or ugly; dark or light; human-shaped or animal-like?
3. Disposition. Are they good or evil; solitary or social; mischievous or helpful; capricious or predictable?
4. Function. What do they do?

ABODE

According to Greek mythology the natural world is inhabited by female deities. Inferior in power and influence to their counterparts dwelling on Mount Olympus, these nymphs—as they are often called—are categorized and named according to their abode and dominion. Dryads preside over forests; oreads over mountains; naiads over springs, rivers, and lakes; nereids over both saltwater and freshwater; and oceanids over the oceans. These minor deities played an important role in the popular religions of ancient Greece and Rome, and contributed substantially to the fairy lore of northern Europe.

In the sixteenth century Paracelsus, introduced in the previous chapter, described four types of elemental beings, differentiated from one another primarily by their places of habitation: gnomes in rocks and soil, salamanders in fire, sylphs in air, and undines in water. This classification according to abode fits well into a tradition of fairy lore widely believed both before and after Paracelsus.

A standard Christian-based hypothesis of the origin of fairies suggests that these are fallen angels, not evil enough for damnation, but not good enough to remain in God's presence, and had thus been cast onto earth. Each became a different type of fairy according to where it landed: elves in the hills, wood nymphs in the forests, household spirits on inhabited buildings, mermaids and mermen in the water, and so forth. Shakespeare's Prospero follows this tradition when he summons "ye elves of hills, brooks, standing lakes, and groves; and ye, that on the sands with printless foot do chase the ebbing Neptune" (*The Tempest,* act 5, scene 1).

Earth

Underground People

Humans, by nature, are earthbound. Many mythologies dictate that the earth is our mother, but our forebears also saw hiding places for mysterious and often sinister beings in the earth's untamed regions: mountains, forests, thickets, swamps, deserts, and underground caverns. Such earth sprites, reflecting the inherent dangers of the wild places they inhabited, were often malevolent. But helpful creatures dwelled there as well, and these may represent survivals of ancient earth deities, such as the Germanic goddess Nerthus described by the Roman historian Tacitus some 2,000 years ago. These deities did not suddenly become extinct with the conversion of Europe to Christianity. In the late nineteenth century, Lady Wilde, a perceptive observer of popular belief, said of Irish fairies: "Earth, lake, and hill are peopled by these fantastic, beautiful gods of earth; the wilful, capricious child-spirits of the world" (p. 142).

In Germany elves and dwarfs are often referred to generically as underground people, or simply earth people; and in Scandinavia similar beings are called hill people. Scottish brownies take their name from their earth-colored skin and clothing; whereas green, the color of vegetation, is associated with fairies everywhere. Gnomes' relationship with the earth, formally documented by Paracelsus and informally featured in countless legends, playfully continues into the twenty-first century in the form of ceramic (or—now more commonly—plastic) garden statues.

Like plants and animals in the natural world, earth sprites often fill specific niches. Ancient burial mounds and similar monuments are reputedly home to a host of supernatural beings, including fairies and elves. Miners everywhere have reported sharing their underground workspace with elfin fellows, known in Cornwall as knockers, in Germany as kobolds and mine monks, and in other places by a multitude of local names. Some sprites are at home only in the forest—even in individual trees. The grain mother, one of Europe's most enduring earth spirits, rules over cultivated land. She obviously represents a survival of prehistoric fertility goddesses.

Trolls

Among the most familiar, but at the same time problematic, of all earth spirits are the Scandinavian trolls. Prominently featured in souvenir shops from Stockholm to Reykjavik, they are grotesquely ugly, but usually reveal a certain whimsical humor. In folktales, for example the famous nineteenth-century Norwegian collection by Peter Christen Asbjørnsen and Jørgen Moe, trolls are typically cast as gigantic ogres with only one redeeming feature: they are usually too stupid to carry out their malicious attacks. Everyone knows the story of "Three Billy Goats Gruff," with the troll under the bridge who waits for the larger billy goat, who—as it turns out—is much too large for the troll to handle.

This view fits into a tradition with roots in Norse mythology where trolls and giants (in many contexts the two words are interchangeable) were the arch enemies of the gods, but often slow-witted. Thor was their principal nemesis, killing many of them with his famous battle hammer. For centuries afterward, folktales featuring trolls often have important events happening on a Thursday (Thor's Day), whereas other days of the week are rarely named.

In addition to being vulnerable to Thor's hammer, trolls had to remain underground during the daytime, because if they were exposed to direct

Garden gnome. Photographed by the author in Bonn, Germany.

sunlight they would either explode or turn to stone. In Iceland, with its many lava flows, it is not difficult to find troll-shaped rocks, which adds credibility to this last belief.

The above-mentioned qualities of trolls are widely known, but they tell only half the story. Parallel to this tradition is one giving trolls a multifaceted role in Scandinavian folklore. An early outside visitor to Sweden, the German Ernst Moritz Arndt, wrote in 1804: "The word *troll* embraces a host of spirits and a mass of witch types.... The name *troll* is very imprecise. As a rule it designates the small forest and mountain spirits that we [Germans], according to popular belief, call the underground people" (Arndt, vol. 3, pp. 7–8). Confirming this view, the pioneering Danish folklorist J. M. Thiele, in his collection *Danmarks Folkesagn* (Denmark's Folk Legends, 1818–23), used "troll folk" as a general heading, encompassing the subcategories "hill folk," "elf folk," and "dwarfs."

Folk legends throughout Scandinavia corroborate this view, with trolls— like the fairies and elves of other countries—playing rolls of many types, even that of a fairy-tale princess. For example, a Swedish legend describes how a man captured a beautiful troll woman by throwing a piece of steel between her and the hill where she resided. Her father, observing what had happened, responded from an opening in the hillside by asking the man if he intended to marry his daughter. Upon hearing an affirmative answer, the father offered generous wedding gifts. The troll kept his promise, giving the bridal pair

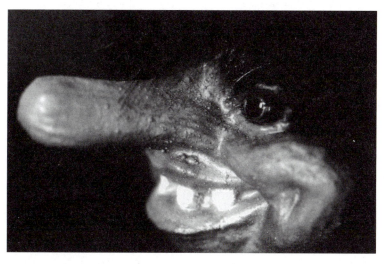

A troll purchased in a souvenir shop in Trondheim, Norway. Photograph by the author.

a large bag of money and numerous copper pots. The man and his troll wife lived happily together, and with time their union was blessed with a number of children (Keightley, pp. 108–109).

Household Spirits

Household and farm spirits form an important subcategory of earth fairies. Typically a single such sprite is bound to a specific domestic building or farm-yard, sometimes for many human generations. They are known by different names: brownie in Scotland, pixie in the west of England, pisky in Cornwall, kobold in Germany, nisse in Denmark, tomte in Sweden, and too many local and dialect names to enumerate. Treated right, they help with chores and generally reward their human hosts with prosperity and good health; but if slighted they can be cruelly vindictive in their reprisals.

In Germany sudden or unexplained wealth is often attributed to a kobold or drake having joined a previously poor household. Drakes, like most crea-tures discussed in this handbook, are shape shifters, and they often gain entry into a household by disguising themselves as cold, wet hens or cats (Gander, pp. 33–39). When an unsuspecting and kind-hearted person car-ries the animal inside to be warmed and dried, the drake establishes himself within the household. He also can assume other shapes, ranging from fiery streaks across the sky to an innocent-looking herdsman applying for work. Once ensconced within the household the drake brings his hosts mixed bless-ings. Frequently mentioned is his ability to gather stores of grain about him, probably from neighbors' barns or unharvested fields. Sometimes the drake presents his hosts with gold. As evidenced by many accounts, neighbors are highly suspicious of wealth attributed to a drake, although simple envy prob-ably contributes to such criticism. Be that as it may, by all accounts a drake's help is demonic in nature, and thus dangerous.

Having a household spirit of any type can be a mixed blessing. Their gen-eral helpfulness is often tempered by mischievous trickery. In a widely dis-tributed family of legends (Christiansen type 7020) the host family grows weary of their supernatural lodger, and they attempt to rid themselves of him by moving to a different house. These stories nearly always conclude with a punch-line ending, giving the unwanted guest the last word.

The Danish account "The Nisse Is Moving Too" is typical: A man who lived in a house occupied by a nisse grew weary of the latter's pranks and thus resolved to move elsewhere. Having already hauled several loads of household goods to the new house, he loaded the cart with the few remaining items, mostly empty tubs and barrels. Turning to say a last farewell to the house, he noticed the nisse comfortably seated in a barrel on the cart. "We're moving today, aren't we!" exclaimed the unwelcome passenger (Thiele, vol. 2, pp. 209–210).

In some instances the plagued man resorts to burning down a house or barn to rid himself of the unwanted guest, but these attempts never succeed. The Grimm brothers tell of a peasant whose barn was inhabited by a kobold whose mischief was no longer tolerable. The man was advised to burn the barn down, so he hauled out all the straw, one cartload at a time. After the last load was removed he locked the kobold inside the barn and set it afire. When the barn was completely ablaze the peasant looked behind him, and there he saw the kobold seated at the rear of the cart. "It was high time that we got out!" shouted the kobold, and then repeated, "It was high time that we got out!" The peasant thus had no choice but to keep the kobold (*German Legends*, no. 73).

Two additional legends about "Unwanted Houseguests" are reproduced under the heading of that name in chapter three.

Water

Traditional cultures everywhere associate water with supernatural beings, and understandably so. Rivers, lakes, and oceans are governed by superhuman forces, constantly changing appearance, and receding or flooding in an often incomprehensible manner. Moreover, water is at the same time life sustaining and life threatening: home to countless living creatures, but a deathtrap for others. As stated above, popular belief explains that among the creatures who thrive there are the spirits who fell into water when cast out of heaven with other fallen angels.

Local stories offer different explanations, but with similar results. According to a Welsh legend, Saint Patrick, originally from Wales, returned to his homeland for a visit, only to be met with insults from his former countrymen for having migrated to Ireland. He responded by transforming his abusers into water creatures, the males into fish and the females into water fairies. To this day Crumlyn Lake is inhabited by their offspring (Sikes, p. 35). John Rhys's claim that most lakes in Wales "were once believed to have had inhabitants of a fairy kind" (p. 582) applies to other regions as well. Lady Gregory quotes one of her Irish informants: "For one [fairy] there's on the land, there's ten on the sea" (p. 13).

The inherent and obvious danger of water has led to supernatural explanations for mishaps of all types, especially death by drowning. A widespread migratory legend, generically titled "The Hour Has Come, but Not the Man" (Christiansen type 4050), depicts a water spirit's right to a human sacrifice each year. Examples from Germany and Wales are reproduced in chapter three. These stories suggest that no human intervention can save an intended victim, once doomed by fate to drown.

Water Bulls and Water Horses

In many instances the sinister water spirit is a shape-shifting creature that can take on almost any appearance, frequently that of a domestic animal. J. F. Campbell cites the example of the water bull, which "is like a common bull, though he is amphibious and supernatural, and has the power of assuming other shapes. . . . There is a water bull in nearly every Scotch loch of any note. Loch Ness is full of them" (vol. 4, p. 300). Also reported on the Isle of Man and in Norway, water bulls often came ashore and caused the death of domestic cows.

Campbell also tells in detail the story of a shape-shifting water horse that played the role of a demon lover (vol. 4, pp. 302–306). His source was the quintessential FOAF (friend of a friend), as modern folklorists playfully have designated such second- and third-hand informants: "The narrator prefaced this story by remarking that it was 'perfectly true,' for he had it from a lobster fisher, who heard it from an old man who witnessed the whole scene."

According to this "perfectly true" story, a servant girl was herding cattle near a loch when a strange man approached and asked her to arrange his hair. She agreed to do this, but took fright when she discovered seaweed growing in his hair. At the first opportunity she fled toward home, with the man—now in the shape of a horse—pursuing her. An old woman saw what was happening and shouted to her to open the bullpen, which she did. The bull attacked the horse, and a fight ensued, not ending until the two animals had driven each other out to sea. The next day the bull's body was found on the shore, but the horse was never seen again.

The Scottish kelpie was a similar shape shifter. Usually seen in the form of a horse, it was known to lure a man to mount it, but then would carry him to his death in a nearby body of water (Keightley, p. 385). Similar creatures were the *njugl* in the Shetland Islands (Nicolson, pp. 58–59), and the *nøkk* in Scandinavia (Kvideland and Sehmsdorf, pp. 252–53). The "Whitsuntide Legend of the Fairy Horses" from Ireland provides an additional example of dangerous animal-shaped beings that inhabit water. Its complete text is printed in chapter three.

Underwater animals are not always evil. There are many legends, especially in Ireland and Wales, depicting cattle and horses that sometimes come ashore and breed with ordinary animals, and often with good results (Rhys, p. 582). The hybrids from these pairings can be vigorous, high-performing animals.

The most famous example of fairy cattle emerging from the sea is the Irish myth of *Bo-Finn, Bo-Ruadh,* and *Bo-Dhu,* the white, the red, and the black cows. The story tells how a mermaid once came ashore and announced the imminent arrival of three sacred cows from beneath the sea. The cows, each a different color, "were destined to fill the land with the most splendid cattle, so that the people should never know want." The mermaid's prophecy came true, and Ireland's cattle have been superior to those of neighboring countries ever since (Wilde, pp. 168–70).

Mermaids, Mermen, and Selkies

The Old English word *mere* (sea) can be compounded with numerous other terms to designate fabled aquatic creatures, with *mermaid* and *merman* being the best known. Indeed, the mermaid's composite human and fish body is a familiar image, but not a universal one. Paracelsus claimed that "water people look like humans, both women and men" (p. 235), a view shared by others as well (Gregory, p. 10; Kuhn and Schwartz, p. 175).

Often referred to as "sea fairies" (Kennedy, p. 109), mermaids and mermen are well known for their romantic entanglements with humans of the opposite sex. These affairs seldom develop into permanent and mutually satisfying relationships. A number of such cases are discussed at length in chapter one. "The Lady of Gollerus" is a well-known Irish legend about marriage between a man and a mermaid. Its full text is printed in chapter three.

A mermaid in a traditional pose. From Richard Huber, *Treasury of Fantastic and Mythological Creatures* (Dover Pictorial Archive).

Selkies (also spelled *silkies*) are a special class of water fairies, native to the oceans surrounding the northernmost British Isles, and extending as far as Iceland. In water they appear as large seals with human features, but they use their sealskins only for transportation to and from their undersea kingdoms, where they live much like humans do on earth. They frequently visit secluded beaches, where they shed their sealskins then dance and frolic in the sand. In a popular group of legends (Christiansen type 4080), a man takes the sealskin of one of the female selkies, thus depriving her of means to return home. From this point forward, the story typically follows the pattern seen in "The Lady of Gollerus," cited in the preceding paragraph.

Undines

Water fairies live in lakes and rivers, as well as in the open sea. The most famous of these are the undines, named by Paracelsus as one of the four classes of elemental beings inhabiting the earth. Although undines have water as their natural home, they function well on land and often marry earthlings. Such spirits are featured in numerous European chapbooks written during the Renaissance, where the heroine is traditionally named Melusine or Melusina. The following account from the Harz Mountains of Germany is typical of the many regional legends about this being:

A knight became lost in the woods, finally coming upon a castle inhab-ited by a beautiful woman, who apparently lived there alone. She gave him shelter, and he fell in love with her, asking her to marry him. She accepted, but only under the condition that every Friday he would allow her to go wherever she wanted, and that he would not follow her. This he promised, and they lived happily together for a long time. One day a stranger came and was given lodging. It was a Friday, and the lady of the house was absent. The husband described his wife's weekly outings, whereupon the guest told him that nothing good could come from such behavior. Alarmed by this remark, the husband set forth to find his wife. He finally discovered her in the cellar, half fish and half human, swimming in a small pond. Seeing her husband, she cast a sad glance at him, and then disappeared. The husband died soon afterward (Ey, pp. 173–76).

Wells and Springs

Fairyland, as noted in the preceding pages, is often deemed to be an under-ground realm. Wells and springs are obvious openings into the earth and can thus serve as gateways to fairyland (Wilde, p. 65). A large number of fairy tales use this motif, giving their heroes and heroines access to fairy realms through wells. The Grimm brothers' "Frau Holle," reprinted in chapter three, is a famous example.

The association of wells with fairies—and also with other earth deities—has led to the veneration of wells. One such place is Clootie Well near the village of Munlochy in Scotland. It is said that this well was originally the home of a fairy, who expected the gift of a piece of cloth (cloot) before allowing a mortal to drink its magic water. Still today the bushes and trees surrounding the well are covered with pieces of cloth left behind by visitors who playfully or seriously continue the ancient custom. Similar traditions are associated with healing wells and springs throughout Europe, although for the most part Christian saints have replaced fairies or pagan deities as the supernatural patrons. The worldwide practice of throwing coins into a fountain for good luck is an obvious survival of the recognition and homage that our ancestors gave to the spirits associated with wells.

Nixes and Nixies

Water sprites throughout Europe are marked by diversity of name, function, and description. Nowhere is this more pronounced than in Germany. A listing of all the regional and dialect names given to supernatural water beings would fill pages. Nix and nixie (male and female) are generic terms that encompass many other designations. In appearance they are often indistinguishable from ordinary humans, except for the wet seams at the bottom of their clothing. They live beneath the waters of deep lakes and rivers, often in places that—in spite of being submerged—closely resemble the habitations of their earthly neighbors. Their acts parallel those of earth fairies throughout Europe. They kidnap children, seduce young men and women, require the services of human midwives, pilfer goods from marketplaces, predict the future, practice shape shifting, and play pranks. In fact, most of their activities have little to do with water, with one important exception: They often cause the death by drowning of unwary humans.

Air

Paracelsus had relatively little to say about sylphs, the elemental beings that he assigned to the air. The folkloric record is similarly sparse, with comparatively few fairy types making their homes in air, especially in relation to the large numbers who live in water or within the earth. This is not to say that terrestrial fairies are earthbound. Fairy cavalcades are often airborne, as is the infamous wild hunt led by Odin. Individual fairies, too, often travel through the air. Peter Pan's companion Tinker Bell is constantly flitting about in the air, and Peter flying away with Wendy and her brothers creates one of the most memorable images in James Barrie's famous story.

Fairies, like witches, can transport themselves through the air astride inanimate objects; but where witches use broomsticks, fairies are more likely to choose the stalk of a bush. Or, like Shakespeare's "airy spirit" Ariel, they can fly about on the back of a bat (*The Tempest,* act 5). In folk narratives fairies are rarely described as having wings, but visual artists regularly portray them with wings, typically shaped like those of a butterfly.

Magic words work also, and these can be learned by humans, as illustrated by the Cornish story, "The Piskies in the Cellar" (Hunt, pp. 88–90): A certain John Sturtridge was walking homeward when he came upon a party of the little people. Hearing one of them shout, "Ho! and away for Par Beach!" he repeated the same cry, then found himself magically transported through the air to the place named. The piskies next cried out, "Ho! and away for Squire Tremain's cellar!" which he also repeated, joining the little people in their raid on the squire's store of drink. He was found there the following morning, muddled by his night of imbibing. John was sentenced to hang, but before the sentence could be carried out, he recalled the magic charm. Shouting "Ho! and away for France!" he disappeared into thin air.

A final group of airborne fairies are the swan maidens, who with the help of feathery robes can fly between earth and distant spheres. Edwin Sidney

Airborne fairy. Woodcut after a drawing by W. H. Brooke, from Thomas Crofton Croker, *Fairy Legends and Traditions* (1826).

Hartland observed: "The myth of the swan maiden is one of the most widely distributed and at the same time one of the most beautiful stories ever evolved from the mind of man" (p. 255). An example of this widespread story is reproduced in chapter three.

Fire

Apart from Paracelsus' salamander, the best-known fairy figure associated with fire is the will-o'-the-wisp, also known by its Latin name *ignis fatuus* (foolish fire) and numerous local names, including jack-o'-lantern. Often explained as the spirits of deceased unbaptized children, these fiery beings were deemed to be malicious (or at best mischievous) creatures that appeared as points or streaks of light on a dark night. Seen at close distance, a will-o'-the-wisp has been described as a human-like creature made of fire from head to toe and having enormously long legs (Kuhn and Schwartz, p. 84). It can appear at sea, where it misleads sailors and fishermen (Gregory, p. 9), but in most cases it lures a confused land wanderer from safe paths. Countless legends depict a hapless (and often intoxicated) traveler struggling homeward on a dark night. Seeing a lantern not far off, he assumes it is being carried by a fellow walker and follows it; but instead of guiding to him safety, the light takes him through swamps and moors, and often to the brink of a cliff. The drunkenness specifically mentioned in many such accounts suggests that a victim's failure to find a safe way home was due more often to the spirit in the drink than one wandering about a field. The spontaneous combustion of marsh gasses provides a rational explanation for the mysterious lights described in these legends.

Many other fairy figures are associated with fire. The Bretons speak of a double apparition named *Sand Yan y Tad* (St. John and Father), carrying at its fingertips five lights, which spin like wheels (Keightley, p. 441). Fairy folk of many descriptions reputedly have set humans' houses and barns afire in revenge for perceived injury or insult (for example, Knoop, p. 79). In a more playful mode, James Barrie's Tinker Bell is introduced to the readers of *Peter Pan* as "a strange light, no bigger than your fist" (ch. 1).

The kobold, a German domestic sprite, was often seen as a wisp of fire leaving or entering a house by way of the chimney. In some regions the kobold is known as a drake (German *Drache*). Both the English and the German words reflect this household spirit's connection with dragons, famous for breathing fire.

Another fiery spirit from Germany is the "burning man," who in some depictions is a ghost from purgatory, but in others is an elemental being with little connection to any Christian beliefs. A similarly ambiguous figure, also well documented in Germany, is the fire rider, a being—sometimes human, sometimes unearthly—who magically can control conflagrations, often extinguishing a house fire simply by walking or riding into or around the burning building. A related apparition with the same name foretells house fires by arriving on the scene wearing a red cap.

APPEARANCE

In chapter one, under the heading "Depictions," I discuss at length the physical appearance of individual fairies. The present discussion is limited to the appearance of entire groups or families, and how physical traits, especially color, correlate with behavior. Fairy observers have never been color blind, and the hue of fairy skin is frequently mentioned, often in a manner that today must be labeled racist. Skin color, according to these views, is a reliable indicator of personality and moral inclination.

One of the earliest commentators to categorize fairy folk by color was Snorri Sturluson, compiler of *The Prose Edda*, one of the primary sourcebooks of Norse mythology. Writing in the early 1220s, Snorri described two families of elves: The light elves, who are "fairer than the sun" inhabit a world called Alfheim; whereas the dark elves are "blacker than pitch" and live down in the earth (p. 26). The light elves have an angelic disposition, and the dark elves—who in many contexts are indistinguishable from dwarfs—are evildoers.

Elsewhere Snorri's simplistic two-color spectrum was further subdivided. Writing in the early twentieth century, A. Haas described four races of underground people that inhabited the Baltic island of Rügen (part of Germany, but with strong Scandinavian ties). Here too skin color is an indicator of behavior:

> The underground people of Rügen were formerly divided into four tribes: the whites, the greens, the browns, and the blacks. The white dwarfs were the royal tribe. They were daintily built, were somewhat mischievous, but were nonetheless good Christians. They lived in the Ralswiek Mountains. Then came the tribe of the green dwarfs, a good-natured people. They were almost as daintily built as the whites and were likewise good Christians. They lived in the vicinity of Zirkow. The tribes of brown and black dwarfs lived up to their names, for they were mean-spirited tricksters with small misshapen figures and over-sized heads. They had no religion, and plagued mankind in every way possible. (pp. 53–54)

DISPOSITION

Humans appear to have a deeply rooted propensity for dichotomies. You are either for me or against me. A decision is either right or wrong. A supernatural power is either good or evil. This tendency manifests itself in our depictions of fairy folk as well. However else we categorize them, we often separate them into groups of good or bad. Perhaps the most famous of these divisions are the Scottish "seelie court" and "unseelie court," from a dialect word designating *blessed*. This division separates fairies into two tribes, one helpful toward humans, the other malicious:

> The good fairies, the seelie court, were well disposed to man, rendering him help in his extremity. They provided bread for the poor householder, and seed corn for the impoverished crofter. Some men invoked their aid in the performance of their daily task.... The bad fairies, the unseelie court, worked much evil. Man must be careful in case he came within their power.... The worst characteristic of the unseelie court was their thieving propensities. They abstracted the goods of mortals and carried them to their subterranean abodes. (McPherson, pp. 98–101)

In other countries commentators made similar mutually exclusive divisions. In Ireland, Lady Wilde observed: "There are two parties amongst the fairy spirits, one a gentle race that loves music and dancing, the other that has obtained power from the devil, and is always trying to work evil" (p. 73). Her compatriot Lady Gregory supported this opinion: "There are two races among the sidhe. One is tall and handsome, gay, and given to jesting and to playing pranks.... The people of the other race are small, malicious, [and] wide-bellied" (p. v). Perhaps the simplest such formulation comes from Germany: "There are two kinds of kobolds: good ones and evil ones" (Temme, p. 57).

Another bipolar division of fairies, but ultimately a more complicated one, is W. B. Yeats' designation of trooping fairies and solitary fairies, based on the observation that fairies—at least those in Ireland—tend either to collect in social groups or to live by themselves. Yeats used this division as the organizing principle for his collection *Fairy and Folk Tales of the Irish Peasantry* (1888).

Trooping fairies live in organized communities, either underground or beneath the sea. They are well known for their singing, circle dances, and cavalcades, and are especially active on the great fairy festivals each year: May Eve (Beltane), Midsummer Eve (summer solstice), and November Eve (Samain). They can be either helpful or harmful to humans. Solitary fairies are mostly harmful to humans, and—as their name indicates—live by themselves. Included in this group are leprechauns and banshees.

FUNCTION

Motifs and Plots

This last category is perhaps the easiest to define, for it describes the acts, rather than the actors. Fairies, it seems, have a limited repertoire of deeds. Their exploits follow patterns that are often predictable, whether performed by a selkie from the Shetland Islands or a forest sprite from Bohemia. That said, there are still far too many standard plots in fairy legends to elucidate them all in a single chapter, so the following selections are but a representative sampling of a much larger whole.

We know about fairies' acts through stories reputedly based on actual experiences and observations. The individual building blocks of such stories are called motifs, and these have been cataloged by the American folklorist Stith Thompson in his six-volume *Motif-Index of Folk-Literature* (1955). He assigns a number to each motif in much the same way that a librarian categorizes books according to a number determined by the Library of Congress or the Dewey Decimal System. This monumental work encompasses many different folklore genres and themes, including fairy lore. Most fairy motifs are listed as subdivisions under the heading F200. The following table, containing references to the visibility of fairies, illustrates how the various subdivisions are organized, each with its own decimal number. Again, this is but a small sampling from a catalog that fills six large volumes.

F235	Visibility of fairies
F235.1	Fairies invisible
F235.2	Fairies visible only at certain times
F235.2.1	Fairies visible only at night
F235.2.2	Fairies visible only at noonday
F235.3	Fairies visible to one person alone
F235.4	Fairies made visible through use of magic object
F235.4.1	Fairies made visible through use of ointment
F235.4.2	Fairies made visible through use of magic soap
F235.4.3	Fairies made visible through use of magic stone on eyes
F235.4.4	Fairies made visible through use of magic water
F235.4.5	Fairies made visible through use of saliva
F235.4.6	Fairies made visible when one carries four-leaf clover
F235.5	Fairies made visible by stepping on certain spot
F235.5.1	Fairies made visible by standing on another's foot
F235.5.2	Fairies made visible when person steps into fairy ring

Numerous additional aspects of fairy lore—always reduced to their simplest terms—are identified and numbered in this motif index.

Motifs are building blocks, elements that can be pieced together in different combinations to construct longer narratives. The resulting stories follow discrete plots, and these too have been described and cataloged by Stith Thompson, following a pattern established by the Finnish folklorist Antti Aarne. Known as the Aarne-Thompson system, this catalog identifies some 2,500 basic plots, assigning to each a type number. However, relatively few of these tales relate specifically to fairy lore. Those that do include types 476* (A Midwife for the Elves), 500 (Guessing the Helper's Name), 503 (The Hunchbacks and the Elves), 503* (Helpful Elves), and 758 (Origin of Elves).

The Aarne-Thompson system was expanded by the Norwegian folklorist Reidar Christiansen to include migratory legends (type numbers 3000–8025), including many dealing with fairies. By way of example, type 6035 legends depict fairies assisting a farmer in his work, and those of type 6045 describe how a drinking cup is stolen from the fairies.

Tasks

In the following pages of this chapter, I identify and discuss a handful of roles typically played by fairies of different types and in different countries. The selection has been somewhat arbitrary, given the variety of activities undertaken by fairies. Each category was chosen because of its universality within the realm of Celtic-Germanic fairy lore.

Bogeys

Adults have long used imaginary fairy-like creatures to frighten children into good behavior. Known generically as bogeys, bogeymen, boogeymen, bugbears, bug-a-boos, and similar names, these spooks are generally of little concern to grownups, but can be terrifying to children.

An unusual (at least by modern standards) statue stands guard in Bern, Switzerland. High on a pedestal at the *Kornhausplatz,* in the center of the old city, stands a dwarf-like ogre, the *Chindlifrässer* (child-eater), surrounded by terrified youngsters. He has captured a half dozen children, who are in his pockets and arms, all awaiting the fate of the one whose head he has taken entirely into his mouth. Since about 1545 this statue has graphically warned Swiss children of the potentially dire consequences of disobedience.

The Swiss are not alone in their use of such primitive psychological pedagogy. Hanns Bächtold-Stäubli, in the index to his *Handwörterbuch des deutschen Aberglaubens* (Handbook of German Superstition), lists no fewer than twenty-eight different supernatural creatures who punish bad German children, often fatally (vol. 4, cols. 1366–74). England too has its share of bogeys and bugbears. In 1584 Reginald Scot cataloged by name the various fairies and spirits used to frighten children of his generation into good behavior. Here is the list, using Scot's original spelling and punctuation:

> In our childhood our mothers maids have so terrified us with … bull beggers, spirits, witches, urchens, elves, hags, fairies, satyrs, pans, faunes, sylens, kit with the cansticke, tritons, centaurs, dwarfes, giants, imps, calcars, conjurors, nymphes, changlings, *Incubus,* Robin good-fellowe, the spoorne, the mare, the man in the oke, the hell waine, the fierdrake, the puckle, Tom thombe, hob gobblin, Tom tumbler, boneles, and such other bugs, that we are afraid of our owne shadowes. (p. 86)

Bogeys often reside in places of potential danger to children. Thus Yorkshire parents formerly convinced their children that a mysterious being named Jenny Green-Teeth or Peg-o'-the-Well lived in nearby bodies of water, and that she would certainly capture and drown any child who approached too closely (Parkinson, pp. 202–203).

Many cultures have counterparts to the European grain mother (called variously *corn mother, rye mother,* and such). Originally a revered deity akin to Demeter, the Greek goddess of agriculture, with time she degenerated into a bogey whose primary function was to frighten children away from cultivated fields. Her name notwithstanding, she is usually portrayed as a very unmotherly type, sometimes with sharp and protruding iron breasts, breasts that kill rather than nurture. One of the many names given to her is the rather indelicate Low German *Tittenwief,* which requires no translation. Her frightening aspect carries from the field into the home, where unruly children are threatened: "Shut your mouth, or the Rye Mother, with her long black tits, will come and take you away!" (Grimm, *German Legends,* no. 90)

Supernatural threats and promises were not limited to children. Throughout Britain brownies, pixies, and Robin Goodfellow served famously as enforcers of household cleanliness. Servants who practiced good housekeeping might expect to find a coin in their shoe the next morning, whereas those guilty of "sluttishness," the fairies' most despised vice, risked pinches and more. Robin Goodfellow speaks for himself in a ballad from Percy's *Reliques of Ancient English Poetry* (vol. 3, pp. 202–203):

> When house or hearth doth sluttish lie,
> I pinch the maidens black and blue;

The bedclothes from the bed pull I,
And lay them naked all to view.
'Twixt sleep and wake,
I do them take,
And on the key-cold floor them throw.
If out they cry,
Then forth I fly,
And loudly laugh out, ho, ho, ho!

Reginald Scot, writing in 1584, wryly claimed that many reported apparitions were actually knaves in white sheets (p. 86). Robin Goodfellow's punishing tricks, especially those involving pinching a sleeping girl then pulling off her bedclothes, probably also belong to this trickster category, and might well be labeled sexual harassment rather than supernatural justice. Nonetheless, a great many accounts do attribute to fairy folk the meting out of deserved punishments and rewards. But the fairies did not continue this system of justice forever. In his famous poem "The Fairies' Farewell" (Gardner, pp. 218–20), written in 1620, the poet Richard Corbet bemoaned the loss of fairy justice:

Farewell, rewards and fairies,
Good housewives now may say,
For now foul sluts in dairies
Do fare as well as they;
And though they sweep their hearths no less
Than maids were wont to do,
Yet who of late for cleanliness
Finds sixpence in her shoe?

Fairy justice is an important component of traditional tales such as "Cinderella" and "Sleeping Beauty." Intervention by fairies rewards the deserving heroes and heroines, but also punishes the wrongdoers. Even Santa Claus, that "jolly old elf," belongs to this tradition, with the promise of desirable presents for good boys and girls, but a stick or a lump of coal for those who have been bad.

Most of the examples in this section fairly obviously belong to fiction rather than belief, especially for mature adults. However, there is much evidence that many fairy beliefs and practices have evolved from ancient myths, which once were accepted with all seriousness. There are many accounts, well into the nineteenth century, of fairies serving as wise and benevolent deities, albeit with a penchant for good-natured mischief. Thus we read that dwarfs inhabiting the famous *Erdmannshöhle* (earth-man's cave) near the village of Hasel in Germany's Black Forest "gave wholesome warnings to the wicked, and helped the good with their work at home and in the field, bringing them prosperity," a condition that existed until the people fell into immorality, causing the dwarfs to abandon them forever (Baader, pp. 17–18).

Smiths

One of the most glaring inconsistencies in European fairy lore is the prescribed use of iron as protection against fairy folk of all kinds, notwithstanding the important role that dwarfs and elves play as smiths. These mutually contradictory claims are found throughout the Germanic-Celtic area, and are documented from the earliest times into the twentieth century.

In a legend from the German island of Rügen, a dwarf made and gave to a peasant an iron plow that the smallest foal, or even a dog, was able to pull through the hardest clay soil with ease (Keightley, pp. 197–200). Grinken the Smith, a dwarf-like wild man who lived underground not far from Münster, Germany, made things from iron so well that they lasted forever. His locks were so ingeniously crafted that no human could open them without the keys (Grimm, *German Legends,* no. 157).

Dwarf smiths feature prominently in Norse mythology, where they are portrayed as working with iron, gold, and other materials. They created golden hair for Thor's wife Sif, after Loki maliciously cut off her natural hair. They constructed the famous ship *Skidbladnir,* which was large enough to carry all the Aesir, fully armed, but designed so ingeniously that when not in use it could be folded up and carried in a pouch. They also made Odin's spear.

The best-known weapon in Norse mythology was Thor's hammer, also crafted by dwarfs. The story of its forging is given in detail in Snorri's *Prose Edda* (pp. 108–109). The dwarf Brokk (whose name means *blacksmith*) worked the bellows while his brother Eitri tended the molten iron. The batch was nearly spoiled because a fly kept stinging Brokk on the eyelids as the work progressed. The fly was actually the shape-shifting demigod Loki, but his attempts to ruin the hammer failed. In the end its only fault was a rather short handle, but otherwise it was a blacksmith's masterpiece. It was totally unbreakable; it would magically return to its owner, no matter how far he threw it; and it could become small enough to fit inside a shirt.

Blacksmithing and fairy lore come together most famously in the legendary lord of elves, Wayland the Smith. Variant spellings of his name include Völund, Weland, Weyland, Welent, Welund, and Wieland. His story is told most completely in the "Lay of Völund" from *The Poetic Edda* (recorded in Iceland in the thirteenth century but based on much older oral tradition). The story opens when Völund, whose skills as a smith were known throughout the northern world, and his two brothers, all sons of a Finnish king, approached

Thor's hammer. From Richard Huber, *Treasury of Fantastic and Mythological Creatures* (Dover Pictorial Archive).

three beautiful women spinning on the shore of a lake. Next to them lay their swanskins, for, reveals the narrator, "they were valkyries." Each woman embraced one of the brothers, and they lived together as married couples for seven years. Then inexplicably the three women flew away. Two brothers left on snowshoes in pursuit of their missing wives, but Völund—hoping that his valkyrie would return—remained home. An unprincipled king captured Völund (whom he called "Lord of Alfs"), lamed him, and then forced him to ply his craft for him. Völund avenged himself by killing two of the king's sons and seducing his daughter. He then made his escape by flying away, using wings that he himself had fashioned in his smithy (pp. 159–67).

Additional information about the legendary smith is contained in the Norse *Thidrik's Saga* (recorded in the mid thirteenth century). Here we discover that he was the son of a giant and the grandson of a mermaid, and that he learned metalworking from the dwarfs. This version of the story too ends when the captive smith creates for himself a set of mechanical wings and flies away. This episode is reminiscent of, and may have been influenced by, the ancient Greek myth of Daedalus, who similarly used self-constructed wings of wax and feathers to escape from the confines of the earth, but then flew too close to the sun. The wax melted and Daedalus plummeted to his death in the sea.

Although in some respects the construction of artificial wings by a skilled human craftsman is a rationalization of traditionally magic events, the northern European accounts cited above—with their background of mermaids, valkyries, swan maidens, dwarfs, and elves—are firmly rooted in fairy lore. Even Völund's Finnish ancestry supports this connection. The medieval Norse referred to the Lapps (who call themselves Sami) as Finns, and this culture has long had a reputation throughout northern Europe for skill in sorcery. Furthermore, a strong tradition exists, especially in the British Isles, suggesting that Lapps are descendants of an ancient fairy race.

Völund, usually spelled Wayland or Weland, is also known in ancient Britain, tales of his exploits having been carried to Britain by the Angles, Saxons, and Jutes. He is mentioned in *Beowulf* and other Anglo-Saxon documents, and his fame lives to this day through the folklore associated with the Neolithic long barrow tomb known as Wayland's Smithy in Oxfordshire. Local tradition dictates that Wayland still inhabits this structure, and if a horse loses its shoe in the vicinity, the rider need only leave the horse and a silver coin at the tomb's entrance. The process is described by a character in Sir Walter Scott's novel *Kenilworth* (ch. 10):

> You must tie your horse to that upright stone that has the ring in't, and then you must whistle three times, and lay me down your silver groat on that other flat stone, walk out of the circle, sit down on the west side of that little thicket of bushes, and take heed you look neither to right nor to left for ten minutes, or so long as you shall hear the hammer clink, and whenever it ceases, say your prayers for the space you could tell a hundred—or count over a hundred, which will do as well—and then come into the circle; you will find your money gone and your horse shod.

Similar legends are told in Scandinavia and Germany. For example, a troll reputedly has his smithy within a mound in the Danish parish of Bur. Anyone needing a piece of iron forged must only leave the iron and a silver shilling atop the mound, speaking the forging instructions aloud. The next morning the coin will have disappeared and the completed work will be there in its place (Thiele, vol. 2, pp. 146–47). Similarly, farmers near Sundwig in northern Germany reportedly placed broken implements, together with appropriate payment, at the mouth of a certain cave. The following morning the items would be there, now flawlessly repaired (Kuhn, vol. 1, p. 148). Near Iburg in northern Germany, the underground people formerly did blacksmith work under like circumstances, and for very little money. However, once a prankster left manure instead of the expected coin, and since then the underground people there have done no more black-smithing for humans (Kuhn and Schwartz, p. 312).

Guardians of Hidden Treasure

Fairies and ghosts are associated everywhere with hidden treasure. The most famous guardian of treasure in German folklore is the dwarf Alberich, the keeper of the famous horde of the Nibelungs, also known as the Volsungs (*Nibelungenlied,* ch. 3). This horde included the fated Ring of Andvari (*Saga of the Volsungs,* ch. 14), thought by some to have been the inspiration for the One Ring in J.R.R. Tolkien's *Lord of the Rings.* Jacob Grimm, a gifted philologist, theorized that the name Alberich evolved through the forms Alberon and Auberon (both French) to Oberon in English (*Deutsche Mythologie,* vol. 1, pp. 374–75). Thus it can be argued that the mythological treasure keeper of the ancient Germans was also the fairy king of medieval and Renaissance England.

Legendry abounds in tales of smaller hordes—akin, for example, to the pot of gold at the end of the rainbow—watched over by individual trolls or dwarfs. One such story, from Sweden, tells how a farmer tricked a troll into revealing his treasure. He first filled a large kettle with old horseshoes and other metal junk, then built a fire, fixing it so the light would shine above the kettle. Thinking that it must be glistening gold, the troll came to investigate. When he saw what was actually there, he said to the farmer, who was standing nearby, "That's nothing to shine a light over! Come with me, and you'll see something different." He took the farmer to his own treasure, a kettle filled with gold and silver. Seizing the opportunity, the farmer threw his knife into the kettle. The presence of steel deprived the troll of his power over the horde, so the farmer was able to claim it for himself, and he was wealthy for the rest of his life (Lindow, pp. 75–76).

The most famous European treasure keepers are the Irish leprechauns, who "know all the secrets of hidden treasure" (Wilde, p. 60). Usually depicted as very small men with wrinkled faces and wearing leather aprons, these wights are also known as shoemakers. The treasures guarded by them are usually considered to be their own savings, a surprising turn, given that cobblers are rarely known for their wealth. However, the rules and expectations of human society do not necessarily apply in fairyland.

Unlike the Swedish troll described above, leprechauns are virtually never tricked into giving up their treasures. From the evidence of numerous legends, it is not overly difficult to capture a leprechaun, but nearly impossible to outwit one. Two patterns emerge in these tales. "The Kildare Lurikeen," reproduced

Leprechaun. Illustration by John D. Batten,
from Joseph Jacobs, *Celtic Fairy Tales*
(1892).

in chapter three, represents the first. Here the captive escapes by diverting the
attention of his captor. Tradition dictates that taking one's eye from a captured
leprechaun for even an instant will give him the opportunity to escape.

In tales following the second pattern, the captor does succeed in tricking
or forcing the leprechaun to reveal the location of buried treasure, say beneath
a particular bush in a field filled with bushes of the same kind. The human,
filled with anticipation, releases the leprechaun. Having no digging tool at
hand, he marks the spot by tying one of his garters around the bush, then
rushes home to fetch a spade. Upon his return he discovers that every bush in
the large field has an identical garter tied around it. An exemplary tale of this
type is "The Field of Boliauns" (Croker, vol. 1, pp. 178–83).

Setting and Predicting the Future

One of the most time-honored and widespread functions of fairy folk is
to foresee—or in some instances to predetermine—the future. The Fates of
ancient Greece and Rome were three goddesses who set, already at the time
of birth, a person's lifespan and his or her allocation of future suffering. Their
collective name has given us not only the English word *fate,* but also—by way
of Latin and French—the word *fairy.* Following this tradition, the heroine of

"Sleeping Beauty" (Aarne-Thompson type 410), one of the world's best-loved fairy tales, is blessed soon after her birth by fairies or wise women. Typically, as in the versions by the Grimm Brothers and Charles Perrault, most of the fairies bestow positive blessings, but one of them delivers a curse, resulting in the famous 100-year sleep.

Other legendary and mythical figures are attended to at birth as well, most famously the British King Arthur. As recorded in about 1200 by the Middle English poet Layamon, at his birth Arthur was received by elves, who blessed him with a glorious future. In modern English:

> So soon he came on earth,
> Elves received him.
> They enchanted that child
> With magic most strong.
> They gave him might
> To be the best of all knights.
> They gave him another thing
> That he should be a rich king.
> They gave him the third
> That he should long live.
> They gave to that kingly child
> Virtues most good.
> That he was most generous
> Of all men alive.
> This the elves him gave (Keightley, p. 321).

Helgi—not well known in the English-speaking world, but a great hero in Norse mythology—was similarly blessed. As we read in *The Saga of the Volsungs* (ch. 8): "When Helgi was born, Norns came and set his destiny, saying that he would become the most famous of all kings." The Norns, like the Greek and Roman Fates, were originally three in number. Their names were Urd, Verdandi, and Skuld (Past, Present, and Future). As Snorri recorded in *The Prose Edda* (p. 44): "There are, however, more Norns, those that come to every child that is born in order to shape its life, and these are beneficent, others belong to the family of the elves, and a third group belongs to the family of the dwarfs."

Traditional beliefs in northern Europe identified a number of other supernatural beings whose primary function was to govern or predict the future. Designated by different names—fetch, wraith, doppelgänger, co-walker, and others—these entities were normally attached to a single individual and made an appearance only in premonition of an imminent life-changing event, most often death itself. These personal spirits are ill defined, but their association with Norns (some of whom were descendents of elves and dwarfs) obviously attaches them to fairy lore.

The banshees of Ireland play a similar role. Like the Fates and the Norns, they too are female. According to most traditions a banshee is connected to a particular family, and she manifests herself, usually by wailing loudly, when a member of the family is about to die. In the words of one commentator: "She may be seen at night as a shrouded woman, ... lamenting with veiled face" (Wilde, pp. 135–37).

Other fairy types play the same role, but only as part of a larger repertoire. For example, will-o'-the-wisps, whose primary activity is to lead unwary travelers astray, also have been known to predict death (Kuhn, vol. 2, p. 23). One of the most famous death predictions by a fairy is described in *The Nibelungenlied*, written in Bavaria or Austria in the early 1200s. A band of warriors en route from Burgundy to Hungary came upon some water fairies bathing in the Danube. Hagen, one of the Burgundians (also called Nibelungs) stole their clothes. One of the fairies offered to predict the outcome of their visit to Hungary, if Hagen would return their clothes. He agreed, but was dissatisfied with her prophecy: "Not one of you shall survive there apart from the king's chaplain." To prove her wrong, while they were ferrying across the Danube Hagen threw the chaplain overboard and attempted to hold him under the water. Although the chaplain

Banshee. Woodcut after a drawing by W. H. Brooke, from Thomas Crofton Croker, *Fairy Legends and Traditions* (1826).

could not swim, he was helped by the hand of the Lord, and he reached dry land safely. Needless to say, the chaplain did not continue onward with the Nibelungs, and it also goes without saying that the rest of the water fairy's predictions came true as well. In Hungary the Nibelungs entered into a great battle with King Etzel (better known as Attila the Hun), and not one of them survived (chs. 25, 38–39).

Fairies are also able to transfer their powers of prophecy to ordinary mortals, as evidenced by the Scottish legend of Thomas Rymer, also known as True Thomas, a historical person who reputedly was carried to fairyland by the Queen of Elfland. Upon his departure she blessed him that henceforth he would be able to speak only the truth. He protested, wisely seeing that such a gift would make diplomatic conversation quite difficult, if not impossible. She gave it to him anyway, and as a consequence, from that time onward whatever he said about the future became an accurate prophecy. The complete text of a ballad relating this famous story is reprinted in chapter three.

WORKS CITED

Aarne, Antti, and Stith Thompson. *The Types of the Folktale.* Helsinki: Suomalainen Tiedeakatemia, 1961.

Arndt, Ernst Moritz. *Reise durch Schweden im Jahr 1804.* 4 vols. Berlin: Lange, 1806.

Baader, Bernhard. *Volkssagen aus dem Lande Baden.* Karlsruhe: Herder, 1852.

Bächtold-Stäubli, Hanns. *Handwörterbuch des deutschen Aberglaubens.* 10 vols. Berlin: de Gruyter, 1927–1942.

Campbell, J. F. *Popular Tales of the West Highlands.* 4 vols. London: Gardner, 1890–93.

Christiansen, Reidar. *The Migratory Legends.* Helsinki: Suomalainen Tiedeakatemia, 1958.

Croker, Thomas Crofton. *Fairy Legends and Traditions of the South of Ireland.* 3 vols. London: Murray, 1825–28.

Ey, August. *Harzmärchenbuch; oder, Sagen und Märchen aus dem Oberharze.* Stade: Steudel, 1862.

Gander, Karl. *Niederlausitzer Volkssagen.* Berlin: Deutsche Schriftsteller-Genossenschaft, 1894.

Gardner, Helen. *The New Oxford Book of English Verse.* Oxford: Oxford UP, 1972.

Gregory, Lady Isabelle Augusta. *Visions and Beliefs in the West of Ireland.* New York and London: Putnam, 1920.

Grimm, Jacob. *Deutsche Mythologie.* 3 vols. Frankfurt am Main: Ullstein, 1981. First published 1835.

Grimm, Jacob and Wilhelm. *The German Legends of the Brothers Grimm.* Trans. Donald Ward. 2 vols. Philadelphia: Institute for the Study of Human Issues, 1981.

Haas, A. *Rügensche Sagen und Märchen.* Stettin: Burmeister, 1903.

Hartland, Edwin Sidney. *The Science of Fairy Tales: An Inquiry into Fairy Mythology.* London: Scott, 1891.

Hunt, Robert. *Popular Romances of the West of England.* London: Hotten, 1871.

Jacobs, Joseph. *Celtic Fairy Tales.* London: Nutt, 1892.

Keightley, Thomas. *The Fairy Mythology.* London: Bohn, 1850.

Kennedy, Patrick. *Legendary Fictions of the Irish Celts.* London: Macmillan, 1891.

Knoop, Otto. *Volkssagen, Erzählungen, Aberglauben, Gebräuche und Märchen aus dem östlichen Hinterpommern.* Poznan, Poland: Jolowicz, 1885.

Kuhn, Adalbert, and Wilhelm Schwartz. *Norddeutsche Sagen, Märchen und Gebräuche.* Leipzig: Brockhaus, 1848.

Kuhn, Adalbert. *Sagen, Gebräuche und Märchen aus Westfalen.* 2 vols. Leipzig: Brockhaus, 1859.

Kvideland, Reimund, and Henning K. Sehmsdorf. *Scandinavian Folk Belief and Legend.* Minneapolis, U of Minnesota P, 1988.

Lindow, John. *Swedish Legends and Folktales.* Berkeley: U of California P, 1978.

McPherson, J. M. *Primitive Beliefs in the North-East of Scotland.* London: Longmans, Green, and Co., 1929.

Nibelungenlied, The, trans. A. T. Hatto. London: Penguin, 1969.

Nicolson, John. *Some Folk-Tales and Legends of Shetland.* Edinburgh: Allan, 1920.

Paracelsus [Theophrastus von Hohenheim]. *Four Treatises.* Ed. Henry E. Sigerist. Baltimore: Johns Hopkins UP, 1996.

Parkinson, Thomas. *Yorkshire Legends and Traditions.* London: Stock, 1888.

Percy, Thomas. *Reliques of Ancient English Poetry.* 3 vols. London: Sonneschein, Lebas, and Lowrey, 1886. First published 1765.

Poetic Edda, The. Transl. Lee M. Hollander. Austin: U of Texas P, 1988.

Rhys, John. *Celtic Folklore: Welsh and Manx.* Oxford: Oxford UP, 1901.

Saga of the Volsungs, The. Trans. Jesse L. Byock. Berkeley: U of California P, 1990.

Scot, Reginald. *The Discoverie of Witchcraft.* New York: Dover, 1972. First published 1584.

Sikes, Wirt. *British Goblins: Welsh Folk-Lore, Fairy Mythology, Legends, and Traditions.* Boston: Osgood, 1881.

Snorri Sturluson. *The Prose Edda.* Berkeley: U of California P, n.d.

Temme, J.D.H. *Die Volkssagen der Altmark.* Berlin: Nicolai, 1839.

Thiele, J. M. *Danmarks Folkesagn.* 3 vols. Copenhagen: Rosenkilde og Bagger, 1968.

Thompson, Stith. *Motif-Index of Folk-Literature: A Classification of Narrative Elements in Folktales, Ballads, Myths, Fables, Mediaeval Romances, Exempla, Fabliaux, Jest-Books, and Local Legends.* Revised edition. 6 vols. Bloomington: Indiana UP, 1955.

Wilde, Lady Francesca. *Ancient Legends, Mystic Charms, and Superstitions of Ireland.* London: Chatto and Windus, 1919. First published 1887.

Yeats, W. B. *Fairy and Folk Tales of Ireland.* New York: Macmillan, 1983. Includes *Fairy and Folk Tales of the Irish Peasantry,* first published 1888, and *Irish Fairy Tales,* first published 1892.

Three
Examples and Texts

INTRODUCTION

The essence of fairy mythology lies in the ability of its stories to elicit and maintain credibility in spite of, or perhaps because of, their miraculous contents. Traditionally told by ordinary people, these legends claim to be true accounts of extraordinary events experienced, if not by the narrators themselves, then at least by members of their own class: friends of friends, and relatives of relatives. The texts reproduced below exemplify a vast body of such tales, most of which were first committed to print in the nineteenth century, following many centuries of oral transmission and preservation. For countless generations these stories survived and grew without the sponsorship of church and state and without the marketing of publishers and booksellers, because they addressed some of life's most difficult questions. They deal with the apparent arbitrariness of many common experiences, especially negative ones, such as poverty, infidelity, sickness, and death. However, they rarely offer simplistic explanations and solutions. The fairies believed to be behind such events were everywhere known to be capricious, but they were at least approachable and somehow very humanlike. In the end, life was still a mystery, but many of the inexplicable powers that directed it were close to home.

With few exceptions the following tales traditionally were presented as authentic experiences to listeners who sincerely believed in their basic premise: that we are surrounded by unseen beings who greatly influence our well-being. In some instances the storylines have been dressed up—made more literary—by well-meaning editors. For example, Thomas Crofton Croker obviously had English book buyers in mind as he formulated his stylized tale "The Lady of Gollerus," which is based on a simple legend told artlessly throughout Europe. Similarly, the anonymous "Fairy Grove" was created for a specific commercial niche, the growing market for children's books. But it is not pure fabrication, consisting instead almost entirely of motifs found in a once-believed mythology: abduction by fairies, accelerated passage of time in fairyland, fairies' insistence on secrecy, and others.

A common feature of fairy legends is their connection to a specific place, and this quality is shared by most of the following accounts. They are not set in a far-away land, but rather at a familiar place still known. At their best fairy legends are too good to stay in one locale. They migrate and assume new frameworks but keep intact their essence and their basic storylines. To illustrate this phenomenon I present the stories in this chapter in pairs, or even in groups of three or four, usually from different places, but still representing very similar beliefs.

ORIGINS

Angels Cast from Heaven (Bohemia)

When God cast out the arrogant angels from heaven, they became the evil spirits that plague mankind, tormenting us and inflicting us with harm. The ones who fell into hell and into caves and abysses became devils and death-maidens. However, those who fell onto the earth became kobolds, imps, dwarfs, thumblings, alps, noon-and-evening-ghosts, and will-o'-the-wisps. Those who fell into the forests became the wood-spirits who live there: the hey-men, the wild-men, the forest-men, the wild-women, and the forest-women. Finally, those who fell into the water became water spirits: water men, mermaids, and merwomen.

- Josef Virgil Grohmann, *Sagen-Buch von Böhmen und Mähren* (Prague: Calve, 1863), p. 108.

- The German names of the spirits mentioned are: *Teufel, Todmädchen, Kobolde, Schrätlein, Zwerge, Daumlinge, Alpe, Mittags- und Abendgespenster, Irrlichter, Waldgeister, Hemänner, wilde Männer, Waldmänner, wilde Weiber, Waldfrauen, Wassergeister, Wassermänner, Meerjungfern, Meerfrauen.* Grohmann does not give this piece a title.

- The historical Kingdom of Bohemia is currently part of the Czech Republic.

The Genesis of the Hidden People (Iceland)

A traveler once lost his way and knew not whither to turn or what to do. At last, after wandering about for some time, he came to a hut that he had never seen before; and on his knocking at the door, an old woman opened it and invited him to come in, which he gladly did.

Inside, the house seemed to be a clean and good one. The old woman led him to the warmest room, where were sitting two young and beautiful girls. Besides these, no one else was in the house. He was well received and kindly treated and, having eaten a good supper, was shown to bed.

He asked whether one of the girls might stay with him, as his companion for the night, and his request was granted.

And now wishing to kiss her, the traveler turned towards her and placed his hand upon her; but his hand sank through her, as if she had been of mist, and though he could well see her lying beside him, he could grasp nothing but the air.

So he asked what this all meant, and she said, "Be not astonished, for I am a spirit. When the devil, in times gone by, made war in heaven, he, with all his armies, was driven into outer darkness. Those who turned their eyes to look after him as he fell were also driven out of heaven; but those who were neither for nor against him were sent to the earth and commanded to dwell there in the rocks and mountains. These are called elves and hidden people. They can live in company with none but their own race. They do either good or evil, which they will, but what they do they do thoroughly. They have no bodies as you other mortals, but can take a human form and be seen of men when they wish. I am one of these fallen spirits, and so you can never hope to embrace me."

To this fate the traveler yielded himself and has handed down to us this story.

- Jón Arnason, *Icelandic Legends,* trans. George E. J. Powell and Eiríkur Magnússon (London: Bentley, 1864), pp. 20–21. Translation slightly revised.

The Underground People (Frisian Islands)

The Lord Jesus came one day to a house where a woman lived who had five beautiful and five ugly children. She hid the five ugly children in the cellar. The Lord Jesus asked her where her other children were. The woman said, "I do not have any more children."

Then the Lord Jesus cursed the five ugly children, saying: "That which is beneath shall remain beneath, and that which is above shall remain above!"

When the woman returned to the cellar, her five ugly children had disappeared. The underground people are their descendants.

- J.G.Th. Grässe, *Sagenbuch des Preussischen Staats,* vol. 1 (Glogau: Flemming, 1871), p. 1092. Aarne-Thompson folktale type 758.

- This legend is from Amrum, one of the North Frisian Islands belonging to Germany.

The First Fairies (Wales)

In our Savior's time there lived a woman whose fortune it was to be possessed of nearly a score of children, and as she saw our blessed Lord approach her dwelling, being ashamed of being so prolific, and that he might not see them all, she concealed about half of them closely, and after his departure, when she went in search of them, to her great surprise found they were all gone. They never afterwards could be discovered, for it was supposed that as a punishment from heaven for hiding what God had given her, she was deprived of them, and it is said these, her offspring, have generated the race called fairies.

- Wirt Sikes, *British Goblins: Welsh Folk-Lore, Fairy Mythology, Legends, and Traditions* (Boston: Osgood, 1881), pp. 133–34. Aarne-Thompson folktale type 758. Sikes does not give this piece a title.

PROSPECTS FOR SALVATION

The Fairy and the Bible Reader (Scotland)

In a Ross-shire narrative, a beautiful green lady is represented as appearing to an old man reading the Bible and seeking to know if for such as her Holy Scripture held out any hope of salvation. The old man spoke kindly to her; but said that in these pages there was no mention of salvation for any but the sinful sons of Adam. She flung her arms over her head, screamed, and plunged into the sea.

- J. F. Campbell, *Popular Tales of the West Highlands,* vol. 2 (London: Gardner, 1890), p. 75. Christiansen migratory legend type 5050.

The Water Nymph (Sweden)

About a mile northwest from Järna Church was located, at one time, a water mill, Snöåqvarn, belonging to the parishioners of Nås.

One Sunday morning, before the church of Järna had a priest of its own, the chaplain of Nås set out for that place and had just arrived at the mill, when he saw a water man sitting in the rapids below it, playing on a fiddle a psalm from a psalm book.

"What good do you think your playing will do you?" said the priest. "You need expect no mercy!"

Sadly the figure ceased playing and broke his fiddle in pieces, whereupon the priest regretted his severe condemnation and again spoke, "God knows, maybe, after all."

"Is that so?" exclaimed the man in joy. "Then I'll pick up my pieces and play better and more charmingly than before."

- Herman Hofberg, *Swedish Fairy Tales,* trans. W. H. Myers (Chicago: Conkey, 1893), pp. 194–95. Christiansen migratory legend type 5050.

- Note in the original text: The water nymphs are noted musicians, their music usually being in a plaintive strain and expressing a longing to be released on the day of judgment. Sometimes, but not so often, they appear in the folklore as the capricious rulers of the streams that they inhabit.

- The places named in this legend are in the province of Dalarna.

FAIRYLAND

The Enchanted Isle (Isle of Man)

Out under the Irish Sea, fifteen or sixteen miles southwest of the Calf, there is an enchanted isle. Long, long ago it was on the surface of the water—that was in the days when Manannan ruled in Man—but when Saint Patrick drove Manannan and his men from the island in the form of three-legged creatures, they came upon this isle. Manannan dropped it to the bottom of the sea, and they were seen no more.

Now it is the home of Manannan Mac y Leirr, Son of the Sea, and he rules it as he used to rule Man. But once in seven years, when Old May Day is on a Sunday, the isle may be seen. It rises up from the sea just before sunrise, like a beautiful vision, and Manannan looks once more at Ellan Vannin [Manx Gaelic for *Isle of Man*]. The hills of the enchanted isle are green; white foam rings it round; and if you are near enough you may see the tossing arms and golden hair of the mermaids by the water's edge washing their glittering jewels, and hear the singing of birds, and smell the fragrant scent of flowers. But as the first rays of the sun rest upon its highest hills, it sinks into the deep, deep sea.

- Sophia Morrison, *Manx Fairy Tales* (London: Nutt, 1911), pp. 121–22.
- The Isle of Man's flag depicts three human legs joined at the thighs like spokes in a wheel.

The Green Isles of the Ocean (Wales)

The people of Pembrokeshire were for a long time puzzled to know where the fairies, or the Children of Rhys the Deep, as they are called in Little

England beyond Wales, lived. They used to attend the markets at Milford Haven and other places regularly. They made their purchases without speaking, laid down their money, and departed, always leaving the exact sum required, which they seemed to know without asking the price of anything. A certain Gruffydd ab Einion was wont to supply them with more corn than anybody else, and there was one special butcher at Milford Haven upon whom they bestowed their patronage exclusively. To ordinary eyes they were invisible, but some keen-sighted persons caught glimpses of them at the markets. No one, however saw them coming or going, and great was the curiosity as to where they lived, for even fairies must make their home somewhere.

One day Gruffydd ab Einion was walking about St. David's churchyard, when he saw islands far out at sea where he had never observed land before. "Ah!" he said, "there are the Green Isles of Ocean, *Gwerddonau Llion,* about which the poets sing. I will go to see them."

He started to go down to the seashore to get a nearer view, but the islands disappeared. He went back to the place where he had seen the vision; he could again see the islands quite distinctly, with houses dotted here and there among green fields. Now, Gruffydd was a very acute man; he cut the turf from which he espied the islands, and took it down to a boat. He stood upon it and, setting sail, before long landed on the shore of one of the islands.

The fairies welcomed him warmly and, after showing him all the wonders of their home, sent him back loaded with presents. They made him, however, leave behind the enchanted turf, and pointed out an underground passage by which he could come to visit them. He continued to be a great friend of Rhys the Deep's children as long as he lived, and the gold they presented him with made him the richest man in West Wales.

- W. Jenkyn Thomas. *The Welsh Fairy Book* (London: Unwin, [1908]), pp. 91–92. Christiansen migratory legend type 4075.

Jemmy Doyle in the Fairy Palace (Ireland)

My father was once coming down Scollagh Gap on a dark night, and all at once he saw, right before him, the lights coming from ever so many windows of a castle and heard the shouts and laughing of people within. The door was wide open, and in he walked; and there on the spot where he had often drunk a tumbler of bad beer, he found himself in a big hall and saw the king and queen of the fairies sitting at the head of a long table, and hundreds of people, all grandly dressed, eating and drinking. The clothes they had on them were of an old fashion, and there were harpers and pipers by themselves up in a gallery, and playing the most delightful old Irish airs. There was nothing to be seen but rich silk dresses, and pearls, and diamonds on the gentlemen and ladies, and rich hangings on the walls, and lamps blazing.

The queen, as soon as she saw my father, cried out, "Welcome, Mr. Doyle. Make room there for Mr. Doyle and let him have the best at the table. Hand Mr. Doyle a tumbler of punch, that will be strong and sweet. Sit down, Mr. Doyle, and make yourself welcome."

So he sat down and took the tumbler, and just as he was going to taste it, his eye fell on the man next him, and he was an old neighbor that was dead twenty years. Says the old neighbor, "For your life, don't touch bit nor sup." The smell was very nice, but he was frightened by what the dead neighbor said, and he began to notice how ghastly some of the fine people looked when they thought he was not minding them.

So his health was drunk, and he was pressed by the queen to fall to, but he had the sense to take the neighbor's advice and only spilled the drink down between his coat and waistcoat.

At last the queen called for a song, and one of the guests sang a very inde- cent one in Irish. He often repeated a verse of it for us, but we didn't know the sense. At last he got sleepy and recollected nothing more, only the rubbing of his legs against the bushes in the knoc (field of gorse) above our place in Cromogue; and we found him asleep next morning in the haggard, with a scent of punch from his mouth. He told us that we would get his knee-buckles on the path at the upper end of the knoc, and there, sure enough, they were found. Heaven be his bed!

- Patrick Kennedy. *Legendary Fictions of the Irish Celts,* 2nd ed. (London: Macmillan, 1891), pp. 104–105. Kennedy's source: "Mrs. K."

ABDUCTED MUSICIANS

Fiddler Lux from Buttwil (Switzerland)

Fiddler Lux (Lukas) had played until midnight at a wedding in the Lucerne village of Hitzkirch and was making his way back to his home village of Buttwil in Aargau. The night was black, and the thick beech forest at the base of Mount Lindenberg, over which his homeward path led, was darker than usual. In the middle of the forest lies the *Geissenrain,* a hill where it is said that a magic castle with all its treasures is buried. The few too many glasses of wedding wine that Lux had consumed gave him brave thoughts, so arriving at this place in the woods, he said, "If I only knew how to get in there, I would certainly fill my pockets."

"Just come with me!" answered a dwarf, who suddenly stood before him. "My people are waiting inside, and you must play for them," continued the dwarf, "but be careful not to make any unreasonable demands when afterward they ask you about your fee!"

Lukas acknowledged what had been said and immediately followed after his little leader. Although he knew the forest well, he had never before seen such eerie paths. They went through the thickest undergrowth, which separated to two sides, as if blown by the wind. Finally they arrived at a brightly lit door in the side of a cliff. It opened by itself, then closed itself behind them. After walking through decorated and brightly lit rooms, they came to a large hall that magnificently glistened as though it were illuminated by a sun. Ladies and gentlemen in old-fashioned costumes promenaded friendlily about.

At a signal from the leader, Lux began to play. The group took up their dance positions, then proceeded to dance more daintily and with better manners than the fiddler had seen all the days of his life. Furthermore, his instrument's tone became more and more magnificent. Dance tunes without end came to him, until finally he himself became enraptured by his own playing. Then suddenly a tall skeleton appeared before him and asked him how much he wanted to be paid. Wisely remembering the earlier warning, the fiddler silently and respectfully held out his hat. The skeleton filled it to the brim with coal. Then the dwarf appeared again and forthwith led the fiddler outside the hall and the mountain.

Now alone in the dark, it was only with difficulty that he found his way back to the footpath without breaking his fiddle against the tree trunks. He finally arrived at his hut, and only then did he notice how heavy the supposed pieces of coal were pressing down against his head. Angrily, he emptied them out in the grass, then went to bed. Tired and out of sorts because of the miserly payment, he slept until late the next day. Finally hunger awakened him, and, as was his custom, he started out for nearest tavern. But when he put on his hat, a beautiful gold coin fell out of its lining and dropped ringing to the floor.

Only now did he understand what his payment had been. Immediately he ran to the front of his house where yesterday, with curses, he had emptied his hat. Still lying there was the entire heap—of coal. Returning to the woods, he long sought yesterday's footpath, but he never again found it. And neither did he ever again find the door or the castle.

- Ernst L. Rochholz, *Schweizersagen aus dem Aargau,* vol. 1, (Aarau: Sauerländer, 1856), no. 221, pp. 311–12).

- The places named in this legend are in northeastern Switzerland.

Touching the Elements (Shetland Islands)

A fiddler belonging to Yell was waylaid and carried off by the trows while on his way to supply music to a Halloween gathering that was being held in a neighboring district. After playing for some considerable time he was allowed to depart and immediately proceeded homewards. When he came to his house, however, he saw with amazement that the roof was off, the walls decayed and crumbling into ruins, and the floor grown over with rank grass. He questioned the neighbors, but they were utter strangers to him and could cast no glimmer of light on the remarkable situation. The place had been in that ruinous condition all their time, they said. He sought out the oldest inhabitant, but even he had no recollection of anyone staying in the place, but he did remember hearing a tale to the effect that at one time the *guidman* [master] of that house had mysteriously disappeared and never returned. It was commonly supposed that the hill-folk had taken him.

The fiddler, of course, knew no one and had nowhere to go, and when the old man asked him to spend the night at his house, he very gladly accepted the invitation. It so happened that the following day was Sacrament Sunday, and they both went to church. The fiddler asked to be permitted to communicate. This request was granted, but no sooner did he touch the "elements" [bread and wine of the Eucharist] than he crumbled into dust.

- John Nicolson, *Some Folk-Tales and Legends of Shetland* (Edinburgh: Allan, 1920), p. 14.
- Yell is one of the Shetland Islands, just north of Mainland, the largest island in the chain.

CAPTURING A FAIRY

Krachöhrle, Where Are You? (Germany)

In the little valley between Wehr and Hasel there was a hole in the ground where a man thought there might be a badger. He turned his dog loose into the hole, then held an open sack next to the opening. Before long something jumped into the sack, which the man immediately tied shut, then lifting it to his back, he went on his way.

Suddenly from nearby a dwarf called out, "Krachöhrle, where are you?"

"On his back, in the sack!" replied a voice from inside the sack.

Then the man knew that instead of a badger he had captured a dwarf, and without delay he set him free.

- Bernhard Baader, *Neugesammelte Volkssagen aus dem Lande Baden* (Karlsruhe: Gessner, 1859), no. 16, pp. 11–12. Christiansen migratory legend type 6010.
- Wehr and Hasel are towns in southwest Germany's Black Forest, near the Swiss border. A prime tourist attraction nearby is the *Erdmannshöhle* (gnome's cavern), rich in folklore about the underground people.

A Fairy Caught (Cornwall)

The following, communicated to me on the 8th of August [1870], is too good to be lost. I therefore give it in my correspondent's own words:

I heard last week of three fairies having been seen in Zennor very recently. A man who lived at the foot of Trendreen hill, in the valley of Treridge, I think, was cutting furze on the hill. Near the middle of the day he saw one of the small people, not more than a foot long, stretched at full length and fast asleep, on a bank of griglans (heath), surrounded by high brakes of furze. The man took off his furze cuff and slipped the little man into it without his waking up, went down to the house, took the little fellow out of the cuff on the hearthstone, when he awakened and seemed quite pleased and at home, beginning to play with the children, who were well pleased with the small body and called him Bobby Griglans.

The old people were very careful not to let Bob out of the house, or be seen by the neighbors, as he promised to show the man where the crocks of gold were buried on the hill. A few days after he was brought from the hill, all the neighbors came with their horses (according to custom) to bring home the winter's reek [pile] of furze, which had to he brought down the hill in trusses on the backs of the horses. That Bob might be safe and out of sight, he and the children were shut up in the barn. Whilst the furze carriers were in to dinner, the prisoners contrived to get out, to have a "courante" [dance] round the furze reek, when they saw a little man and woman, not much larger than Bob, searching into every hole and corner among the trusses that were dropped round the unfinished reek. The little woman was wringing her hands and crying, "O my dear and tender Skilly-widden, wherever canst ah (thou) be gone to? Shall I ever east eyes on thee again?"

"Go 'e back," says Bob to the children. "My father and mother are come here too." He then cried out, "Here I am, mammy!" By the time the words were out of his mouth, the little man and woman, with their precious Skilly-widden, were nowhere to be seen, and there has been no sight nor sign of them since. The children got a sound thrashing for letting Skillywidden escape.

- Robert Hunt, *Popular Romances of the West of England* (London: Hotten, 1871), pp. 450–51. Christiansen migratory legend type 6010.
- Zennor is a fishing village on the Cornish coast and is also famed for mermaid sightings.
- Furze, also called gorse, is a yellow-blossomed bush traditionally harvested for fuel and fodder.

The Kildare Lurikeen (Ireland)

A young girl that lived in sight of Castle Carberry, near Edenderry, was going for a pitcher of water to the neighboring well one summer morning, when who should she see sitting in a sheltery nook under an old thorn, but the lurikeen, working like vengeance at a little old brogue only fit for the foot of a fairy like himself. There he was, boring his holes and jerking his waxed ends, with his little three-cornered hat with gold lace, his knee breeches, his jug of beer by his side, and his pipe in his mouth. He was so busy at his work and so taken up with an old ballad he was singing in Irish, that he did not mind Breedheen till she had him by the scruff o' the neck, as if he was in a vice.

"Ah, what are you doin'?" says he, turning his head round as well as he could. "Dear, dear! to think of such a purty colleen ketchin' a body, as if he was afther robbin' a hen roost! What did I do to be thrated in such an undecent manner? The very vulgarest young ruffin in the townland could do no worse. Come, come, Miss Bridget, take your hands off, sit down, and us have a chat, like two respectable people."

"Ah, Mr. Lurikeen, I don't care a wisp of *borrach* [coarse tow] for your politeness. It's your money I want, and I won't take hand or eye from you till you put me in possession of a fine lob of it."

"Money, indeed! Ah! where would a poor cobbler like me get it? Anyhow there's no money hereabouts, and if you'll only let go my arms, I'll turn my pockets inside out, and open the drawer of my seat, and give you leave to keep every halfpenny you'll find."

"That won't do; my eyes'll keep going through you like darning needles till I have the gold. Begonies, if you don't make haste, I'll carry you, head and pluck, into the village, and there you'll have thirty pair of eyes on you instead of one."

"Well, well! Was ever a poor cobbler so circumvented! And if it was an ignorant, ugly bosthoon that done it, I would not wonder; but a decent, comely girl, that can read her *Poor Man's Manual* at the chapel, and—"

"You may throw your compliments on the stream there. They won't do for me, I tell you. The gold, the gold, the gold! Don't take up my time with your blarney."

"Well, if there's any to be got, it's undher the ould castle it is. We must have a walk for it. Just put me down and we'll get on."

"Put you down indeed! I know a trick worth two of that. I'll carry you."

"Well, how suspicious we are! Do you see the castle from this?"

Bridget was about turning her eyes from the little man to where she knew the castle stood, but she bethought herself in time.

They went up a little hillside, and the lurikeen was quite reconciled and laughed and joked; but just as they got to the brow, he looked up over the ditch, gave a great screech and shouted just as if a bugle horn was blew at her ears, "Oh, murdher! Castle Carberry is afire."

Poor Biddy gave a great start and looked up towards the castle. The same moment she missed the weight of the lurikeen, and when her eyes fell where he was a moment before, there was no more sign of him than if everything that passed was a dream.

- Patrick Kennedy, *Legendary Fictions of the Irish Celts* (London: Macmillan, 1891), pp. 117–18.

- The lurikeen, better known as the leprechaun, has two functions in Irish folklore: shoemaker and guardian of buried treasure. The ruins of Castle Carberry (modern spelling, *Carbury*) are in County Kildare. The town of Edenderry lies some four miles to the west in County Offaly.

CHANGELINGS

The Rye-Mother (Germany)

In the year 1662 a woman from Saalfeld told Praetorius the following story: A nobleman from there forced one of his subjects, a woman who had given birth less than six weeks earlier, to help bind sheaves during the harvest. The woman, who was still nursing her baby, took it with her to the field. In order better to perform her work, she laid the child on the ground. Some time later, the nobleman, who was present there, saw an earth-woman with a child come and exchange it for the peasant woman's child. The false child began to cry. The peasant woman hurried to it in order to nurse it, but the nobleman held her back, saying that he would tell her the reason in good time. The woman thought that he was doing this in order to make her work harder, which caused her great concern. Meanwhile, the child cried incessantly, until finally the rye-mother returned, picked up the crying child and laid the stolen child back in its place.

After seeing all of this transpire, the nobleman summoned the peasant woman and told her to return home. And from that time forth he resolved to never again force a woman who had recently given birth to work.

- Jacob and Wilhelm Grimm, *Deutsche Sagen*, vol. 1 (Berlin: Nicolai, 1816), no. 90. The Grimms' source: Johannes Praetorius, a penname for Hans Schulz (1630–80). Christiansen migratory legend type 5085.
- Saalfeld is in Thuringia in east-central Germany.

The Father of Eighteen Elves (Iceland)

At a certain farm, long ago, it happened that all the household were out one day, making hay, except the farmer's wife and her only child, a boy of four years. He was a strong, handsome, lusty little fellow, who could already speak almost as well as his elders and was looked upon by his parents with great pride and hope. As his mother had plenty of other work to do besides watching him, she was obliged to leave him alone for a short time, while she went down to the brook to wash the milk pails. So she left him playing in the door of the cottage and came back again as soon as she had placed the milk pails to dry.

As soon as she spoke to the child, it began to cry in a strange and unnatural way, which amazed her not a little, as it had always been so quiet and sweet tempered. When she tried to make the child speak to her, as it normally did, it only yelled the more, and so it went on for a long time, always crying and never would be soothed, till the mother was in despair at so remarkable a change in her boy, who now seemed to have lost his senses.

Filled with grief, she went to ask the advice of a learned and skillful woman in the neighborhood and confided to her all her trouble. Her neighbor asked her all sorts of questions: How long ago this change in the child's manner had happened; what his mother thought to be the cause of it; and so forth. To all of which the wretched woman gave the best answers she could.

At last the wise woman said, "Do you not think, my friend, that the child you now have is a changeling? Without doubt it was put at your cottage door in the place of your son, while you were washing the milk pails."

"I know not," replied the other, "but advise me how to find it out."

So the wise woman said, "I will tell you. Place the child where he may see something he has never seen before and let him fancy himself alone. As soon as he believes no one to be near him, he will speak. But you must listen attentively, and if the child says something that declares him to be a changeling, then beat him without mercy."

That was the wise woman's advice, and her neighbor, with many thanks for it, went home. When she got to her house, she set a cauldron in the middle of the hearth, and taking a number of rods, bound them end to end, and at the bottom of them fastened a porridge spoon. This she stuck into the cauldron in such a way that the new handle she had made for it reached right up the chimney. As soon as she had prepared everything, she fetched the child and, placing him on the floor of the kitchen, left him and went out, taking care, however, to leave the door ajar, so that she could hear and see all that went on.

When she had left the room, the child began to walk round and round the cauldron and eye it carefully, and after a while he said, "Well! I am old enough, as anybody may guess from my beard, and the father of eighteen elves, but never in all my life, have I seen so long a spoon to so small a pot."

On hearing this the farmer's wife waited not a moment, but rushed into the room and snatching up a bundle of firewood flogged the changeling with it, till he kicked and screamed again.

In the midst of all this, the door opened, and a strange woman, bearing in her arms a beautiful boy, entered and said, "See how we differ! I cherish and love your son, while you beat and abuse my husband." With these words, she gave back to the farmer's wife her own son, and taking the changeling by the hand, disappeared with him.

But the little boy grew up to manhood, and fulfilled all the hope and promise of his youth.

- Jón Arnason, *Icelandic Legends,* trans. by George E. J. Powell and Eiríkur Magnússon (London: Bentley, 1864), pp. 41–44. Translation slightly revised. Christiansen migratory legend type 5085.

MIDWIVES

Midwife for a Nixie (Germany)

A midwife in Westerhausen was sitting one evening at home when someone knocked on her window and shouted that she should come outside. She did so, and there stood a nix, who told her to follow him. They walked to the Beck [a deep pond near Westerhausen], and the nix took a rod and struck the water with it. The water separated, and with dry feet they walked to the bottom.

Here the woman helped the nix's wife deliver a child. To thank the midwife, the nixie told her that when the nix asked her how she should be paid, instead of money, she should ask for some of the sweepings.

Then the midwife bathed the new baby, and while doing so she heard the nix's other children—there were five of them—running around and asking their father, "Shall we pinch her? Shall we pinch her?" But the father told them not to.

When the midwife was finished the nix asked, "What shall I pay you?"

Following the wife's advice, she requested some of the sweepings from behind the door.

"God told you to say that," said the nix, giving her what she wanted. Then he took her back home, and when she looked at the sweepings, they had turned to pure gold.

- Adalbert Kuhn and Wilhelm Schwartz, *Norddeutsche Sagen, Märchen und Gebräuche* (Leipzig: Brockhaus, 1848), pp. 173–74. Christiansen migratory legend type 5070.
- Westerhausen is a village near Halberstadt in northern Germany.
- The water spirit in this legend is identified in the original German as the *Nickelmann,* translated here as the generic *nix* (female *nixie*).

The Midwife of Listowel (Ireland)

There was an old woman, a midwife, who lived in a little house by herself between this and Listowel. One evening there was a knock at the door. She opened it, and what should she see but a man who said she was wanted, and to go with him quickly. He begged her to hurry. She made herself ready at once, the man waiting outside. When she was ready the man sprang on a fine, large horse and put her up behind him. Away raced the horse then. They went a great distance in such a short time that it seemed to her only two or three miles.

They came to a splendid large house and went in. The old woman found a beautiful lady inside. No other woman was to be seen. A child was born soon, and the man brought a vial of ointment, told the old woman to rub it on the child, but to have a great care and not touch her own self with it. She obeyed him and had no intention of touching herself, but on a sudden her left eye itched. She raised her hand and rubbed the eye with one finger. Some of the ointment was on her finger, and that instant she saw great crowds of people around her, men and women. She knew that she was in a fort among fairies and was frightened, but had courage enough not to show it and finished her work.

The man came to her then and said, "I will take you home now."

He opened the door, went out, sprang to the saddle, and reached his hand to her, but her eye was opened now and she saw that in place of a horse it was an old plow beam that was before her. She was more in dread then than ever, but took her seat, and away went the plow beam as swiftly as the very best horse in the kingdom. The man left her down at her own door, and she saw no more of him.

Some time after there was a great fair at Listowel. The old midwife went to the fair, and there were big crowds of people on every side of her. The old woman looked around for a while and what did she see but the man who had taken her away on a plow beam. He was hurrying around, going in and out among the people, and no one knowing he was in it but the old woman.

At last the finest young girl at the fair screamed and fell in a faint—the fairy had thrust something into her side. A crowd gathered around the young girl. The old woman, who had seen all, made her way to the girl, examined her side and drew a pin from it. The girl recovered.

A little later the fairy made his way to the old woman. "Have you ever seen me before?" asked he.

"Oh, maybe I have," said she.

"Do you remember that I took you to a fort to attend a young woman?"

"I do."

"When you anointed the child did you touch any part of yourself with the ointment I gave you?"

"I did without knowing it; my eye itched and I rubbed it with my finger."

"Which eye?"

"The left."

The moment she said that he struck her left eye and took the sight from it. She went home blind of one eye and was that way the rest of her life.

- Jeremiah Curtin, *Irish Tales of the Fairies and the Ghost World* (Boston: Little, Brown, 1895), pp. 43–45. Christiansen migratory legend type 5070.

- Listowel is a town in County Kerry.

ANCIENT MONUMENTS

Legend of the Rollright Stones (England)

Not far from the borders of Gloucestershire and Oxfordshire, and within the latter county, is the pretty village of Rollright and near the village, up a hill, stands a circle of small stones and one larger stone, such as our Celtic antiquaries say were raised by the druids.

As soon as the druids left them, the fairies, who never failed to take possession of their deserted shrines, seemed to have had an especial care over these stones, and anyone who ventures to meddle with them is sure to meet with some very great misfortune.

The old people of the village, however, who generally know most about these matters, say the stones were once a king and his knights, who were going to make war on the King of England. And they assert that, according to old prophecies, had they ever reached Long Compton, the King of England must inevitably have been dethroned, and this king would have reigned in his place. But when they came to the village of Rollright they were suddenly turned into stones in the place where they now stand.

Be this as it may, there was once a farmer in the village who wanted a large stone to put in a particular position in an outhouse he was building in his farmyard, and he thought that one of the old knights would be just the thing for him. In spite of all the warnings of his neighbors he determined to have the stone he wanted, and he put four horses to his best wagon and proceeded up the hill. With much labor he succeeded in getting the stone into his wagon, and though the road lay downhill, it was so heavy that his wagon was broken and his horses were killed by the labor of drawing it home. Nothing daunted by all these mishaps, the farmer raised the stone to the place it was to occupy in his new building.

From this moment everything went wrong with him. His crops failed year after year. His cattle died one after another. He was obliged to mortgage his land and to sell his wagons and horses, till at last he had left only one poor broken-down horse which nobody would buy and one old crazy cart.

The author examining the Rollright Stone Circle in Oxfordshire, England. Photograph by Patricia Ashliman.

Suddenly the thought came into his head that all his misfortunes might be owing to the identical stone which he had brought from the circle at the top of the hill. He thought he would try to get it back again, and his only horse was put to the cart. To his surprise he got the stone down and lifted it into the cart with very little trouble, and, as soon as it was in, the horse, which could scarcely bear along its own limbs, now drew it up the hill of its own accord with as little trouble as another horse would draw an empty cart on level ground, until it came to the very spot where the stone had formerly stood beside its companions.

The stone was soon in its place, and the horse and cart returned home, and from that moment the farmer's affairs began to improve, till in a short time he was a richer and more substantial man than he had ever been before.

- Edwin Sidney Hartland, *English Fairy and Other Folk Tales* (London: Scott, 1890), pp. 151–52. Hartland's source: *Folk-Lore Record,* vol. 2, p. 177.

- The Rollright stone circle was probably erected about 3,000 B.C.E. and thus predates by millennia the druids to whom it is here attributed. This monument is near the town of Chipping Norton in Oxfordshire. There are three parts to the Rollright complex: the circle itself (about 100 feet in diameter and consisting today of seventy-seven upright stones), a nearby solitary monolith (the king stone), and a group of five standing stones (the whispering knights) about 400 yards from the circle. The king stone has been severely deformed by countless individuals who have—for centuries—chipped off fragments to serve as good-luck charms, suggesting a belief quite contrary to the views reflected in the above legend.

The Gnoll Fairy Stone (Wales)

Fairies were constantly seen on a fine evening by *Clwyda'r Banwan* (the Banwan Gates), dancing within the rings; but since the wonderful stone (on which was written fairy language in their characters, for nobody had ever understood them) had been removed from the center of the largest circle to Gnoll gardens, nobody had ever seen the fairies. But they had their revenge; for no sooner had the grotto, which cost Lady Mackworth thousands of pounds, been finished, than one evening—oh! I shall never forget it!—there was thunder and lightning and rain, such as was never seen or heard before; and next morning the grotto had disappeared, for the hill behind it fell over it and has hidden it forever; and woe betide the man that will dare to clear away the earth. When the storm abated we all heard the fairies laughing heartily.

- J. O. Westwood, "Early Inscribed Stones of Wales," *Archaeologia Cambrensis,* series 3, vol. 11 (1865), pp. 60–61.

- This account was given by a gardener who claimed to have personally experienced the event. In about 1835 the stone—according to modern scholars a Roman grave marker—was removed from its original site and placed in a garden grotto at the Gnoll, an estate overlooking Neath, a town in south Wales. Soon afterward, the grotto was buried beneath a landslide, giving rise to the tradition that fairies had taken their revenge for the stone's removal. In spite of the gardener's warning, the stone was recovered and since 1922 has been on display in the Swansea Museum. The "fairy language" mentioned above is a badly weathered Latin inscription.

DEATH OF AN UNDERGROUND PERSON

The Troll Turned Cat (Denmark)

Pedersborg lies a quarter of a mile from Sorø, and a little farther on is the town of Lyng. Between these two towns is a hill called Brøndøj, said to be inhabited by the troll people. One of these was a jealous old troll, whom they called Knurremurre (Rumble-grumble), because he often caused so much turmoil within the hill. Once Knurremurre came to suspect a friendship between his young wife and a young troll, and he became so angry that he threatened to kill the younger one. The latter, accordingly, thought it would be best to leave the hill. Turning himself into a ruddy tomcat, he went to the town of Lyng, where he established himself in the house of a poor man named Plat.

Here he lived for a long time. Every day he got milk and porridge, always lying about in an easy chair beside the stove. One evening Plat came home, and as he entered the room the cat was sitting in his usual place, licking porridge out of a pot. "Mother," said the man, "let me tell you what happened to me on the road. Just as I was passing Brøndøj, a troll came out and said to me, "Listen, Plat, tell your cat that Knurremurre is dead."

The moment the cat heard these words, he stood up on his hind legs and tipped the pot onto the floor. He then rushed out the door, saying, "What! Is Knurremurre dead? Then I certainly may go home at once!"

- Thomas Keightley, *The Fairy Mythology* (London: Bohn, 1850), pp. 120–21. Translation revised. Keightley's source: J. M. Thiele, *Danmarks Folkesagn* (1843). Thiele names this piece simply "Brøndøj" after the hill inhabited by the trolls. Aarne-Thompson folktale type 113A; Christiansen migratory legend type 6060B.

- The places named in this legend are on the island of Zealand.

Prilling and Pralling Is Dead (Germany)

The servant of Landholder Gireck (whose residence in Plau was on Elden Street where Master Mason Büttner's house now stands) was once hauling a load of manure to a field abutting Gall Mountain. He had just unloaded the manure and was about to put the sideboards back onto the wagon when he heard his name being called from the mountain, together with the words, "When you get home say that Prilling and Pralling is dead." Back at home, he had scarcely related this experience and repeated the words, when they heard groaning and crying coming from the house's cellar. They investigated, but found nothing but a pewter mug, of a kind that had never before been seen in Plau. The master of the house kept the mug, and when he later moved to Hamburg he took it with him. About seventy years ago someone from Plau saw it there.

- Karl Bartsch, *Sagen, Märchen und Gebräuche aus* Meklenburg [Mecklenburg], vol. 1 (Vienna: Braumüller, 1879), pp. 42–43. Christiansen migratory legend type 6060B.

- Plau is located midway between Hamburg and Berlin.

LIVING ABOVE THE FAIRIES

Raginal (Denmark)

A farmer fell into poverty because he could not keep any cows in his stalls, the necks of all having been broken one after another. He therefore left the farm, which was sold to another. When the new proprietor came into the cow-shed one evening and saw that everything was in a dubious state, he exclaimed, "Good evening, Raginal!"

Whereupon a voice answered, "What? Do you know me?"

"Yes, I have known you for many a year!"

"If," said the troll, who dwelled beneath, "you will move your cowshed to some other place, you shall become a wealthy man. I have my habitation under the cows, and their filth falls down on my table every day, so that I have been obliged to break their necks."

The man removed the cowshed and thrived from that time.

- Benjamin Thorpe, *Northern Mythology: From Pagan Faith to Local Legends.* (Ware, Hertfordshire: Wordsworth, 2001), p. 333. First published 1851. Thorpe's source is J. M. Thiele, *Danmarks Folkesagn* (1843). Christiansen migratory legend type 5075. Translation revised.

Why Deunant Has the Front Door in the Back (Wales)

The cattle of the farmer living at Deunant, close to Aberdaron, were grievously afflicted with the "short disease," which is the malady known in English as the black quarter. Naturally, he thought they were bewitched. One night before going to bed he was standing a few steps in front of his house, meditating over his trouble. "I cannot imagine why the cattle do not get better," said he out loud to himself.

"I will tell you," said a squeaky little voice close by him. The farmer turned in the direction of the sound and saw a tiny little man, looking very angrily at him. "It is," continued the manikin, "because your family keeps on annoying mine so much."

"How is that?" asked the farmer, surprised and puzzled.

"They are always throwing the slops from your house down the chimney of my house," said the little man.

"That cannot be," retorted the farmer. "There is no house within a mile of mine."

"Put your foot on mine," said the small stranger, "and you will see that what I say is true."

The farmer, complying, put his foot on the other's foot, and he could clearly see that all the slops thrown out of his house went down the chimney of the other's house, which stood far below in a street he had never seen before. Directly he took his foot off the other's, however, there was no sign of house or chimney. "Well, indeed, I am very sorry," said the farmer. "What can I do to make up for the annoyance which my family has caused you?"

The tiny little man was satisfied by the farmer's apology, and he said, "You had better wall up the door on this side of your house and make another in the other side. If you do that, your slops will no longer be a nuisance to my family and myself." Having said this he vanished in the dusk of the night.

The farmer obeyed, and his cattle recovered. Ever after he was a most prosperous man, and nobody was so successful as he in rearing stock in all Lleyn. Unless they have pulled it down to build a new one, you can see the house with the front door at the back.

- W. Jenkyn Thomas. *The Welsh Fairy Book* (London: Unwin, [1908]), pp. 159–62. Christiansen migratory legend type 5075.

- Aberdaron is a fishing village located at the tip of the Lleyn Peninsula in northern Wales.

A fairy domicile beneath a house in Deunant, Wales. Illustration by Willy Pogány, from W. Jenkyn Thomas, *The Welsh Fairy Book* (1907).

UNWANTED HOUSEGUESTS

The Cluricaune (Ireland)

Mr. Harris, a Quaker, had a cluricaune in his family. It was very diminutive in form. If any of the servants, as they sometimes do through negligence, left the beer barrel running, little Wildbeam (for that was his name) would wedge himself into the cock and stop it at the risk of being smothered, until someone came to turn the key. In return for such services, the cook was in the habit, by her master's orders, of leaving a good dinner in the cellar for little Wildbeam.

One Friday it so happened that she had nothing to leave but part of a herring and some cold potatoes, when just at midnight something pulled her out of bed, and, having brought her with irresistible force to the top of the cellar stairs, she was seized by the heels and dragged down them. At every knock her head received against the stairs, the cluricaune, who was standing at the door, would shout out:

Molly Jones, Molly Jones,
Potato skins and herring bones!
I'll knock your head against the stones!
Molly Jones, Molly Jones.

The poor cook was so much bruised by that night's adventure, she was confined to her bed for three weeks after.

In consequence of this piece of violent conduct, Mr. Harris wished much to get rid of his fairy attendant; and being told if he removed to any house beyond a running stream, that the cluricaune could not follow him, he took a house and had all his furniture packed on carts for the purpose of removing. The last articles brought out were the cellar furniture; and when the cart was completely loaded with casks and barrels, the cluricaune was seen to jump into it, and fixing himself in the bung-hole of an empty cask, cried out to Mr. Harris, "Here, master! Here we go, all together!"

"What!" said Mr. Harris. "Dost thou go also?"

"Yes, to be sure, master," replied little Wildbeam. "Here we go, all together."

"In that case, friend," said Mr. Harris, "let the carts be unpacked. We are just as well where we are."

Mr. Harris died soon after, but it is said the cluricaune still attends the Harris family.

- Thomas Crofton Croker, *Fairy Legends and Traditions of the South of* Ireland, vol. 1 (London: Murray, 1825), pp. 140–42). Christiansen migratory legend type 7020.
- *Cluricaune* is an alternate designation for the leprechaun.

The Kobold (Germany)

In the vicinity of Köpenick a servant had a kobold who had become a nuisance for him, so he wanted to get rid of him. Therefore he decided to move away, leaving the kobold behind. The evening before moving day he walked by the spring. Seeing the kobold sitting there, he asked "What are you doing here?"

"Oh," said the kobold, "I am washing out my rags, because we are moving tomorrow, you know."

Thus the servant saw that he would have to keep him, and he took the kobold with him.

- Adalbert Kuhn and Wilhelm Schwartz, *Norddeutsche Sagen, Märchen und Gebräuche* (Leipzig: Brockhaus, 1848), p. 82. Christiansen migratory legend type 7020.
- Köpenick is today a suburb of Berlin.

HELPFUL ELVES

The Shoemaker and the Elves (Germany)

A shoemaker had become so poor that he had only leather enough for a single pair of shoes. He cut them out one evening, then went to bed, intending to finish them the next morning. When he got up and returned to his work he found the shoes on his workbench, beautifully finished. A customer soon came by and paid so much for the shoes that the shoemaker was able to buy enough leather for two more pairs of shoes, and that evening he cut them out as well. Upon returning to his work the next morning, they too were already finished, and he sold them for enough money to buy leather for four pairs of shoes. And so it continued. However many shoes the shoemaker would cut out in the evening, the same number were finished the following morning. He soon became a wealthy man.

One evening shortly before Christmas, just before going to bed, and having already cut out a good many shoes, he said to his wife, "Let us stay up tonight and see who is doing our work."

So they lit a candle, then hid themselves behind some clothes that were hanging in a corner of the room. At midnight two cute little naked men

The shoemaker and his wife observe the helpful elves. Illustration by Walter Crane, from Jacob and Wilhelm Grimm, *Household Stories* (1886).

appeared. Sitting down at the workbench, they picked up the cut-out pieces and worked so unbelievably quickly and nimbly that the amazed shoemaker could not take his eyes from them. Nor did they stop until they had finished everything. Then they skipped away, and it was still a long time before daybreak.

The woman said to her husband, "The little men have made us wealthy. We must show them our thanks. I feel sorry for them that they have to go about without any clothes and freeze. I want to sew some shirts, jackets, undershirts, and trousers for them, and knit a pair of stockings for each of them, and you should make a pair of shoes for each of them."

The husband agreed to this, and when everything was finished they set it out in the evening. Wanting to see what the little men would do, they again hid themselves. At midnight the little ones came as usual. They seemed to be very happy when they saw the clothes lying there, and they very quickly put them on. Then they began to hop and jump and dance, and they danced right out the door, and they never came back again.

- Jacob and Wilhelm Grimm, *Kinder- und Hausmärchen,* vol. 1 (Berlin: Realschulbuchhandlung, 1812), no. 39/1. The Grimms' source was Dorothea (Dortchen) Wild, who later married Wilhelm. Aarne-Thompson folktale type 503*. Christiansen migratory legend type 7015.

- My translation follows the text of the first edition. In later editions the Grimm brothers altered most of their stories, including this account, typically making them more dramatic and literary.

Hob Thrust (England)

Once upon a time there was a poor shoemaker who could not earn enough to keep himself and his family. This grieved him very much, but one morning when he came downstairs he found a piece of leather which he had cut out already made into a pair of shoes, which were beautifully finished. He sold these shoes the same day and with the money he bought as much leather as would make two pairs of shoes. The next morning he found that this leather too had been made into shoes, but he did not know who had done it. In this way his stock of shoes kept always getting bigger.

He very much wished to know who had made the shoes, so he told his wife he would stay up all night and watch, and then he found Hob Thrust at work upon the leather. As soon as Hob Thrust had finished a pair of shoes the shoemaker took them and put them into a cupboard. Immediately after that Hob Thrust finished another pair, which the shoemaker also took up and put away. Then he made first one pair of shoes and then another so fast that the little shop was soon filled with them, and as there was no more room in the house the shoemaker threw the shoes out of the window as fast as Hob Thrust could make them.

Hob Thrust also worked for farmers in the night. One morning when a farmer woke he found that the hay upon a rough piece of stony ground was newly mown. This had happened several times before, so one day he said he would stay up all night and watch. Then he saw it was Hob Thrust who mowed the hay; so on the following day he drove some iron gavelocks [crowbars] and harrow teeth into the ground. On the next night Hob Thrust came to mow the hay again, when his scythe struck against a gavelock. He merely said, "Umph, a dock," and cut through it with his scythe. And when his scythe struck against a harrow tooth, he said, "Umph, a dock," and cut straight through it.

- Sidney Oldall Addy, *Household Tales with Other Traditional Remains: Collected in the Counties of York, Lincoln, Derby, and Nottingham* (London: Nutt, 1895), no. 38, pp. 39–40. Aarne-Thompson folktale type 503*.

- Note by Addy: "From Dore, in Derbyshire. . . . The first part of this story is identical with the first part of the Grimms' tale of "The Elves," no. 39. But it is certain that this tale about Hob Thrust was not borrowed from Grimm, because it has given rise to a proverbial saying in the neighborhood of Sheffield where knives are made. When a man is heard to boast of the number of knives or other articles which he can make in a day, the rejoinder is, 'Ah, tha can mak 'em faster than Hob Thrust can throw shoes out o' t' window.' In his capacity as the farmer's friend Hob Thrust reminds us of Thor."

- Both parts of this tale are garbled versions of traditional tales. The first part seems to combine elements of "The Shoemaker and the Elves," told in an uncontaminated version by the Grimms, and "The Sorcerer's Apprentice" (Aarne-Thompson type 325*). In the latter tale a naïve individual gains supernatural assistance for some task, typically carrying water, but then cannot make the magic helper stop. Part two of "Hob Thrust" is reminiscent of the widespread tale of the mowing contest with an ogre (Aarne-Thompson type 1090).

THE HUMPBACKS AND THE ELVES

Billy Beg, Tom Beg, and the Fairies (Isle of Man)

Not far from Dalby, Billy Beg and Tom Beg, two humpback cobblers, lived together on a lonely croft. Billy Beg was sharper and cleverer than Tom Beg, who was always at his command. One day Billy Beg gave Tom a staff, and quoth he, "Tom Beg, go to the mountain and fetch home the white sheep."

Tom Beg took the staff and went to the mountain, but he could not find the white sheep. At last, when he was far from home and dusk was coming on, he began to think that he had best go back. The night was fine, and stars and a small crescent moon were in the sky. No sound was to be heard but the curlew's sharp whistle. Tom was hastening home and had almost reached Glen Rushen, when a gray mist gathered and he lost his way. But it was not long before the mist cleared, and Tom Beg found himself in a green glen such as he had never seen before, though he thought he knew every glen within five miles of him, for he was born and reared in the neighborhood. He was marveling and wondering where he could be, when he heard a faraway sound drawing nearer to him.

"Aw," said he to himself, "there's more than myself afoot on the mountains tonight. I'll have company."

The sound grew louder. First it was like the humming of bees, then like the rushing of Glen Meay waterfall, and last it was like the marching and the murmur of a crowd. It was the fairy host. Of a sudden the glen was full of fine horses and of little people riding on them, with the lights on their red caps shining like the stars above and making the night as bright as day. There was the blowing of horns, the waving of flags, the playing of music, and the barking of many little dogs. Tom Beg thought that he had never seen anything so splendid as all he saw there. In the midst of the drilling and dancing and singing one of them spied Tom, and then Tom saw coming towards him the grandest little man he had ever set eyes upon, dressed in gold and silver and silk shining like a raven's wing.

"It is a bad time you have chosen to come this way," said the little man, who was the king.

"Yes, but it is not here that I'm wishing to be though," said Tom.

Then said the king, "Are you one of us tonight, Tom?"

"I am surely," said Tom.

" Then," said the king, "it will be your duty to take the password. You must stand at the foot of the glen, and as each regiment goes by, you must take the password. It is Monday, Tuesday, Wednesday, Thursday, Friday, Saturday."

"I'll do that with a heart and a half," said Tom.

At daybreak the fiddlers took up their fiddles; the fairy army set itself in order; the fiddlers played before them out of the glen; and sweet that music was. Each regiment gave the password to Tom as it went by: Monday, Tuesday, Wednesday, Thursday, Friday, Saturday; and last of all came the king, and he too gave it: Monday, Tuesday, Wednesday, Thursday, Friday, Saturday.

Then he called in Manx to one of his men, "Take the hump from this fellow's back," and before the words were out of his mouth the hump was whisked off Tom Beg's back and thrown into the hedge.

How proud now was Tom, who so found himself the straightest man in the Isle of Man! He went down the mountain and came home early in the morning with light heart and eager step. Billy Beg wondered greatly when he saw Tom Beg so straight and strong, and when Tom Beg had rested and refreshed himself he told his story how he had met the fairies who came every night to Glen Rushen to drill.

The next night Billy Beg set off along the mountain road and came at last to the green glen. About midnight he heard the trampling of horses, the lashing of whips, the barking of dogs, and a great hullabaloo, and, behold, the fairies and their king, their dogs and their horses, all at drill in the glen as Tom Beg had said.

When they saw the humpback they all stopped, and one came forward and very crossly asked his business.

"I am one of yourselves for the night and should be glad to do you some service," said Billy Beg.

So he was set to take the password: Monday, Tuesday, Wednesday, Thursday, Friday, Saturday. And at daybreak the King said, "It's time for us to be off," and up came regiment after regiment giving Billy Beg the password: Monday, Tuesday, Wednesday, Thursday, Friday, Saturday. Last of all came the king with his men. and gave the password also: Monday, Tuesday, Wednesday, Thursday, Friday, Saturday, "AND SUNDAY," says Billy Beg, thinking himself clever.

Then there was a great outcry. "Get the hump that was taken off that fellow's back last night and put it on this man's back," said the king, with flashing eyes, pointing to the hump that lay under the hedge.

Before the words were well out of his mouth the hump was clapped onto Billy Beg's back.

"Now," said the king, "be off, and if ever I find you here again, I will clap another hump onto your front!"

And on that they all marched away with one great shout and left poor Billy Beg standing where they had found him, with a hump growing on each shoulder. And he came home next day dragging one foot after another, with a wizened face and as cross as two sticks, with his two humps on his back, and if they are not off, they are there still.

- Sophia Morrison, *Manx Fairy Tales* (London: Nutt, 1911), pp. 56–61. Aarne-Thompson folktale type 503.

The Fairies and the Humpback (Scotland)

A man who was a humpback once met the fairies dancing, and danced with their queen; and he sang with them, "Monday, Tuesday, Wednesday," so well that they took off his hump, and he returned home a straight-bodied man.

Then a tailor went past the same place and was also admitted by the fairies to their dance. He caught the fairy queen by the waist, and she resented his familiarity. And in singing he added "Thursday" to their song and spoilt it. To pay the tailor for his rudeness and ill manners, the dancers took up the hump they had just removed from the first man and clapped it on his back, and the conceited fellow went home a humpback.

- W. Y. Evans-Wentz, *The Fairy Faith in Celtic Countries* (London: Frowde, 1911), p. 92. Evans-Wentz's source was a protestant minister serving on the island of Benbecula in the Outer Hebrides. Aarne-Thompson folktale type 503.

GUESSING THE HELPER'S NAME

Rumpelstiltskin (Germany)

Once upon a time there was a miller who was poor, but who had a beautiful daughter. Now it happened that he got into a conversation with the king and said to him, "I have a daughter who knows the art of turning straw into gold."

So the king immediately sent for the miller's daughter and ordered her to turn a whole room full of straw into gold in one night. And if she could not do it, she would have to die. She was locked in the room, and she sat there and cried, because for her life she did not know how the straw would turn into gold.

Then suddenly a little man appeared before her and said, "What will you give me, if I turn this all into gold?" She took off her necklace and gave it to the little man, and he did what he had promised.

The next morning the king found the room filled with gold, and his heart became even more greedy. He put the miller's daughter into an even larger room filled with straw and told her to turn it into gold. The little man came again. She gave him a ring from her hand, and he turned it all into gold. The third night the king had her locked in a third room, which was larger than the first two, and entirely filled with straw. "If you succeed this time, I'll make you my wife," he said.

Then the little man came and said, "I'll do it again, but you must promise me the first child that you have with the king."

In her distress she made the promise, and when the king saw that this straw too had been turned into gold, he took the miller's daughter as his wife. Soon

Rumpelstiltskin. Illustration by Walter Crane, from Jacob and
Wilhelm Grimm, *Household Stories* (1886).

thereafter the queen delivered a child. Then the little man appeared before
her and demanded the child that had been promised him. The queen begged
him to let her keep the child, offering him great riches in its place. Finally he
said, "I'll be back to get the child in three days. But if by then you know my
name, you can keep the child.!"

For two days the queen pondered what the little man's name might be,
but she could not think of anything and became very sad. On the third day
the king came home from a hunt and told her how, two days earlier, while
hunting deep in a dark forest, he had come upon a little house. A comical
little man was there, jumping about as if on one leg, and crying out:

> Today I'll bake; tomorrow I'll brew.
> Then I'll fetch the queen's new child.
> It is good that no one knows
> Rumpelstiltskin is my name.

The queen was overjoyed to hear this. Then the dangerous little man
arrived and asked, "Your majesty, what is my name?"

"Is your name Conrad?"

"No."

"Is your name Heinrich?"

"No."

"Then could your name be Rumpelstiltskin?"

"The devil told you that!" shouted the little man. He ran away angrily and
never came back.

- Jacob and Wilhelm Grimm, *Kinder- und Hausmärchen,* vol. 1 (Berlin:
  Realschulbuchhandlung, 1812), vol. 1, no. 55. Aarne-Thompson folktale
  type 500.

- My translation is based on the first edition. The Grimms altered this tale con-
  siderably in succeeding editions. The most notable change is the introduction

Tom Tit Tot by Arthur Rackham, from Flora
Annie Steel, *English Fairy Tales* (1918).

of the spinning wheel as a device for turning straw into gold. Further, in later
editions the queen discovers the dwarf's name through a messenger whom she
herself sends forth to collect strange names, not through her husband's chance
meeting with the little man.

Tom Tit Tot (England)

Once upon a time there was a woman, and she baked five pies. And when
they came out of the oven, they were that overbaked the crusts were too hard
to eat. So she says to her daughter, "Darter," says she, "put you them there
pies on the shelf, and leave 'em there a little, and they'll come again." She
meant, you know, the crust would get soft.

But the girl, she says to herself, "Well, if they'll come again, I'll eat 'em
now." And she set to work and ate 'em all, first and last.

Well, come suppertime the woman said, "Go you, and get one o' them
there pies. I dare say they've come again now."

The girl went and she looked, and there was nothing but the dishes. So back she came and says she, "Noo, they ain't come again."

"Not one of 'em?" says the mother.

"Not one of 'em," says she.

"Well, come again, or not come again," said the woman, "I'll have one for supper."

"But you can't, if they ain't come," said the girl.

"But I can," says she. "Go you, and bring the best of 'em."

"Best or worst," says the girl, "I've ate 'em all, and you can't have one till that's come again."

Well, the woman she was done, and she took her spinning to the door to spin, and as she span she sang:

My darter ha' ate five, five pies today.
My darter ha' ate five, five pies today.

The king was coming down the street, and he heard her sing, but what she sang he couldn't hear, so he stopped and said, "What was that you were singing, my good woman?"

The woman was ashamed to let him hear what her daughter had been doing, so she sang, instead of that:

My darter ha' spun five, five skeins today.
My darter ha' spun five, five skeins today.

"Stars o' mine!" said the king, "I never heard tell of anyone that could do that." Then he said, "Look you here, I want a wife, and I'll marry your daughter. But look you here," says he, "eleven months out of the year she shall have all she likes to eat, and all the gowns she likes to get, and all the company she likes to keep; but the last month of the year she'll have to spin five skeins every day, and if she don't I shall kill her."

"All right," says the woman; for she thought what a grand marriage that was. And as for the five skeins, when the time came, there'd be plenty of ways of getting out of it, and likeliest, he'd have forgotten all about it.

Well, so they were married. And for eleven months the girl had all she liked to eat, and all the gowns she liked to get, and all the company she liked to keep. But when the time was getting over, she began to think about the skeins and to wonder if he had 'em in mind. But not one word did he say about 'em, and she thought he'd wholly forgotten 'em. However, the last day of the last month he takes her to a room she'd never set eyes on before. There was nothing in it but a spinning wheel and a stool. And, says he, "Now, my dear, here you'll be shut in tomorrow with some victuals and some flax, and if you haven't spun five skeins by the night, your head'll go off." And away he went about his business.

Well, she was that frightened, she'd always been such a gatless [careless] girl, that she didn't so much as know how to spin, and what was she to do tomorrow with no one to come nigh her to help her? She sate down on a stool in the kitchen, and law! how she did cry! However, all of a sudden she heard a sort of a knocking low down on the door. She upped and oped it, and what should she see but a small little black thing with a long tail. That looked up at her right curious, and that said, "What are you a-crying for?"

"What's that to you?" says she.

"Never you mind," that said, "but tell me what you're a-crying for."

"That won't do me no good if I do," says she.

"You don't know that," that said, and twirled that's tail round.

"Well," says she, "that won't do no harm, if that don't do no good," and she upped and told about the pies, and the skeins, and everything.

"This is what I'll do," says the little black thing. "I'll come to your window every morning and take the flax and bring it spun at night."

"What's your pay?" says she.

That looked out of the corner of that's eyes, and that said, "I'll give you three guesses every night to guess my name, and if you haven't guessed it before the month's up you shall be mine."

Well, she thought, she'd be sure to guess that's name before the month was up. "All right," says she, "I agree."

"All right," that says, and law! how that twirled that's tail.

Well, the next day, her husband took her into the room, and there was the flax and the day's food. "Now, there's the flax," says he, "and if that ain't spun up this night, off goes your head." And then he went out and locked the door. He'd hardly gone, when there was a knocking against the window. She upped and she oped it, and there sure enough was the little old thing sitting on the ledge.

"Where's the flax?" says he.

"Here it be," says she. And she gave it to him. Well, come the evening a knocking came again to the window. She upped and she oped it, and there was the little old thing with five skeins of flax on his arm.

"Here it be," says he, and he gave it to her. "Now, what's my name?" says he.

"What, is that Bill?" says she.

"Noo, that ain't," says he, and he twirled his tail.

"Is that Ned?" says she.

"Noo, that ain't," says he, and he twirled his tail.

"Well, is that Mark?" says she.

"Noo, that ain't," says he, and he twirled his tail harder, and away he flew.

Well, when her husband came in, there were the five skeins ready for him. "I see I shan't have to kill you tonight, my dear," says he. "You'll have your food and your flax in the morning," says he, and away he goes. Well, every day the flax and the food were brought, and every day that there little black impet used to come mornings and evenings. And all the day the girl sate trying to think of names to say to it when it came at night. But she never hit on the right one. And as it got towards the end of the month, the impet began to look so maliceful, and that twirled that's tail faster and faster each time she gave a guess.

At last it came to the last day but one. The impet came at night along with the five skeins, and that said, "What, ain't you got my name yet?"

"Is that Nicodemus?" says she.

"Noo, 'tain't," that says.

"Is that Sammle?" says she.

"Noo, 'tain't," that says.

"A-well, is that Methusalem?" says she.

"Noo, 'tain't that neither," that says.

Then that looks at her with that's eyes like a coal of fire, and that says, "Woman, there's only tomorrow night, and then you'll be mine!" And away it flew.

Well, she felt that horrid. However, she heard the king coming along the passage. In he came, and when he sees the five skeins, he says, says he, "Well, my dear," says he. "I don't see but what you'll have your skeins ready tomorrow night as well, and as I reckon I shan't have to kill you, I'll have supper in here tonight." So they brought supper, and another stool for him, and down the two sate.

Well, he hadn't eaten but a mouthful or so, when he stops and begins to laugh.

"What is it?" says she.

"A-why," says he, "I was out a-hunting today, and I got away to a place in the wood I'd never seen before. And there was an old chalk pit. And I heard a kind of a sort of humming. So I got off my hobby, and I went right quiet to the pit, and I looked down. Well, what should there be but the funniest little black thing you ever set eyes on. And what was that doing, but that had a little spinning wheel, and that was spinning wonderful fast, and twirling that's tail. And as that span, that sang:

Nimmy nimmy not
My name's Tom Tit Tot.

Well, when the girl heard this, she felt as if she could have jumped out of her skin for joy, but she didn't say a word. Next day that there little thing looked so maliceful when he came for the flax. And when night came she

The heroine guesses the name of Tom Tit Tot. Illustration by John D. Batten, from Joseph Jacobs, *English Fairy Tales* (1898).

heard that knocking against the window panes. She oped the window, and that come right in on the ledge. That was grinning from ear to ear, and Oo! that's tail was twirling round so fast. "What's my name?" that says, as that gave her the skeins.

"Is that Solomon?" she says, pretending to be afeard.

"Noo, 'tain't," that says, and that came further into the room.

"Well, is that Zebedee?" says she again.

"Noo, 'tain't," says the impet. And then that laughed and twirled that's tail till you couldn't hardly see it.

"Take time, woman," that says; "next guess, and you're mine." And that stretched out that's black hands at her.

Well, she backed a step or two, and she looked at it, and then she laughed out, and says she, pointing her finger at it:

Nimmy nimmy not
Your name's Tom Tit Tot.

Well, when that heard her, that gave an awful shriek and away that flew into the dark, and she never saw it any more.

- Joseph Jacobs, *English Fairy Tales* (London: Nutt, 1898), pp. 1–8. Aarne-Thompson folktale type 500.

Esbern Snare and the Kalundborg Church (Denmark)

When Esbern Snare was about building a church in Kalundborg, he saw clearly that his means were not fully adequate to the task. But a troll came to him and offered his services; and Esbern Snare made an agreement with him on these conditions, that he should be able to tell the troll's name when the church was finished; or in case he could not, that he should give him his heart and his eyes.

The work now went on rapidly, and the troll set the church on stone pillars; but when all was nearly done, and there was only half a pillar wanting in the church, Esbern began to get frightened, for the name of the troll was yet unknown to him.

One day he was going about the fields all alone, and in great anxiety on account of the perilous state he was in, when, tired and depressed, by reason of his exceeding grief and affliction, he laid him down on Ulshøj bank to rest himself a while. While he was lying there, he heard a troll-woman within the hill saying these words:

> Lie still, baby mine!
> Tomorrow cometh Fin,
> Father thine,
> And giveth thee
> Esbern Snare's
> Eyes and heart to play with.

When Esbern heard this, he recovered his spirits, and went back to the church. The troll was just then coming with the half pillar that was wanting from the church; but when Esbern saw him, he hailed him by his name, and called him "Fin." The troll was so enraged at this, that he went off with the half pillar through the air, and this is the reason that the church has but three pillars and a half.

- Thomas Keightley, *The Fairy Mythology* (London: Bohn, 1850), pp. 116–17. Christiansen migratory legend type 7065.
- Kalundborg (also spelled *Kallundborg*) is a city in northwestern Zealand. Esbern Snare's famous church, the *Frue Kirke,* built in 1170, still stands.
- John Greenleaf Whittier retold this legend in a ballad titled "Kallundborg Church."

SEDUCED BY A FAIRY

Connla and the Fairy Maiden (Ireland)

Connla of the Fiery Hair was son of Conn of the Hundred Fights. One day as he stood by the side of his father on the height of Usna, he saw a maiden clad in strange attire coming towards him. "Whence comest thou, maiden?" said Connla.

"I come from the Plains of the Ever Living," she said, "there where there is neither death nor sin. There we keep holiday always, nor need we help from any in our joy. And in all our pleasure we have no strife. And because we have our homes in the round green hills, men call us the Hill Folk."

The king and all with him wondered much to hear a voice when they saw no one. For save Connla alone, none saw the fairy maiden.

"To whom art thou talking, my son?" said Conn the king.

Then the maiden answered, "Connla speaks to a young, fair maid, whom neither death nor old age awaits. I love Connla, and now I call him away to the Plain of Pleasure, where Boadag is king for aye, nor has there been complaint or sorrow in that land since he has held the kingship. Oh, come with me, Connla of the Fiery Hair, ruddy as the dawn with thy tawny skin. A fairy crown awaits thee to grace thy comely face and royal form. Come,

Connla follows the fairy maiden. Illustration by John D. Batten, from Joseph Jacobs, *Celtic Fairy Tales* (1892).

and never shall thy comeliness fade, nor thy youth, till the last awful day of judgment."

The king in fear at what the maiden said, which he heard, though he could not see her, called aloud to his druid, Coran by name. "Oh, Coran of the many spells," he said, "and of the cunning magic, I call upon thy aid. A task is upon me too great for all my skill and wit, greater than any laid upon me since I seized the kingship. A maiden unseen has met us, and by her power would take from me my dear, my comely son. If thou help not, he will be taken from thy king by woman's wiles and witchery."

Then Coran the druid stood forth and chanted his spells towards the spot where the maiden's voice had been heard. And none heard her voice again, nor could Connla see her longer. Only as she vanished before the druid's mighty spell, she threw an apple to Connla.

For a whole month from that day Connla would take nothing, either to eat or to drink, save only from that apple. But as he ate, it grew again and always kept whole. And all the while there grew within him a mighty yearning and longing after the maiden he had seen.

But when the last day of the month of waiting came, Connla stood by the side of the king, his father, on the Plain of Arcomin, and again he saw the maiden come towards him, and again she spoke to him.

"'Tis a glorious place, forsooth, that Connla holds among short-lived mortals awaiting the day of death. But now the folk of life, the ever-living ones, beg and bid thee come to Moy Mell, the Plain of Pleasure, for they have learnt to know thee, seeing thee in thy home among thy dear ones."

When Conn the king heard the maiden's voice he called to his men aloud and said, "Summon swift my druid Coran, for I see she has again this day the power of speech."

Then the maiden said, "Oh, mighty Conn, fighter of a hundred fights, the druid's power is little loved; it has little honor in the mighty land, peopled with so many of the upright. When the Law will come, it will do away with the druid's magic spells that come from the lips of the false black demon."

Then Conn the king observed that since the maiden came Connla his son spoke to none that spoke to him. So Conn of the Hundred Fights said to him, "Is it to thy mind what the woman says, my son?"

"'Tis hard upon me," then said Connla. "I love my own folk above all things; but yet, but yet a longing seizes me for the maiden."

When the maiden heard this, she answered and said, "The ocean is not so strong as the waves of thy longing. Come with me in my curragh, the gleaming, straight-gliding crystal canoe. Soon we can reach Boadag's realm. I see the bright sun sink, yet far as it is, we can reach it before dark. There is, too, another land worthy of thy journey, a land joyous to all that seek it. Only wives and maidens dwell there. If thou wilt, we can seek it and live there alone together in joy."

When the maiden ceased to speak, Connla of the Fiery Hair rushed away from them and sprang into the curragh, the gleaming, straight-gliding crystal canoe. And then they all, king and court, saw it glide away over the bright sea towards the setting sun. Away and away, till eye could see it no longer, and Connla and the fairy maiden went their way on the sea, and were no more seen, nor did any know where they came.

- Joseph Jacobs, *Celtic Fairy Tales* (London: Nutt, 1892), pp. 1–4. Jacobs source: the Irish epic *Book of the Dun Cow,* written before 1106.

The Old Age of Oisin (Ireland)

After the fatal battle of Gavra the only surviving warrior, Oisin, son of Fion, was borne away on the Atlantic waves by the Lady Niav of resplendent beauty, and for a hundred and fifty years he enjoyed her sweet society in the Land of Youth below the waters. Getting at last tired of this monotony of happiness, he expressed a wish to revisit the land where his youth and manhood had been spent, and the loving Niav was obliged to consent. She wept bitterly on seeing him mount the white steed, and warned him that if his feet touched earth, he would never see her nor Tir na n'Og again, and that his strength would be no more than that of a newly-born child.

Alas! Fion and his heroes were scarcely remembered on the plains and by the streams of Erin. The fortress of Almuin was a mound and moat overgrown with docks and thistles, and moss had covered the huge casting-stones of the Fianna. Where strong mounds and ditches once secured armed warriors from their foes, he found unchecked entrance, and prayers and hymns recited and sung in stone buildings surmounted by cross and spire. He saw fewer spears and many more sickles than in the days of Fion, and near the Pass of Wattles (Dublin) he found Patrick the missionary raising a lowly house of worship.

As he sorrowfully rode up the Glen of Thrushes (Glann a Smoll), a crowd of men striving to raise a huge stone on a low wagon, craved his aid. Stooping, he heaved the mass onto the car, but in doing so the girth snapped, the saddle turned round, away flew the white steed, and the last of the heroes lay on the hillside, a grizzly-haired, feeble man.

- Patrick Kennedy, *Legendary Fictions of the Irish Celts* (London: Macmillan, 1891), pp. 212–13.
- Oisin (usually spelled *Ossian* in English) was a legendary Gaelic hero and poet.

True Thomas is seduced by the Queen of Elfland. From a placard commemorating the event near Melrose, Scotland. Photograph by the author.

True Thomas (Scotland)

True Thomas lay on Huntlie bank,	
A ferlie he spied wi' his ee,	ferlie = marvel; ee = eye
And there he saw a lady bright,	
Come riding down by the Eildon Tree.	
Her shirt was o the grass-green silk,	
Her mantle o the velvet fyne,	
At ilka tett of her horse's mane	ilka tett = every lock
Hang fifty siller bells and nine.	siller = silver
True Thomas, he pulld aff his cap,	aff = off
And louted low down to his knee:	louted = bent
"All hail, thou mighty Queen of Heaven!	
For thy peer on earth I never did see."	
"O no, O no, Thomas," she said,	
"That name does not belang to me;	belang = belong
I am but the queen of fair Elfland,	
That am hither come to visit thee.	
"Harp and carp, Thomas," she said,	carp = sing

"Harp and carp along wi me,
And if ye dare to kiss my lips,
Sure of your bodie I will be."
"Betide me weal, betide me woe,   weal = well
That weird shall never daunton me;"   weird = fate; daunton = daunt
Syne he has kissed her rosy lips,   syne = then
All underneath the Eildon Tree.
"Now, ye maun go wi me," she said,   maun = must
"True Thomas, ye maun go wi me,   weal = good
And ye maun serve me seven years,
Thro weal or woe, as may chance to be."
She mounted on her milk-white steed,
She's taen True Thomas up behind,   taen = taken
And aye wheneer her bridle rung,
The steed flew swifter than the wind.
O they rade on, and farther on—   rade = rode
The steed gaed swifter than the wind—   gaed = went
Untill they reached a desart wide,   desart = desert
And living land was left behind.
"Light down, light down, now, True
Thomas,
And lean your head upon my knee;
Abide and rest a little space,
And I will shew you ferlies three.   ferlies = marvels
"O see ye not yon narrow road,
So thick beset with thorns and briers?
That is the path of righteousness,
Tho after it but few enquires.
"And see not ye that braid braid road,   braid = broad
That lies across that lily leven?   lily leven = lovely glade
That is the path of wickedness,
Tho some call it the road to heaven.
"And see not ye that bonny road,
That winds about the fernie brae?   fernie brae = ferny bank
That is the road to fair Elfland,
Where thou and I this night maun gae.   maun gae = must go
"But, Thomas, ye maun hold your   maun = must
tongue,
Whatever ye may hear or see,

For, if you speak word in Elflyn land,
Ye'll neer get back to your ain countrie."   ain = own
O they rade on, and farther on,   rade = rode
And they waded thro rivers aboon the knee,   aboon = above
And they saw neither sun nor moon,
But they heard the roaring of the sea.
It was mirk mirk night, and there was   mirk = dark; nae = no;
nae stern light,   stern = star
And they waded thro red blude to the knee;   blude = blood
For a' the blude that's shed on earth
Rins thro the springs o that countrie.   rins = runs
Syne they came on to a garden green,   syne = then
And she pu'd an apple frae a tree: pu'd = pulled; frae = from
"Take this for thy wages, True Thomas,
It will give the tongue that can never lie."
"My tongue is mine ain," True   ain = own
Thomas said;
"A gudely gift ye wad gie to me!   gudely = goodly; wad = would
I neither dought to buy nor sell,   dought to = could
At fair or tryst where I may be.   tryst = market
"I dought neither speak to prince or peer,   dought = could
Nor ask of grace from fair ladye:"
"Now hold thy peace," the lady said,
"For as I say, so must it be."
He has gotten a coat of the even cloth,   even = smooth
And a pair of shoes of velvet green,
And till seven years were gane and past   gane = gone
True Thomas on earth was never seen.

- Francis James Child, *The English and Scottish Popular Ballads,* vol. 1, part 2 (Boston: Houghton, Mifflin, 1884) no. 37C, pp. 325–26. Child's source: Sir Walter Scott, *Minstrelsy of the Scottish Border* (1802).

- True Thomas—also known as Thomas the Rhymer, Thomas Rymer, Thomas Learmont, or Thomas of Erceldoune—was a historical person who lived in southern Scotland in the thirteenth century. According to legend, Thomas had the gift of prophecy, a consequence of the fairy's gift that he could speak only the truth.

- The Eildon Tree disappeared long ago, but a monument near the town of Melrose marks the spot where it formerly stood.

MERMAIDS

A Fatal Encounter (Isle of Man)

Not far from this [a stone cross between Ballifietcher and Lahnclegere], is the Fairies' Saddle, a stone termed so, as I suppose, from the similitude it has of a saddle. It seems to lie loose on the edge of a small rock, and, the wise natives of Man tell you, is every night made use of by the fairies, but what kind of horses they are, on whose backs this is put, I could never find any who pretended to resolve me.

In a creek between two high rocks, which overlook the sea on this side of the island, they tell you also, that mermen and mermaids have been frequently seen. Many surprising stories of these amphibious creatures have I been told here, as well as at Port Iron; but the strangest of all is this:

A very beautiful mermaid, say they, became so much enamored of a young man who used to tend his sheep on these rocks, that she would frequently come and sit down by him, bring him pieces of coral, fine pearls, and—what were yet greater curiosities, and of infinitely more value, had they fallen into the hands of a person who knew their worth—shells of various forms and figures, and so glorious in their color and shine that they even dazzled the eye that looked upon them.

Her presents were accompanied with smiles, battings on the cheek, and all the harks of a most sincere and tender passion; but one day throwing her arms more than ordinarily eager about him, he began to be frighted that she had a design to draw him into the sea, and struggled till he disengaged himself, and then ran a good many paces from her; which behavior she resented so highly, it seems, that she took up a stone, and after throwing it at him, glided into her more proper element, and was never seen on land again. But the poor youth, though but slightly hit with the stone, felt from that moment so excessive a pain in his bowels, that the cry was never out of his mouth for seven days, at the end of which he died.

- George Waldron, *A Description of the Isle of Man* (Douglas: Manx Society, 1865) pp. 65–66. First published 1731. Waldron does not give this account a title.

Calmed by an Irish Song (Ireland)

There is no luck if you meet a mermaid and you're out at sea, but storms will come, or some ill will happen.

There was a ship on the way to America, and a mermaid was seen following it, and the bad weather began to come.

And the captain said, "It must be some man in the ship she's following, and if we knew which one it was, we'd put him out to her and save ourselves."

So they drew lots, and the lot fell on one man, and then the captain was sorry for him, and said he'd give him a chance till tomorrow. And the next day she was following them still, and they drew lots again, and the lot fell on the same man. But the captain said he'd give him a third chance, but the third day the lot fell on him again.

And when they were going to throw him out he said, "Let me alone for a while."

And he went to the end of the ship and he began to sing a song in Irish, and when he sang, the mermaid began to be quiet and to rock like as if she was asleep. So he went on singing till they came to America, and just as they got to the land the ship was thrown up into the air, and came down on the water again. There's a man told me that was surely true.

- Lady Augusta Gregory, *Visions and Beliefs in the West of Ireland* (New York and London: Putman, 1920), pp. 10–11. Lady Gregory does not give this account a title. Her source: John Corley.

FAIRY TABOOS

Wild Edric (England)

Shropshire men must have been well acquainted with the fairies five hundred years ago. It was reported then that our famous champion Wild Edric had had an elf-maiden for his wife. One day, we are told, when he was returning from hunting in the forest of Clun, he lost his way and wandered about till nightfall, alone, save for one young page. At last he saw the lights of a very large house in the distance, towards which he turned his steps, and when he had reached it, he beheld within a large company of noble ladies dancing. They were exceedingly beautiful, taller and larger than women of the human race, and dressed in gracefully shaped linen garments. They circled round with smooth and easy motion, singing a soft low song of which the hunter could not understand the words.

Among them was one maiden who excelled all the others in beauty, at the sight of whom our hero's heart was inflamed with love. Forgetting the fears of enchantment, which at the first moment had seized him, he hurried round the house, seeking an entrance, and having found it, he rushed in, and snatched the maiden who was the object of his passion from her place in the moving circle. The dancers assailed him with teeth and nails, but backed by his page, he escaped at length from their hands, and succeeded in carrying off his fair captive.

For three whole days not his utmost caresses and persuasions could prevail on her to utter a single word, but on the fourth day she suddenly broke the silence. "Good luck to you, my dear!" said she, "and you will be lucky too, and enjoy health and peace and plenty, as long as you do not reproach me on account of my sisters, or the place from which you snatched me away, or anything connected with it. For on the day when you do so you will lose both your bride and your good fortune; and when I am taken away from you, you will pine away quickly to an early death."

He pledged himself by all that was most sacred to be ever faithful and constant in his love for her, and they were solemnly wedded in the presence of all the nobles from far and near, whom Edric invited to their bridal feast.

At that time William the Norman was newly made king of England, who, hearing of this wonder, desired both to see the lady, and to test the truth of the tale; and bade the newly married pair to London, where he was holding his court. Thither then they went, and many witnesses from their own country with them, who brought with them the testimony of others who could not present themselves to the king. But the marvelous beauty of the lady was the best of all proofs of her superhuman origin. And the king let them return in peace, wondering greatly.

Many years passed happily by, till one evening Edric returned late from hunting and could not find his wife. He sought her and called for her for some time in vain. At last she appeared.

"I suppose," began he, with angry looks, "it is your sisters who have detained you such a long time, have they not?"

The rest of his upbraiding was addressed to thin air, for the moment her sisters were mentioned she vanished. Edric's grief was overwhelming. He sought the place where he had found her at first, but no tears, no laments of his could call her back. He cried out day and night against his own folly, and pined away and died of sorrow, as his wife had long before foretold.

- Charlotte Sophia Burne, *Shropshire Folk-Lore* (London: Trübner, 1883), pp. 59–60. Burne's source: Walter Mapes, a twelfth-century chronicler.
- William the Conqueror (here called *the Norman*) was crowned king of England in 1066.

Touched by Iron (Wales)

The son of a farmer on Drws Coed farm was one foggy day looking after his father's sheep, when crossing a marshy meadow he beheld a little lady behind some rising ground. She had yellow hair, blue eyes, and rosy cheeks.

He approached her and asked permission to converse; whereupon she smiled sweetly and said to him, "Idol of my hopes, you have come at last!"

They there and then began to "keep company" and met each other daily here and there along the farm meadows. His intentions were honorable; he desired her to marry him. He was sometimes absent for days together, no one knew where, and his friends whispered about that he had been witched.

Around the Turf Lake (Llyn y Dywarchen) was a grove of trees, and under one of these one day the fairy promised to be his. The consent of her father was now necessary. One moonlight night an appointment was made to meet in this wood. The father and daughter did not appear till the moon had disappeared behind the hill. Then they both came. The fairy father immediately gave his consent to the marriage, on one condition, namely, that her future husband should never hit her with iron.

"If ever thou dost touch her flesh with iron she shall be no more thine, but she shall return to her own."

They were married—a good-looking pair. Large sums of money were brought by her, the night before the wedding, to Drws Coed. The shepherd lad became wealthy, they had several handsome children, and they were very happy.

After some years, they were one day out riding, when her horse sank in a deep mire, and by the assistance of her husband, in her hurry to remount, she was struck on her knee by the stirrup of the saddle. Immediately voices were heard singing on the brow of the hill, and she disappeared, leaving all her children behind.

She and her mother devised a plan by which she could see her beloved, but as she was not allowed to walk the earth with man, they floated a large turf on the lake, and on this turf she stood for hours at a time holding converse with her husband. This continued until his death.

- Wirt Sikes, *British Goblins: Welsh Folk-lore, Fairy Mythology, Legends, and Traditions* (Boston: Osgood, 1881), pp. 44–45. Sikes does not give this account a title.
- Llyn y Dywarchen is a lake in Snowdonia National Park, North Wales.

FAIRY BRIDES

The Swan Maiden (Sweden)

A young peasant in the parish of Mellby, who often amused himself with hunting, saw one day three swans flying toward him, which settled down upon the strand of a sound nearby. Approaching the place, he was astonished at seeing the three swans divest themselves of their feathery attire, which they threw into the grass, and three maidens of dazzling beauty step forth and spring into the water. After sporting in the waves awhile they returned to the land, where they resumed their former garb and shape and flew away in the same direction from which they came.

One of them, the youngest and fairest, had, in the meantime, so smitten the young hunter that neither night nor day could he tear his thoughts from the bright image. His mother, noticing that something was wrong with her son, and that the chase, which had formerly been his favorite pleasure, had lost its attractions, asked him finally the cause of his melancholy, whereupon he related to her what he had seen and declared that there was no longer any happiness in this life for him if he could not possess the fair swan maiden.

"Nothing is easier," said the mother. "Go at sunset next Thursday evening to the place where you last saw her. When the three swans come, give attention to where your chosen one lays her feathery garb, take it, and hasten away."

The young man listened to his mother's instructions, and, betaking himself the following Thursday evening to a convenient hiding place near the sound, he waited, with impatience, the coming of the swans. The sun was just sinking behind the trees when the young man's ears were greeted by a whizzing in the air, and the three swans settled down upon the beach, as on their former visit.

As soon as they had laid off their swan attire they were again transformed into the most beautiful maidens, and, springing out upon the white sand, they were soon enjoying themselves in the water. From his hiding place the young hunter had taken careful note of where his enchantress had laid her swan feathers. Stealing softly forth, he took them and returned to his place of concealment in the surrounding foliage.

Soon thereafter two of the swans were heard to fly away, but the third, in search of her clothes, discovered the young man, before whom, believing him responsible for their disappearance, she fell upon her knees and prayed that her swan attire might be returned to her. The hunter was, however, unwilling to yield the beautiful prize, and, casting a cloak around her shoulders, carried her home.

Preparations were soon made for a magnificent wedding, which took place in due form, and the young couple dwelt lovingly and contentedly together.

One Thursday evening, seven years later, the hunter related to her how he had sought and won his wife. He brought forth and showed her, also, the white swan feathers of her former days. No sooner were they placed in her hands than she was transformed once more into a swan, and instantly took flight through the open window. In breathless astonishment, the man stared wildly after his rapidly vanishing wife, and before a year and a day had passed, he was laid, with his longings and sorrows, in his allotted place in the village churchyard.

- Herman Hofberg, *Swedish Fairy Tales,* trans. W. H. Myers (Chicago: Conkey, 1893), pp. 35–38. Aarne-Thompson folktale type 400*.
- Mellby (also spelled *Mjällby*) is in the province Blekinge in southern Sweden.

The Lady of Gollerus (Ireland)

On the shore of Smerwick harbor, one fine summer's morning, just at daybreak, stood Dick Fitzgerald "shoghing the dudeen," which may be translated, smoking his pipe. The sun was gradually rising behind the lofty Brandon, the dark sea was getting green in the light, and the mists clearing away out of the valleys went rolling and curling like the smoke from the corner of Dick's mouth.

"'Tis just the pattern of a pretty morning," said Dick, taking the pipe from between his lips and looking towards the distant ocean, which lay as still and tranquil as a tomb of polished marble. "Well, to be sure," continued he, after a pause, "'tis mighty lonesome to be talking to one's self by way of company, and not to have another soul to answer one—nothing but the child of one's own voice, the echo! I know this, that if I had the luck, or maybe the misfortune," said Dick, with a melancholy smile, "to have the woman, it would not be this way with me! And what in the wide world is a man without a wife? He's no more, surely, than a bottle without a drop of drink in it, or dancing without music, or the left leg of a scissors, or a fishing line without a hook, or any other matter that is no ways complete. Is it not so?" said Dick Fitzgerald, casting his eyes towards a rock upon the strand, which, though it could not speak, stood up as firm and looked as bold as ever Kerry witness did.

But what was his astonishment at beholding, just at the foot of that rock, a beautiful young creature combing her hair, which was of a sea-green color; and now the salt water shining on it appeared, in the morning light, like melted butter upon cabbage.

Dick guessed at once that she was a merrow, although he had never seen one before, for he spied the *cohuleen druith,* or little enchanted cap, which the sea people use for diving down into the ocean, lying upon the strand near her; and he had heard that if once he could possess himself of the cap, she would lose the power of going away into the water; so he seized it with

Dick falls in love with a merrow. Woodcut after a drawing by W. H. Brooke, from Thomas Crofton Croker, *Fairy Legends and Traditions* (1826).

all speed, and she, hearing the noise, turned her head about as natural as any Christian.

When the merrow saw that her little diving cap was gone, the salt tears—doubly salt, no doubt, from her—came trickling down her cheeks, and she began a low mournful cry with just the tender voice of a newborn infant. Dick, although he knew well enough what she was crying for, determined to keep the *cohuleen druith,* let her cry never so much, to see what luck would come out of it. Yet he could not help pitying her; and when the dumb thing looked up in his face, and her cheeks all moist with tears, 'twas enough to make anyone feel, let alone Dick, who had ever and always, like most of his countrymen, a mighty tender heart of his own.

"Don't cry, my darling," said Dick Fitzgerald; but the merrow, like any bold child, only cried the more for that.

Dick sat himself down by her side, and took hold of her hand, by way of comforting her. 'Twas in no particular an ugly hand, only there was a small web between the fingers, as there is in a duck's foot; but 'twas as thin and as white as the skin between egg and shell.

"What's your name, my darling?" says Dick, thinking to make her conversant with him; but he got no answer; and he was certain sure now, either that she could not speak, or did not understand him. He therefore squeezed her hand in his, as the only way he had of talking to her. It's the universal language; and there's not a woman in the world, be she fish or lady, that does not understand it.

The merrow did not seem much displeased at this mode of conversation, and, making an end of her whining all at once, "Man," says she, looking up in Dick Fitzgerald's face, "Man, will you eat me?"

"By all the red petticoats and check aprons between Dingle and Tralee," cried Dick, jumping up in amazement, "I'd as soon eat myself, my jewel! Is it I eat you, my pet? Now, 'twas some ugly ill-looking thief of a fish put that notion into your own pretty head, with the nice green hair down upon it, that is so cleanly combed out this morning!"

"Man," said the merrow, "what will you do with me, if you won't eat me?"

Dick's thoughts were running on a wife. He saw, at the first glimpse, that she was handsome; but since she spoke, and spoke too like any real woman, he was fairly in love with her. 'Twas the neat way she called him "man" that settled the matter entirely.

"Fish," says Dick, trying to speak to her after her own short fashion. "Fish," says he, "here's my word, fresh and fasting, for you this blessed morning, that I'll make you Mistress Fitzgerald before all the world, and that's what I'll do."

"Never say the word twice." says she. "I'm ready and willing to be yours, Mister Fitzgerald; but stop, if you please, 'till I twist up my hair."

It was some time before she had settled it entirely to her liking, for she guessed, I suppose, that she was going among strangers, where she would be looked at. When that was done, the merrow put the comb in her pocket, and then bent down her head and whispered some words to the water that was close to the foot of the rock.

Dick saw the murmur of the words upon the top of the sea, going out towards the wide ocean, just like a breath of wind rippling along, and, says he, in the greatest wonder, "Is it speaking you are, my darling, to the saltwater?"

"It's nothing else," says she, quite carelessly, "I'm just sending word home to my father, not to be waiting breakfast for me, just to keep him from being uneasy in his mind."

"And who's your father, my duck?" says Dick.

"What!" said the merrow, "Did you never hear of my father? He's the king of the waves, to be sure!"

"And yourself, then, is a real king's daughter?" said Dick, opening his two eyes to take a full and true survey of his wife that was to be. "Oh, I'm nothing else but a made man with you, and a king your father. To be sure he has all the money that's down in the bottom of the sea!"

"Money," repeated the merrow, "what's money?"

"'Tis no bad thing to have when one wants it," replied Dick; "and maybe now the fishes have the understanding to bring up whatever you bid them?"

"Oh! yes," said the merrow, "they bring me what I want."

"To speak the truth," said Dick, "'tis a straw bed I have at home before you, and that, I'm thinking, is no ways fitting for a king's daughter; so if 'twould not be displeasing to you, just to mention, a nice featherbed, with a pair of new blankets—but what am I talking about? Maybe you have not such things as beds down under the water?"

"By all means," said she, "Mr. Fitzgerald—plenty of beds at your service. I've fourteen oyster beds of my own, not to mention one just planting for the rearing of young ones."

"You have," says Dick, scratching his head and looking a little puzzled. "'Tis a featherbed I was speaking of, but clearly, yours is the very cut of a decent plan, to have bed and supper so handy to each other, that a person, when they'd have the one, need never ask for the other."

However, bed or no bed, money or no money, Dick Fitzgerald determined to marry the merrow, and the merrow had given her consent. Away they went, therefore, across the strand, from Gollerus to Ballinrunnig, where Father Fitzgibbon happened to be that morning.

"There are two words to this bargain, Dick Fitzgerald," said his Reverence, looking mighty glum. "And is it a fishy woman you'd marry? The Lord preserve us! Send the scaly creature home to her own people, that's my advice to you, wherever she came from."

Dick had the *cohuleen druith* in his hand, and was about to give it back to the merrow, who looked covetously at it, but he thought for a moment, and then, says he, "Please your Reverence, she's a king's daughter."

"If she was the daughter of fifty kings," said Father Fitzgibbon, "I tell you, you can't marry her, she being a fish."

"Please your Reverence," said Dick again, in an undertone, "she is as mild and as beautiful as the moon."

"If she was as mild and as beautiful as the sun, moon, and stars, all put together, I tell you, Dick Fitzgerald," said the priest, stamping his right foot, "you can't marry her, she being a fish!"

"But she has all the gold that's down in the sea only for the asking, and I'm a made man if I marry her; and," said Dick, looking up slyly, "I can make it worth any one's while to do the job."

"Oh! That alters the case entirely," replied the priest. "Why there's some reason now in what you say. Why didn't you tell me this before? Marry her by all means, if she was ten times a fish. Money, you know, is not to be refused in these bad times, and I may as well have the hansel of it as another, that maybe would not take half the pains in counseling you as I have done."

So Father Fitzgibbon married Dick Fitzgerald to the merrow, and like any loving couple, they returned to Gollerus well pleased with each other. Everything prospered with Dick. He was at the sunny side of the world; the merrow made the best of wives, and they lived together in the greatest contentment.

It was wonderful to see, considering where she had been brought up, how she would busy herself about the house, and how well she nursed the children; for, at the end of three years, there were as many young Fitzgeralds—two boys and a girl.

In short, Dick was a happy man, and so he might have continued to the end of his days, if he had only the sense to take proper care of what he had got. Many another man, however, beside Dick, has not had wit enough to do that.

One day when Dick was obliged to go to Tralee, he left the wife minding the children at home after him, and thinking she had plenty to do without disturbing his fishing tackle.

Dick was no sooner gone than Mrs. Fitzgerald set about cleaning up the house, and chancing to pull down a fishing net, what should she find behind it in a hole in the wall but her own *cohuleen druith*.

She took it out and looked at it, and then she thought of her father the king, and her mother the queen, and her brothers and sisters, and she felt a longing to go back to them.

She sat down on a little stool and thought over the happy days she had spent under the sea; then she looked at her children, and thought on the love and affection of poor Dick, and how it would break his heart to lose her. "But," says she, "he won't lose me entirely, for I'll come back to him again, and who can blame me for going to see my father and my mother after being so long away from them?"

She got up and went towards the door, but came back again to look once more at the child that was sleeping in the cradle. She kissed it gently, and as she kissed it a tear trembled for an instant in her eye and then fell on its rosy cheek. She wiped away the tear, and turning to the eldest little girl, told her to take good care of her brothers and to be a good child herself until she came back.

The merrow then went down to the strand. The sea was lying calm and smooth, just heaving and glittering in the sun, and she thought she heard a faint sweet singing, inviting her to come down. All her old ideas and feelings came flooding over her mind. Dick and her children were at the instant forgotten, and placing the *cohuleen druith* on her head, she plunged in.

Dick came home in the evening, and missing his wife, he asked Kathelin, his little girl, what had become of her mother, but she could not tell him. He then enquired of the neighbors, and he learned that she was seen going towards the strand with a strange looking thing like a cocked hat in her hand. He returned to his cabin to search for the *cohuleen druith*. It was gone, and the truth now flashed upon him.

Year after year did Dick Fitzgerald wait, expecting the return of his wife, but he never saw her more. Dick never married again, always thinking that the merrow would sooner or later return to him, and nothing could ever persuade him but that her father the king kept her below by main force; "for," said Dick, "she surely would not of herself give up her husband and her children."

While she was with him, she was so good a wife in every respect, that to this day she is spoken of in the tradition of the country as the pattern for one, under the name of the Lady of Gollerus.

- Thomas Crofton Croker, *Fairy Legends and Traditions of the South of Ireland,* vol. 2 (London: Murray, 1828), pp. 3–13. Christiansen migratory legend type 4080.
- Smerwick Harbor is at the tip of Dingle Peninsula in southwest Ireland. Gollerus is a small village on the eastern side of the harbor.
- Croker gives the name of the enchanted cap as *cohuleen driuth,* but I have preferred the more standard spelling *cohuleen druith.*

FAIRY ANIMALS

The White Cow of Mitchell's Fold (England)

On the Corndon Hill, a bare moorland in the extreme west of Shropshire, stands a half-ruined stone circle known as Mitchell's Fold. And thereto hangs a tale.

In times gone by, before anyone now living can remember, there was once a dreadful famine all about this country, and the people had like to have been clemmed [nearly starved to death]. There were many more living in this part then than what there are now, and times were very bad indeed. And all they had to depend upon was that there used to come a fairy cow upon the hill, up at Mitchell's Fold, night and morning, to be milked. A beautiful pure white cow she was, and no matter how many came to milk her, there was always enough for all, so long as everyone that came only took one pailful.

It was in this way: If anyone was to milk her dry, she would go away and never come again; but so long as everyone took only a pailful apiece, she never would be dry. They might take whatever sort of vessel they liked to milk her into, so long as it was only one apiece, she would always fill it.

Well, and at last there came an old witch, Mitchell her name was. A bad old woman she was, and did a deal of harm, and had a spite against everybody. And she brought a riddle [sieve], and milked the cow into that, and of course the poor thing couldn't fill it. And the old woman milked her, and milked her, and at last she milked her dry, and the cow was never seen there again, not after.

Folks say she went off into Warwickshire like a crazy thing, and turned into the wild dun cow that Guy Earl of Warwick killed; but anyhow they say she was sadly missed in this country, and many died after she was gone, and there's never been so many living about here, not since.

But the old woman got her punishment. She was turned into one of those stones on the hillside, and all the other stones were put up round her to keep her in, and that's how the place came to be called Mitchell's Fold, because her name was Mitchell, you see.

There used to be more stones than there are now, but they have been taken away at one time or another. It's best not to meddle with such places. There was a farmer lived by there, and he blew up some of them and took away the pieces to put round his horse pond, but he never did no good after.

- Charlotte Sophia Burne, *Shropshire Folk-Lore* (London: Trübner, 1883), pp. 39–40.
- For additional legends about fairies' association with prehistoric structures see the section "Ancient Monuments" earlier in this chapter.

The Hedley Kow (England)

The Hedley Kow was a bogie, mischievous rather than malignant, which haunted the village of Hedley, near Ebchester. His appearance was never very alarming, and he used to end his frolics with a horselaugh at the expense of his victims.... Two adventures with the Hedley Kow are thus related:

A farmer named Forster, who lived near Hedley, went out into the field one morning and caught, as he believed, his own grey horse. After putting the harness on, and yoking him to the cart, Forster was about to drive off, when the creature slipped away from the limmers "like a knotless thread," and set up a great nicker as he flung up his heels and scoured away, revealing himself clearly as the Hedley Kow.

Again, two young men of Newlands, near Ebchester, went out one evening to meet their sweethearts and, arriving at the trysting place, saw them, as it appeared, a short distance before them. The girls walked on for two or three miles; the lads followed, quite unable to overtake them, till at last they found themselves up to their knees in a bog and their beguilers vanished, with a loud "Ha! ha!" The young men got clear of the mire and ran homewards as fast as they could, the bogie at their heels hooting and mocking them. In crossing the Derwent they fell into the water, mistook each other for the sprite, and finally reached home separately, each telling a fearful tale of having been chased by the Hedley Kow and nearly drowned in the Derwent.

Surely this northern sprite is closely akin to Robin Goodfellow, whom Ben Jonson introduced to us as speaking thus:

> Sometimes I meete them like a man,
> Sometimes an ox, sometimes a hound,
> And to a horse I turn me can,
> To trip and trot about them round.
>
> But if to ride
> My backe they stride,
> More swift than wind away I go:
> O'er the hedge and lands,
> Through pools and ponds,
> I whirry laughing, Ho! ho! ho!

- William Henderson, *Notes on the Folk-Lore of the Northern Counties of England and the Borders* (London: Longmans, Green, and Company, 1866), pp. 234–35.
- Hedley, Ebchester, and Newlands are in County Durham.

Whitsuntide Legend of the Fairy Horses (Ireland)

There was a widow woman with one son, who had a nice farm of her own close to a lake, and she took great pains in the cultivation of the land, and her corn was the best in the whole country. But when nearly ripe and just fit for cutting, she found to her dismay that every night it was trampled down and cruelly damaged; yet no one could tell by what means it was done.

So she set her son to watch. And at midnight he heard a great noise and a rushing of waves on the beach, and up out of the lake came a great troop of horses, who began to graze the corn and trample it down madly with their hoofs.

When he told all this to his mother she bade him watch the next night also, but to take several of the men with him furnished with bridles, and when the horses rose from the lake they were to fling the bridles over as many as they could catch.

Now at midnight there was the same noise heard again, and the rush of the waves, and in an instant all the field was filled with the fairy horses, grazing the corn and trampling it down. The men pursued them, but only succeeded in capturing one, and he was the noblest of the lot. The rest all plunged back into the lake. However, the men brought home the captured horse to the widow, and he was put in the stable and grew big and strong, and never another horse came up out of the lake, nor was the corn touched after that night of his capture. But when a year had passed by, the widow said it was a shame to keep so fine a horse idle, and she bade the young man, her son, take him out to the hunt that was held that day by all the great gentry of the country, for it was Whitsuntide.

And, in truth, the horse carried him splendidly at the hunt, and everyone admired both the fine young rider and his steed. But as he was returning home, when they came within sight of the lake from which the fairy steed had risen, he began to plunge violently, and finally threw his rider. And the young man's foot being unfortunately caught in the stirrup, he was dragged along till he was torn limb from limb, while the horse still continued galloping on madly to the water, leaving some fragment of the unhappy lad after him on the road, till they reached the margin of the lake, when the horse shook off the last limb of the dead youth from him, and plunging into the waves disappeared from sight.

The people reverently gathered up the remains of the dead, and erected a monument of stones over the lad in a field by the edge of the lake; and every one that passes by still lays a stone and says a prayer that the spirit of the dead may rest in peace.

The phantom horses were never seen again, but the lake has an evil reputation even to this day amongst the people; and no one would venture a boat on it after sundown at Whitsuntide, or during the time of the ripening of the corn, or when the harvest is ready for the sickle, for strange sounds are heard at night, like the wild galloping of a horse across the meadow, along with the cries as of a man in his death agony.

- Lady Jane Francesca Wilde, *Ancient Legends, Mystic Charms, and Superstitions of Ireland* (London: Chatto and Windus, 1919), pp. 108–109.

- Lady Wilde prefaces this legend with the following commentary: Whitsuntide is a very fatal and unlucky time. Especially beware of water then, for there is an evil spirit in it, and no one should venture to bathe, nor to sail in a boat for fear of being drowned; nor to go on a journey where water has to be crossed. And everything in the house must be sprinkled with holy water at Whitsuntide to keep away the fairies who at that season are very active and malicious, and bewitch the cattle, and carry off the young children, and come up from the sea to hold strange midnight revels, when they kill with their fairy darts the unhappy mortal who crosses their path and pries at their mysteries.

- Whitsuntide is the week beginning with the Christian feast of Whitsunday (also known as Pentecost), the fiftieth day after Easter.

WATER SPIRITS DEMAND A SACRIFICE

The Hour Is Here! (Germany)

In the vicinity of Schöneiche not far from Rüdersdorf a group of people were making merry on the bank of a small pond when suddenly they heard someone clapping his hands and a voice calling from the water, "The hour is here, and the person is not here yet!" This was repeated several times.

A short time later an apprentice came along the path, then hurried to the bank of the pond to quench his thirst. One of the merrymakers went to him and held him away from the water, telling him what they had heard. Thus the apprentice changed his mind and went with the merrymakers to a tavern in Schöneiche, where he ordered a glass of beer. He had scarcely brought it to his lips when he collapsed on the floor and died.

- A. Kuhn and W. Schwartz, *Norddeutsche Sagen, Märchen und Gebräuche* (Leipzig: Brockhaus, 1848), pp. 80–81. Kuhn's and Schwartz's source: "Oral from Friedrichshagen near Köpenick." Christiansen migratory legend type 4050.
- The places named in this legend are all near Berlin.

The Hour Is Come, but the Man Is Not (Wales)

As a man from the village of Llanegryn was returning in the dusk of the evening across the mountain from Dolgelley, he heard, when hard by Llyn Gwernan, a voice crying out from the water, "Daeth yr awr ond ni itheth y dyn! (The hour is come, but the man is not!)"

As the villager went on his way a little distance, what should meet him but a man of insane appearance, and with nothing on but his shirt. As he saw the man making full pelt for the waters of the lake, he rushed at him to prevent him from proceeding any further. But as to the sequel there is some doubt. One version makes the villager conduct the man back about a mile from the lake to a farm house called Dyffrydan, which was on the former's way home. Others seem to think that the man in his shirt rushed irresistibly into the lake, and this I have no doubt comes nearer the end of the story in its original form.

- John Rhys, *Celtic Folklore: Welsh and Manx*, (Oxford: Oxford UP, 1901), p. 243. Christiansen migratory legend type 4050.
- Llanegryn, Dolgelley (also spelled *Dolgellau*), and Llyn Gwernan (Lake Gwernan) are in North Wales.

WILL-O'-THE-WISP

The Ellylldan (Wales)

The Ellylldan is a species of elf exactly corresponding to the English will-o'-wisp. . . . Pwca, or Pooka, is but another name for the Ellylldan, as our Puck is another name for the will-o'-wisp; but in both cases the shorter term has a more poetic flavor and a wider latitude. . . . The most familiar form of the Pwca story is one which I have encountered in several localities, varying so little in its details that each account would be interchangeable with another by the alteration of local names. This form presents a peasant who is returning home from his work, or from a fair, when he sees a light traveling before him. Looking closer he perceives that it is carried by a dusky little figure, holding a lantern or candle at arm's length over its head. He follows it for several miles and suddenly finds himself on the brink of a frightful precipice. From far down below, there rises to his ears the sound of a foaming torrent. At the same moment the little goblin with the lantern springs across the chasm, alighting on the opposite side, raises the light again high over its head, utters a loud and malicious laugh, blows out its candle, and disappears up the opposite hill, leaving the awestruck peasant to get home as best he can.

- Wirt Sikes, *British Goblins: Welsh Folk-Lore, Fairy Mythology, Legends, and Traditions* (Boston: Osgood, 1881), pp. 18–24.
- Some scholars believe that Shakespeare drew inspiration from the Welsh fairy featured here for his Puck in *A Midsummer Night's Dream*.

Will-o'-the-Wisp (Germany)

The will-o'-the-wisp is a mischievous gnome who leads people astray at nighttime or in the fog, causing them to loose their way and end up in a swamp. He does this foremost with inquisitive people who purposely follow him. The best way to avoid him or to render him harmless is to stay away from the footpaths where he has power and always to keep one foot in a wagon rut. He helps some people who have lost their way by leading them home, if they speak to him kindly and offer him a generous payment.

Once a person who had lost his way offered him two silver groschens if he would lead him home safely. The will-o'-the-wisp agreed, and finally they arrived at the lost man's house. Happy that he was no longer in need of help, he thanked his guide; but instead of the promised payment, he gave him only a small copper coin. The will-o'-the-wisp accepted it, then asked if he could now find his way home by himself.

He answered, "Yes! I can already see my open front door." But stepping toward it, he fell into some water, for everything he had seen had been only an illusion.

The will-o'-the-wisp takes special delight in tormenting drunks making their way homeward from a fair or an evening of drinking. He leads them astray, and when in their drunkenness they can go no further, preferring instead to sleep off their binge out of doors, then he burns them on the soles of their feet.

In some regions the people believe that wills-o'-the-wisp are the souls of children who died without being baptized. They are seen especially atop graveyard walls. They disappear when one throws a handful of graveyard soil at them.

- Karl Haupt, *Sagenbuch der Lausitz,* vol. 1 (Leipzig: Engelmann, 1862), pp. 58–59.

THIEVING FAIRIES

The Three Cows (England)

There was a farmer, and he had three cows, fine fat beauties they were. One was called Facey, the other Diamond, and the third Beauty. One morning he went into his cowshed, and there he found Facey so thin that the wind would have blown her away. Her skin hung loose about her, all her flesh was gone, and she stared out of her great eyes as though she'd seen a ghost, and what was more, the fireplace in the kitchen was one great pile of wood-ash. Well, he was bothered with it; he could not see how all this had come about.

Next morning his wife went out to the shed, and see! Diamond was for all the world as wisht a looking creature as Facey—nothing but a bag of bones, all the flesh gone, and half a rick of wood was gone, too, but the fireplace was piled up three feet high with white wood ashes. The farmer determined to watch the third night; so he hid in a closet which opened out of the parlor, and he left the door just ajar, that he might see what passed.

Tick, tick went the clock, and the farmer was nearly tired of waiting; he had to bite his little finger to keep himself awake, when suddenly the door of his house flew open, and in rushed maybe a thousand pixies, laughing and dancing and dragging at Beauty's halter till they had brought the cow into the middle of the room. The farmer really thought he should have died with fright, and so perhaps he would, had not curiosity kept him alive.

Tick, tick went the clock, but he did not hear it now. He was too intent staring at the pixies and his last beautiful cow. He saw them throw her down, fall on her, and kill her; then with their knives they ripped her open, and flayed her as clean as a whistle. Then out ran some of the little people and brought in firewood and made a roaring blaze on the hearth, and there they cooked the flesh of the cow. They baked and they boiled, they stewed and they fried.

"Take care," cried one, who seemed to be the king. "Let no bone be broken."

Well, when they had all eaten, and had devoured every scrap of beef on the cow, they began playing games with the bones, tossing them one to another. One little leg bone fell close to the closet door, and the farmer was so afraid lest the pixies should come there and find him in their search for the bone, that he put out his hand and drew it in to him. Then he saw the king stand on the table and say, "Gather the bones!"

Round and round flew the imps, picking up the bones. "Arrange them," said the king; and they placed them all in their proper positions in the hide of the cow. Then they folded the skin over them, and the king struck the heap of bone and skin with his rod. Whisht! Up sprang the cow and lowed dismally. It was alive again; but alas! as the pixies dragged it back to its stall, it halted in the off forefoot, for a bone was missing.

> The cock crew,
> Away they flew.

And the farmer crept trembling to bed.

- William Henderson, *Notes on the Folk-Lore of the Northern Counties of England and the Borders* (London: Longmans, Green, and Company, 1866), pp. 321–22. Henderson's source: Sabine Baring-Gould, who collected this tale in Devonshire.

Riechert the Smith (Germany)

A cultivated field adjoins the east side of Dwarf Mountain near Dardesheim. Once a smith by the name of Riechert planted peas in this field. He noticed that frequently someone picked the peas just as they were at their best. In order to catch the thief he built a little hut on the field, then kept watch in it day and night. He did not see anything during the daytime, but every morning he discovered that in spite of his standing guard some of his crop had been stolen. Angry at his lack of success, he decided to thresh the remaining peas right in the field. He set to work at daybreak. He had not threshed out half the peas when he heard pitiful screams. Investigating, he saw one of the dwarfs lying on the ground beneath the peas. Riechert had crushed his skull with his threshing flail, and because his fog cap had been knocked off, the dwarf was now visible. He quickly fled back into the mountain.

- Jacob and Wilhelm Grimm, *Deutsche Sagen,* vol. 1 (Berlin: Nicolai, 1816), no. 156. The Grimms' source: Johann Karl Christoph, *Volcks-Sagen* (1800).
- Dardesheim is a village northwest of Halberstadt in central Germany. The fog cap (German *Nebelkappe* or *Tarnkappe*), with its ability to make its wearer invisible, is a common feature of German dwarf lore.

NIGHT-MARES

The Alp (Germany)

A cabinetmaker in Bühl slept in a bed in his workshop. Several nights in a row something laid itself onto his chest and pressed against him until he could hardly breathe. After talking the matter over with a friend, the next night he lay awake in bed. At the stroke of twelve a cat slipped in through a hole. The cabinetmaker quickly stopped up the hole, caught the cat, and nailed down one of its paws. Then he went to sleep.

The next morning he found a beautiful naked woman in the cat's place. One of her hands was nailed down. She pleased him so much that he married her.

One day, after she had borne him three children, she was with him in his workshop, when he said to her, "Look, that is where you came in!" and he opened the hole that had been stopped up until now.

The woman suddenly turned into a cat, ran out through the opening, and she was never seen again.

- Bernhard Baader, *Volkssagen aus dem Lande Baden und den angrenzenden Gegenden* (Karlsruhe: Herder, 1851), no. 136, p. 126.
- Bühl is a town in southwest Germany. The closest larger city is Baden-Baden.

A Charm to Control the Night-Mare (England)

S. George, S. George, our ladies knight,
He walkt by daie, so did he by night.

Untill such time as he her found,
He hir beat and he hir bound,
Untill hir troth she to him plight,
She would not come to him that night.

- Reginald Scot, *Discoverie of Witchcraft* (New York: Dover, 1972), p. 49. First published 1584. This charm is also found in James Orchard Halliwell-Phillipps, *Popular Rhymes and Nursery Tales* (London: Smith, 1849), p. 213.

A Shetland Charm (Shetland Islands)

Arthur Knight
He rade a' night,
Wi' open swird
An' candle light.

He sought da mare;
He fan' da mare;
He bund da mare
Wi' her ain hair.

And made da mare
Ta swear:
'At she should never
Bide a' night
Whar ever she heard
O' Arthur Knight.

- G. F. Black and Northcote W. Thomas, *County Folk-Lore*, vol. 3: *Examples of Printed Folk-Lore Concerning the Orkney & Shetland Islands* (London: Folk-Lore Society, 1903), p. 145. Black's source: Karl Blind, *Nineteenth Century* (1879).

FAIRY TALES FOR CHILDREN

Frau Holle (Germany)

A widow had two daughters; the one was beautiful and industrious, the other ugly and lazy. The mother greatly favored the ugly, lazy girl. The other one had to do all the work and was truly a Cinderella. One day while pulling a bucket of water from the well she leaned over too far and fell in. Recovering, she found herself in a beautiful meadow. The sun was shining, and there were thousands of flowers. She walked along and soon came to an oven full of bread. The bread called out, "Take me out, or I'll burn! I've been thoroughly baked for a long time!" The girl took the bread from the oven and walked further until she came to a tree laden with ripe apples.

"Shake me! Shake me! We apples are all ripe!" cried the tree, and the girl shook the tree until the apples fell as though it were raining apples. When none were left in the tree, she continued on her way.

Finally she came to a small house. An old woman was peering out from inside. She had very large teeth, which frightened the girl, and she wanted to run away. But the old woman called out to her, "Don't be afraid, dear child. Stay here with me, and if you do my housework in an orderly fashion, it will go well with you. Only you must take care to make my bed well and shake it until the feathers fly, then it will snow in the world. I am Frau Holle."

Because the old woman spoke so kindly to her, the girl agreed and started in her service. She took care of everything to her satisfaction and always shook her featherbed vigorously. Therefore she had a good life with her: no angry words and cooked meals every day. Now after she had been with Frau Holle for a time, her heart saddened. Even though she was many thousands of times better off here than at home, still she had a yearning for home. Finally she said to the old woman, "I have such a longing for home, and even though I am very well off here, I cannot stay longer."

Frau Holle said, "You are right, and because you have served me so faithfully, I will take you back myself." With that she took her by the hand and led her to a large gate. The gate opened, and while the girl was standing under it, an immense rain of gold fell, and all the gold stuck to her, so that she was completely covered with it. "This is yours because you have been so industrious," said Frau Holle. With that the gate closed, and the girl found herself above in the world. She went home to her mother, and because she arrived all covered with gold, she was well received.

When the mother heard how she had come to the great wealth, she wanted to achieve the same fortune for the other, the ugly and lazy daughter. She made her go and jump into the well. Like the other one, she too awoke in a beautiful meadow, and she walked along the same path. When she came to the oven, the bread cried again, "Oh, take me out, take me out, or else I'll burn! I've been thoroughly baked for a long time!" But the lazy one answered, "As if I would want to get all dirty," and walked away. Soon she came to the apple tree. It cried out, "Oh, shake me, shake me, we apples are all ripe." But she answered, "Oh yes, one could fall on my head," and with that she walked on.

When she came to Frau Holle's house, she was not afraid, because she had already heard about her large teeth, and she immediately began to work for her. On the first day she forced herself, was industrious and obeyed Frau Holle, when she said something to her, because she was thinking about all the gold that she would give her. But on the second day she already began to be lazy, on the third day even more so, then she didn't even want to get up in the morning. She did not make the bed for Frau Holle, the way she was supposed to, and she did not shake it until the feathers flew.

Frau Holle soon became tired of this and dismissed her of her duties. This is just what the lazy girl wanted, for she thought that she would now get the rain of gold. Frau Holle led her too to the gate. She stood beneath it, but instead of gold, a large kettle full of pitch spilled over her. "That is the reward for your services," said Frau Holle, and closed the gate. Then the lazy girl returned home, entirely covered with pitch, and it would not come off as long as she lived.

- Jacob and Wilhelm Grimm, *Kinder- und Hausmärchen,* vol. 1 (Berlin: Realschulbuchhandlung, 1812), no. 24. The Grimms' source: Dorothea (Dortchen) Wild. Aarne-Thompson folktale type 480.

- My translation follows the text of the first edition. In later editions the Grimm brothers altered most of their stories, including this account.

The Fairy Grove; or, The Little Black Dog (England)

"I hope," said a woodman one day to his wife, "that the children will not run into that fir grove by the side of the river. Who they are that have come to live there, I cannot tell, but I am sure it looks more dark and gloomy than ever; and some queer looking beings are to be seen lurking about it."

That very evening little Mary and her playfellow little Martin were playing at hoop in the valley. "Where can he be hid?" said she. "He must have gone into the fir grove," and down she ran to look. Just then she spied a little dog, who wagged his tail and led her towards the grove.

For a while she gazed on the fairy scene around her, till at last one of the little dancers ran up to her, and said, "So you have come to see us at last? We have often seen you play about and wished to have you with us."

Then they led her about with them and showed her all their sports, and Mary was borne in their arms everywhere they went.

Sometimes they went to look at the royal stores, for little dwarfs were always employed in searching the earth for gold.

"And who are you?" said Mary one day.

"We are what are called elves in your world," said one whose name was Gossamer, who had become her dearest friend. "We are told you talk a great deal about us. Some of our tribes like to work you mischief, but we who live here seek only to be happy. We meddle little with mankind, but when we do, it is to do them good."

"And where is your queen?" said little Mary.

Mary and Gossamer. Woodcut from the
anonymous *Fairy Grove* (ca. 1840).

"Hush! Hush! You cannot see or know her. You must leave us before she
comes back, which will now be very soon, for mortal step cannot come where
she is."

Soon afterwards Gossamer told Mary the time was come to bid her farewell. She then gave her a ring in token of friendship and led her to the edge
of the grove.

"Think of me," said she, "but beware you tell not what you have seen, or
try to visit any of us again, for if you do, we shall leave the grove and come
back no more."

Turning round, Mary saw nothing but the gloomy fir grove she had known
before. "How frightened my father and mother will be!" thought she as she
looked at the sun, which had risen some time. She hastened homewards,
wondering, however, as she went along, to see that the leaves, which were
yesterday so fresh and green, were now falling dry and yellow around her.
The cottage too seemed changed, and when she went in, there sat her father

looking some years older than when she saw him last; and her mother, whom she hardly knew, was by his side, and also a young man.

"Father," said Mary, "who is this?"

"Who are you that call me father?" said he. "Are you—no you cannot be—our long-lost Mary?"

But they soon saw that it was their Mary. And the young man who was her old friend and playfellow Martin, said, "No wonder you had forgotten me in seven years. Do not you remember how we parted seven years ago while playing in the field? We thought you were quite lost; but we are glad to see that someone has taken care of you and brought you home at last."

Little by little she came to herself, thought of her story as a mere dream, and soon became Martin's bride. Everything seemed to thrive around them; and Mary called her first little girl Elfie, in memory of her friends. The little thing was loved by everyone.

It was pretty and very good tempered. Mary thought that it was very like a little elf; and all without knowing why, called it the fairy child.

One day as Mary was dressing her she found a piece of gold hanging round her neck by a silken thread, and knew it to be the same sort as she had seen in the hands of the fairy dwarfs. Elfie seemed sorry at its being seen, and said that she had found it in the garden. But Mary watched her, and soon found that she went every afternoon to sit by herself in a shady place behind the house. So one day she hid herself to see what the child did there, and to her great surprise, Gossamer was sitting by her side.

"Dear Elfie," she was saying, "your mother and I used to sit thus when she was young and lived among us. Oh! if you could but come and do so too! But since our queen came to us, it cannot be; yet I will come and see you and talk to you while you are a child. But when you grow up we must part forever."

Then she plucked one of the roses that grew around them, and breathed gently upon it, and said, "Take this for my sake. It will keep its freshness a whole year."

Then Mary loved her little Elfie more than ever, and when she found that she spent some hours of almost every day with the elf, she used to hide herself and watch them without being seen, till one day when Gossamer was bearing her little friend through the air from tree to tree, her mother was so frightened least the child should fall, that she could not help screaming out, and Gossamer set her gently on the ground and seemed angry and flew away.

Mary one day told her husband the whole story; and to show him all she said was true, she took him to see Elfie and the fairy, but no sooner did Gossamer know that he was there than she changed herself into a raven and flew off into the fir grove.

In the morning all the neighbors flocked around, asking what the noise and bustle of last night could mean. Mary and her husband knew what was the matter, and bewailed their folly, for they foresaw that their kind neighbors [the fairies] to whom they owed all their luck, were gone forever.

- *The Fairy Grove; or, The Little Black Dog* (London: Marks, ca. 1840), an anonymous eight-page pamphlet illustrated with five woodcuts.

DEPARTURE

Departure of the Dwarfs (Germany/Bohemia)

The inhabitants of Dittersbach tell that dwarfs lived in the nearby mountains in the time before the large bell was poured (which happened in the year 1514). They often came into the village and affixed themselves to houses and rooms, so that people became quite accustomed to them. However, after the bell was rung, the hard sound of the metal—which they could not stand—drove them away, and now there is no longer any trace of them.

The dwarfs who lived on the broad mountain near Zittau were also driven away by the ringing of bells. At their departure they enlisted a peasant from the nearby village of Hainewalde with two wagons to drive them across the Bohemian border. Both wagons were stuffed full, with dwarfs hanging on every crossbar and spoke. They rewarded the peasant very generously, so that he became a rich man. To this day his descendants still benefit from his fortune. In departing the dwarfs said that they would return only after the bells had been done away with, and after Saxony returned to Bohemia. Then, they believed, the times would be better.

- Karl Haupt, *Sagenbuch der Lausitz,* vol. 1 (Leipzig: Engelmann, 1862), no. 31, p. 36.
- Dittersbach (Czech *Jetrichovice*) is in the present-day Czech Republic. Zittau and Hainewalde are in eastern Germany near its borders with Poland and the Czech Republic.

Departure of the Trolls from Vendsyssel (Denmark)

One evening after sunset there came a strange man to the ferry of Sund. He engaged all the ferryboats there to go backwards and forwards the whole night long between that place and Vendsyssel, without the people's knowing what lading they had. He told them that they should take their freight on board half a mile to the east of Sund, near the alehouse at the bridge of Lange.

At the appointed time the man was at that place, and the ferrymen, though unable to see anything, perceived very clearly that the boats sunk deeper and deeper, so that they easily concluded that they had gotten a very heavy freight on board. The ferryboats passed in this manner to and fro the whole night long; and though they got every trip a fresh cargo, the strange man never left them, but stayed to have everything regulated by his directions.

When morning was breaking they received the payment they had agreed for, and they then ventured to inquire what it was they had been bringing over, but on that head their employer would give them no satisfaction. But there happened to be among the ferrymen a smart fellow who knew more about these matters than the others. He jumped on shore, took the clay from under his right foot, and put it into his cap, and when he had set it on his head he perceived that all the sand hills east of Aalborg were completely covered with little troll people, who had all pointed red caps on their heads. Ever since that time there have been no dwarfs seen in Vendsyssel.

- Thomas Keightley, *The Fairy Mythology: Illustrative of the Romance and Superstition of Various Countries* (London: Bohn, 1850), pp. 127–28.

- Note by Keightley: The story is told by the ferrymen to travelers.

- Vendsyssel and Aalborg are in northern Jutland.

Four
Scholarship and Belief

ORIGINS

Norse and Germanic Mythology

Fairy accounts, from the Middle Ages to the present, often ask, "What are fairies, and where do they come from?" Diverse theories, often mutually contradictory, present themselves as answers. One of the oldest such accounts is part of the creation myth found in the *Prose Edda* (pp. 41–42), written by the Icelander Snorri Sturlusson in the 1220s but based on much older oral traditions. Here we learn that the dark elves of Norse mythology first appeared as maggots in the giant Ymir's rotting body. With time and by the decree of unnamed gods, they became humanlike in appearance and understanding, although they lived beneath the earth. There is little to distinguish these dark elves of Norse mythology from the dwarfs of the same belief system. Indeed, one of the dwarfs in the *Prose Edda* is named Alf, which means *elf*.

Another ancient document presenting a theory about the origin of elves is *Beowulf*. Based on Germanic traditions brought to Britain by Anglo-Saxon invaders in the mid fifth century, this work, as now comprised, was composed by an unnamed English poet, probably before the Viking raid at Lindisfarne in 793. The author, reflecting the folk belief of his era, associates elves with other demonic beings, including the monster Grendel, and states that such creatures are descendants of the biblical Cain: "From him [Cain] sprang every misbegotten thing, monsters and elves and the walking dead, and also those giants who fought against God time and again" (lines 111–114). This reference to the Bible in an otherwise heathen work is an example of how Christian concepts crept into the indigenous mythologies of recent converts.

Eve's Hidden Children

A pseudo-biblical explanation for fairy origins is the story of "Eve's Hidden Children" (Aarne-Thompson folktale type 758), found throughout Europe and as far abroad as the Philippines. A Danish version, published by J. M. Thiele in 1843, is typical:

> One day while Eve was washing her children at a spring, the Lord suddenly appeared before her. Frightened, she hid the children who were not yet washed. The Lord asked her if all her children were there, and she answered yes, not wanting him to see that some were not yet washed. Then the Lord said that the children she had hidden from him should from then on be hidden from mankind. The unclean children instantly disappeared and were hidden in the hills. From these have descended all the underground people. (vol. 2, pp. 141–42)

Two additional versions of this tale, one from the Frisian Islands and one from Wales, are reproduced in chapter three of this handbook. In spite of its biblical context, the story's playful tone suggests that it was told less as factual history and more as a parable illustrating a moral value (Do not be ashamed of your less attractive offspring).

Fallen Angels

Another biblical explanation for the existence of sundry earth sprites derives from the reference in *Revelation* (ch. 12) to a war in heaven, after which Satan and his followers were cast out onto the earth. According to widespread popular belief, the worst of these sinners were relegated to hell, whereas those with lesser sins were scattered across the earth to become fairies, elves, mermaids, brownies, and such, with their names, appearance, and future activities determined by where they landed: woods, fields, mountains, seas, or inhabited dwellings. Thus earth, sea, forest, and domestic sprites of all sorts share a common ancestry. This folk theology finds advocates across Europe, for example in Bohemia (Grohmann, p. 108), Denmark (Thiele, vol. 2, p. 141), Iceland (Árnason, pp. 20–21), Ireland (Kennedy, p. 128), Scotland (Gregor, p. 59), and Sweden (Hofberg, p. 56).

From the Middle Ages through the nineteenth century a large number of commentators have claimed that various fairies and dwarfs—even those who apparently serve humans well—are satanic demons, or even "the devil himself" (Knoop, p. 78). This pessimistic view derives from medieval theology. Unable or unwilling to convince early converts to Christianity that

Cast-out angel. Detail from a painting by Hieronymus Bosch (ca. 1500). From Richard Huber, *Treasury of Fantastic and Mythological Creatures* (Dover Pictorial Archive).

the indigenous deities honored and feared by their ancestors were unreal, churchmen proclaimed that major gods, for example Odin or Thor, actually existed, but that they were evil spirits, to be shunned and feared. Similarly, the host of lesser deities designated today as fairies, elves, pixies, and such were also identified as devils.

This view resulted in confusion as to what sort of supernatural beings were responsible for various misfortunes that befall humans. For example, throughout Europe and for many centuries fairies were blamed for stealing human children and replacing them with their own misshapen offspring (changelings). However, Martin Luther, writing in the sixteenth century, stated explicitly that it was Satan himself who was responsible for the malformed children known as changelings (vol. 4, pp. 357–58).

Witchcraft

This identification of fairies with devils led quite naturally to the association of fairies with witches, who according to medieval theology were mortal humans who had gained supernatural power through a pact with the devil. A simple example from folklore is presented by the whirlwinds of dust, commonly called *dust devils*. In many nations these are said to be caused by the devil himself, or fairies, or witches (Gregor, p. 65; Croker, vol. 1, p. 71; Rhys, p. 590).

Joan of Arc

Tragically, the perceived association of fairy lore with demonic sorcery was used as evidence in numerous witchcraft trials during the notorious persecutions that cast a shadow across Europe from the middle ages well into the eighteenth century. The most infamous such case is the heresy trial conducted against Joan of Arc in 1431. Central in this proceeding were the inquisitors' attempts to determine the source of Joan's visions. From the court record it is clear that they suspected her of having communed with fairies. According to the transcript of the proceedings of February 21, 1431, she was specifically asked about her knowledge of a tree, popularly called "The Fairies' Tree," near her native village, Domrémy-la-Pucelle. She stated that her godmother had claimed to have seen fairies at that place, and she admitted that as a child she herself had placed garlands on the tree and had sung and danced there, explaining, however, that these activities were merely games, not otherworldly rituals. She explicitly denied the rumor, then current in her village, that she had received her mission at "The Fairies' Tree" (http://www.stjoan-center. com/Trials/sec03.html). The tragic outcome of her trial is well known. Found guilty of heresy, she was burned to death on May 30, 1431. Nearly 500 years later, May 16, 1920, she was canonized as a saint.

Bessie Dunlop, Alison Pearson, and Anne Jeffries

Similar trials elsewhere in Europe show further theological and legal attempts to identify fairy belief with witchcraft, as illustrated by the following three examples, two from Scotland and one from Cornwall. Sir Walter Scott, in his *Letters on Demonology and Witchcraft* (pp. 91–96), relates in some detail the legal proceedings against two of his compatriots: Bessie Dunlop, formally charged with sorcery and witchcraft in 1576, and Alison Pearson, similarly accused in 1588. Both women confessed to having received otherworldly assistance for the purpose of treating the ill and other beneficent endeavors. Both defendants claimed to have received aid from fairyland through intermediaries, men known to their respective communities but now deceased. Furthermore, each woman described personal visits from the Queen of Fairies herself. Although their alleged contacts with the fairies brought only good to their fellow humans, both women were found guilty of witchcraft and burned at the stake.

A generation later a Cornish case had a happier outcome. According to contemporary documentation, in 1645 Anne Jeffries, a nineteen-year-old domestic servant, had an encounter with the "airy people." The immediate consequence was a trance-like seizure, but upon recovering she found herself able to cure diverse illnesses and injuries. Charged with witchcraft, Anne was incarcerated in 1646 and held without nourishment. She claimed that fairies fed her during her imprisonment, and she suffered no apparent ill effects from this harsh treatment. Ultimately she was released for lack of evidence and lived to old age (Hunt, pp. 127–29, 468–70).

Reginald Scot

A remarkably brave and insightful writer for his time, Reginald Scot wrote *The Discoverie of Witchcraft* in 1584. Although Scot's main purpose was to expose the superstitions and theological fallacies leading to the cruel witch trials of his generation, he also dedicated several passages to the debunking of certain fairy beliefs. In so doing he did not depart from his book's announced theme, for fairies and witches belonged together in popular opinion. It seems that in many areas fairy belief waned before the general belief in witchcraft did. Scot can thus argue that witches will soon go the way of fairies: "And know you this, by the way, that heretofore Robin Goodfellow, and Hobgoblin were as terrible, and also as credible to the people, as hags and witches be now; and in time to come, a witch will be as much derided and condemned, and as plainly perceived, as the illusion and knavery of Robin Goodfellow" (p. 74).

Scot claims that many miraculous happenings attributed to witches or fairies were nothing more than brazen trickery. Robin Goodfellow, the infamous fairy trickster, is often only a human trickster in a white sheet: "But certainly, some one knave in a white sheet hath cozened [deceived] and abused many thousands that way."

In other instances, the supernatural events are only self delusion on the part of the observers. His list of those who are particularly susceptible to such fantasies has a decidedly anti-feminine bias: "But you shall understand, that these bugs specially are spied and feared of [by] sick folk, children, women, and cowards, which through weakness of mind and body, are shaken with vain dreams and continual fear" (p. 86).

King James

Scot's exposé of the witchcraft delusion so angered King James VI of Scotland (who in 1603 became King James I of England) that he ordered the book to be burned, then wrote his own *Daemonologie* (1597) to refute it. This is the same King James who sponsored the English translation of the Bible that became the standard scripture for many generations of English-speaking Protestants.

James's *Daemonologie* stands beside the *Malleus Maleficarum* (Witches' Hammer, ca. 1486) of Heinrich Kraemer and Johann Sprenger as one of the most notorious and hateful books ever written. James, a fervent believer in the divine right of kings and in his branch of Protestant Christianity, followed unwaveringly in the steps of his Catholic predecessors Kraemer and Sprenger. Decrying what he saw as a Satan-sent plague of witches in Great Britain, he defended every traditional method of defeating it, including torture, the acceptance of dubious evidence, and cruel execution.

Like his adversary Scot, James too included a good bit of fairy lore in his book. But where Scot saw fairy appearances as pranks or delusions, James interpreted them as apparitions sent by Satan to deceive humankind. In his opinion even the good Scottish brownie, whose help many a householder had come to rely upon, was an inherently evil spirit masquerading as "an angel of light" (p. 65). He discussed other fairy types as well, always with the same conclusion: they are evil spirits sent by the devil (pp. 73–77).

Ancestral Spirits

Closely related to the medieval theological position that fairies are fallen angels or evil spirits is the popular view that they are spirits of deceased pagans who refused to accept Christianity, a theory that found support especially in Celtic areas. For example, Lewis Spence, writing in the early twentieth century, observed that Breton peasants saw in the corrigans (water fairies) "pagan princesses of Brittany who would have none of Christianity when the holy apostles brought it to Armorica, and who must dwell here under a ban, outcast and abhorred" (p. 56). Other views are not quite so severe:

> The Small People are believed by some to be the spirits of the people who inhabited Cornwall many thousands of years ago—long, long before the birth of Christ. They were not good enough to inherit the joys of heaven, but they were too good to be condemned to eternal fires.... When they first came into this land, they were much larger than they are now, but ever since the birth of Christ they have been getting smaller and smaller. Eventually they will turn into *muryans* (ants), and at last be lost from the face of the earth." (Hunt, pp. 80–81)

Even gentler is the Welsh view that fairies were the souls of certain druids, unworthy of Christian salvation but not wicked enough to be cast into hell, so they were assigned to the "green fairy islands" between Wales and Ireland (Sikes, pp. 8–9).

Belief systems throughout Europe identify certain fairy types with specific classes of deceased humans, often with no allusions of personal guilt. Many German legends define will-o'-the-wisps as the spirits of children who died before baptism (for example, Kuhn, vol. 2, p. 23; Kuhn and Schwartz, pp. 425–26; Temme, p. 80). Similarly, Cornish piskies have been called "the spirits of dead-born children" (Evans-Wentz, p. 183). Another class of ghost-fairies are the *willis* (variously spelled), featured in Adolphe Charles Adam's ballet *Giselle* (1841). These, according to Austrian and Slavic folklore, are the spirits of engaged women who died before marriage, then torment mortal men with their seductive dancing.

In some traditions spirits of those who suffer death in a specified manner do not actually become fairies, but they do reside with them. W. Y. Evans-Wentz reported the view from Ireland that "people killed and murdered in war stay on earth till their time is up, and they are among the good people" (p. 32). Furthermore, the deceased are not necessarily victims of a particular act of violence. "The dead are often seen among them," reported Lady Gregory (p. vi), referring to statements made by Irish compatriots who claimed to have visited fairyland. In a sense, fairyland thus becomes a heathen counterpart to Christianity's purgatory, an intermediate domicile for spirits awaiting final judgment.

The association of fairies with the dead, particularly at ancient burial sites, has been documented in numerous cultures and across many centuries. They are often depicted as inhabiting such places, sharing space with corpses, ghosts, and devils. For example, the Icelandic *Bard's Saga,* written in the fourteenth century, describes attempts to break open and loot a king's burial mound. Initial efforts failed, with each day's excavation filling itself in the following night. Finally a priest was recruited, who—armed with holy water and a crucifix—succeeded in keeping the mound open. Inside they discovered the rotting corpse of the king, mysteriously moving about and talking, and with him "trolls and evil spirits, fiends and fairy folk" (Hreinsson, vol. 2, p. 263).

Ghosts

In some traditions, fairies are not merely *associated* with the dead; they *are* the spirits of the dead. Ireland is especially rich in such legends and beliefs. The following statement by a schoolmaster, recorded in the early twentieth century, is typical: "There is implicit belief here in the gentry [fairies], especially among the old people. They consider them the spirits of their departed relations and friends, who visit them in joy and in sorrow" (Evans-Wentz, p. 58). What then distinguishes fairies from ghosts? Evans-Wentz answers the question straightforwardly: "The attributes of a ghost—that is to say, the spirit of a dead man—are indistinguishable from those of a fairy" (p. 438).

Every community has its tales of local places haunted by the ghosts of former inhabitants. In some instances, as just noted, the ghost behaves exactly like a fairy. Kobolds, Germany's most famous household spirits, are believed by some to be ghosts of individuals murdered in the house where they now reside (Grimm, *German Legends,* no. 72).

"The Cauld Lad of Hilton" is one of England's best-known fairy legends. In former times Hilton (also spelled Hylton) Castle had a brownie or house spirit called the Cauld Lad. Unlike most brownies, he did more mischief than good, so the servants—knowledgeable about fairy lore—banished him by presenting him with a new suit of clothes. Some claimed that he was "the spirit of a servant whom one of the barons had killed unintentionally in a fit of passion" (Keightly, pp. 296–97). This legend is still told in Sunderland, where the castle, now in ruins, is located.

In other instances—following a typical ghost-story tradition—the fairy creature is forced by unnamed powers to haunt a particular site as punishment for a crime or shortcoming. "The Kildare Pooka" provides a good example. It tells of an Irish household that was haunted by a pooka. Every night he would noisily finish whatever chores had been left undone. When confronted, the apparition confessed that a generation earlier he had been a servant in the same household, but because of his laziness, when his time came for the other world he was punished with the task of laboring there every night. His beneficiaries, themselves lazy servants, decided to reward him with a new coat. However, in presenting him with the garment they unwittingly broke the spell, for—as he subsequently revealed—the curse was only to last until some mortal paid him for his service. The pooka never returned (Kennedy, pp. 114–16).

Indigenous Peoples

Not all theories of fairy origins are theological in nature. Many nineteenth-century commentators theorized that fairies were real people, descendants of a dark-skinned, small-statured race that was literally driven underground by waves of more advanced invaders. This would explain fairies' traditional fear of iron, a material exploited for weapons and tools by their enemies, and one that seemed magical to people still living in a stone-age culture.

In Britain the ancient race most frequently named in this context were the Picts. John Rhys claims that by the late nineteenth century much Scottish fairy lore had come to be attributed to the historical Picts (pp. 679–80). Nowhere was this more true than in the northern islands. The trows (underground fairies) of Shetland and Orkney were held by some to be progeny of the Picts (Nicolson, p. 11), a view reinforced by the existence of ancient dwellings attributed to this people and often constructed with very low doors and passageways. Furthermore, in many instances centuries of soil buildup and drifting sand had completely buried these structures, making it all the more believable that they had been inhabited by underground people.

One such site is Skara Brae on the mainland of Orkney, unearthed in 1850. At first it was thought to be an abandoned Pictish settlement, but it later proved to be a Neolithic village some 5,000 years old. According to modern theories, the low entryways and passages were designed to conserve heat and to aid in the village's defense, rather than to accommodate its diminutive inhabitants, whether Picts or fairies.

Andrew Lang takes special delight in discrediting the theory that fairies were the descendants of ancient Picts (here called Pechts) by referring to the legend, still current in the late nineteenth century, that they were the builders of the Glasgow Cathedral. The Scots, he concludes, accustomed to centuries of mediocre architecture since the Middle Ages, "looked on the cathedral as no work of ordinary human beings. It was a creation of the Pechts" (p. xix).

Other countries have similar legends explaining the origin of their underground people. Some German traditions purport that that country's dwarfs and elves are descendants of the ancient Wends and Celts (Grimm, *Deutsche Mythologie,* vol. 3, p. 131). Similarly, in northeastern Germany among the many names given to underground people is *kleine Heiden* (little heathens— Gander, p. 41).

Some folk traditions extend the succession of cultural defeats even further into the past. According to these, humans, with their superior religion and technology, supplanted the elves and dwarfs, who many generations earlier had supplanted an even less advanced culture, that of the giants (Keightley, p. 179). As proof that giants formerly existed, one needed only to consider the many prehistoric monuments constructed from very large stones that are found throughout Europe. In the words of Saxo Grammaticus, writing in about 1208: "That the country of Denmark was once cultivated and worked by giants, is attested by the enormous stones attached to the barrows and caves of the ancients" (p. 12). As is widely documented, after the giants (or whoever their creators were) abandoned these stone monuments, elves, trolls, and other such folk took possession of them (Hartland, pp. 151–52; Lady Wilde, p. 142).

Foreigners and Extraterrestrials

Even more common than theories finding fairy origins in indigenous populations are those seeing in foreign invaders or visitors the forebears of fairies. In Britain the latter were sometimes seen as descendants of Finns, a designation for the Sami or Lapps, and a culture known throughout Europe for occult traditions (Lang, pp. xx–xi).

In 2002 the present writer heard a theory expressed by a bed-and-breakfast host in Cornwall that piskies were the descendants of captured Turkish traders. Ordinary humans without special powers, with time these ethnic Turks evolved into bogeymen whose primary function now is to frighten children into good behavior.

In the late eighteenth century a Reverend Peter Roberts advanced the hypothesis that Welsh fairies were remnants of an Irish raiding party that had been left behind in a hostile land. Fearing capture, they camouflaged themselves with green clothing, hid themselves in caves by day, and sent their children out at night to scavenge for food (Sikes, pp. 129–30). In Wales fairies also have been identified with Gypsies (Rhys, p. 106).

The Cornish mine spirits known as buccas or knockers were said to be "the souls of the Jews who formerly worked the tin mines of Cornwall" (Hunt, p. 82). Similarly, in northeastern Germany underground people sometimes were called *Jüdchen* or *Jüdelchen* (little Jews—Gander, p. 41). Germans, especially in the Alpine regions and in mining areas in central Germany, attributed many elf-acts to Italians (usually referred to as Venetians), who—according to legend—had migrated northward to seek underground riches. Adalbert Kuhn and Wilhelm Schwartz offer typical examples of this belief (pp. 197–99).

The ultimate foreigners are extraterrestrials, and long before interplanetary travel became a proven possibility, ordinary people were postulating that at least some fairy types originated beyond this earth, a secular version of the theological claim that fairies are spirits exiled from heaven. Patrick Waters, an Irish tailor interviewed by W. Y. Evans-Wentz in 1908 and again in 1909, classified various fairy tribes, concluding, "The gentry are the most noble tribe of all; and they are a big race who came from other planets" (p. 53).

Many modern UFO enthusiasts hold similar views, interpreting ancient fairy traditions as evidence for earth visitations by intelligent beings from outer space. See, for example, Janet Bord's chapter "UFO Entities and Fairies: Are They the Same?" (pp. 106–29). Recent claims of human abduction by extraterrestrials often bear a striking resemblance to traditional legends of abduction by fairies.

Fantasies

No discussion of fairy origins would be complete without the admission that some (skeptics will say *all*) fairy accounts are nothing more than fantasies or dreams. Even stories told by true believers sometimes contain evidence that the supernatural events described in them may have been more imagined than actually experienced. And a skeptic, relating the same story, will skew the details to emphasize the logical weakness of its underlying foundation. The following two legends tell essentially the same story, the first one with a rationalized ending, devoid of any supernatural conclusions; the second with a mysterious ending that leaves quite open the possibility of supernatural intervention.

In his *Irish Popular Superstitions,* W. R. Wilde recounts an example of "popular superstitious prejudice" in the words of "a person who was present at the transaction." In the year 1818, Mary, the wife of Daniel Kelly, died suddenly and from no apparent cause. Her husband and friends were convinced that she had been carried away by the fairies, leaving in her place an image intended to deceive the mourners. Some three weeks after the burial the widower and the dead woman's brothers, hoping to expose the fairies' deception, dug up the coffin. They expected to find inside "a birch broom, a log of wood, or the skeleton of some deformed monster," but instead "they found in it what they had put into it, but in a much more advanced state of decomposition" (p. 127). The editor's sarcastic conclusion makes this a suitable place to point out that W. R. Wilde and his wife Lady Wilde—also an important and often satirical commentator on folklore—were the parents of Oscar Wilde, an Irish dramatist known for his irreverent irony.

A similar legend from Scotland ends quite differently. Its setting is Kintraw, near Kilmartin in Argyll, and in the shadow of a hill known as "Fairies' Hill." A young woman died suddenly, leaving a husband and two or three young children. The Sunday after the funeral the widower went to church, leaving the children home alone. On his return the children reported that during his absence their mother had visited them, combing their hair and dressing them. This event repeated itself on the two following Sundays At her last appearance the mother revealed that she was a captive of the fairies, and that if her coffin were opened, it would be found to contain nothing but a withered leaf. The widower asked the minister for

A drunken man surrounded by pixies in a cellar. Illustration by C.E. Brock, from Edwin Sidney Hartland, *English Fairy and other Folk Tales* (1890).

advice, who ridiculed the existence of fairies and refused to allow the coffin to be opened. A short time afterward the minister was found dead near the Fairies' Hill. Many thought that he had been killed by the fairies to avenge his scornful remarks (Archibald Campbell, pp. 71–72). This story thus offers an explanation for two otherwise inexplicable deaths while at the same time supporting a community's belief in fairies.

Intoxication

Fairy legends often mention—even emphasize—that the leading character was intoxicated at the time of his or her miraculous encounter. For example, in Germany will-o'-the-wisps "take special pleasure in playing tricks on the intoxicated" (Haupt, vol. 1, p. 59). "Jemmy Doyle in the Fairy Palace" and "Fiddler Lux from Buttwil" both emphasize the leading characters' drinking habits. The full texts of these legends are reproduced in chapter three. Such accounts usually leave unanswered the question as to whether the spirit in the drink enabled contact with supernatural sprites, or whether it produced fantasies that existed only in the participants' imagination.

Thomas Crofton Croker, in his inimitable style, admits openly that the term *fairy struck,* in addition to designating a fairy-induced paralysis, "has also a convivial acceptation, the fairies being not unfrequently made to bear the blame of the effects arising from too copious a sacrifice to the jolly god" (vol. 1, p. 115).

As an example he offers the case of one Morty Sullivan who provisioned himself with a full bottle of whiskey and then set forth on a pilgrimage to a secluded chapel. Underway he was joined by a mysterious old woman who offered him a horse to ride. He foolishly mounted it, but it was a spirit horse or a pooka, and it flung him over a steep cliff, where he was discovered, badly bruised, the following morning by a band of pilgrims. Croker concludes that "those incredulous of supernatural appearances" will attribute Morty's fall to the contents of his bottle rather than to the intervention of a fairy horse (vol. 1, pp. 241–47).

Sometimes an editor's cynicism shines through the literal text, as evidenced in Lady Wilde's masterful use of irony in reporting marvelous events. For example, she tells how a man spent the night away from home, claiming to have been abducted by the fairies; then she concludes with the observation that "wicked people might laugh and jeer and say he was drunk" (p. 93). She does not say whether she herself is one of those skeptical "wicked people."

John Rhys tells how a Welshman, returning home from the Beddgelert fair in a "rather merry" condition, came upon a luxurious mansion. Knowing that no such house existed on his way, he determined that he was lost, and knocked on the door to request lodging for the night. He was ushered into a room filled with merrymakers. As the festivities waned, he was led to a splendid chamber, where he fell asleep in a bed of down. But when he awoke the next morning he found himself lying in a swamp, with a clump of rushes for a pillow and only the open sky for a cover (pp. 99–100).

Some stories end with a "stinger," a punch-line remark that verifies the intoxicated person's observations. Lady Gregory (pp. 195–96) tells of a drunken man who one night, too unsteady to negotiate his way home, fell asleep by the roadside. In the night he heard *them* (a common circumlocution for fairies) planning to steal the white horse of a certain rich man in town. At daybreak

A fairy horse gives his victim a wild ride. Woodcut after a drawing by W. H. Brooke, from Thomas Crofton Croker, *Fairy Legends and Traditions* (1826).

he reported the incident to the intended victim, but the latter only laughed at him, saying, "I'll pay no attention to what a drunkard dreams." But when the rich man later went to his stable, the white horse had disappeared. Stripped of its concluding supernatural embellishment, this legend and many more like it may well have their roots in the confused recollections of hapless drunks.

Imagination

Fantasies need not have their origins in intoxication. We are quite capable of imagining things with or without alcoholic stimulation. Thomas Crofton Croker prefaces his story "The Crookened Back" with the observation that in relating this tale the storyteller gave "full scope to her memory, or her imagination, or both." The resulting tale describes an attack by a pooka which left the first-person narrator with a crooked back. While no one can doubt her injury, Croker, with his introductory remarks about imagination, gives his readers grounds to question its cause (vol. 1, pp. 264–72).

Other collectors and editors go even further. Lady Wilde admits that Irish fairies are an invention of those who believe in them: "The Irish seem to have created this strange fairy race after their own image, for in all things they strangely resemble the Irish character" (p. 142).

Dreams

Dreams, too, produce stories that are at least temporarily believed, however unusual their content. A large number of fairy legends end with the participant waking from a long sleep, thus presenting the possibility that the events were only dreamed and not literally experienced. A parallel situation is presented by the magical plot of Lewis Carroll's *Alice's Adventures in Wonderland,* which turns out to be a dream, although the reader discovers this only in the book's final pages.

John Rhys presents a dream-like sequence of events in his story of a man who lost his way one night and wandered into a bog. He struggled for some time when a beautiful woman appeared before him and pulled him to safety. She gave him "a jolly sweet kiss" and led him to a house, where he spent the night singing and dancing with her. The next morning he was wakened, not by the woman's kiss, but by a shepherd's dog licking his lips. He found himself lying in a sheepfold, with no sign of the previous night's beautiful woman (pp. 149–50).

Archibald Campbell tells of a woman from Tiree (one of the Inner Hebrides Islands), fatigued from preparing wool, who one night wished aloud, "O that someone would come from land or sea, from far or near, to help me with the work of making this cloth." Immediately a strange-looking woman entered the house and began spinning, soon to be joined by numerous others, "till the house was quite full of fairies, men and women, each at work." Fearful that the house would be permanently occupied by these now unwelcome helpers, she called out, "Burg Hill [the name of a nearby fairy hill] is on fire!" The fairies, fearing for the safety of their kin, rushed away, and the woman regained possession of her house. Campbell presents this story with sympathy, but does add a rational explanation: "The over-sensitive, anxious, over-worked goodwife fell asleep, and her dream took the form of the incidents that are here mentioned" (pp. 54–69).

Similarities between dream images and fairy tales have long been noted by students of that literary genre, as well as by psychologists, giving rise to the idea that dreams and accounts of fairy encounters may derive from the same mental processes. No one commented on this topic more elegantly than William Shakespeare. His unforgettable Puck, at the conclusion of *A Midsummer Night's Dream* (act 5, scene 2), admits the possibility that the fairy tale so famously told there may be nothing more than a dream:

> If we shadows have offended,
> Think but this, and all is mended,
> That you have but slumber'd here

While these visions did appear.
And this weak and idle theme,
No more yielding but a dream.

FAIRY MYTHOLOGY

A Complete and Connected Whole

The relative uniformity in northern Europe of stories and customs concerning normally invisible fairy-like creatures (by whatever name) suggests that this lore was once part of a widespread and sincerely felt belief system, which Jacob and Wilhelm Grimm referred to as "a complete and connected whole" (Croker, vol. 3, p. 54). Today we commonly regard fairy tales as fantasy and fiction, viewed in much the same light as myths featuring ancient deities and heroes, such as Zeus and Heracles. However, both sets of beliefs originally emanated from deeply believed religious convictions.

Fairy belief in northern Europe, although never sponsored by a formal organization, was widespread and deep. It was a religion of the people, without an official priesthood or authoritative catechism. Predating Christianity by untold centuries, it offered otherworldly explanations (and sometimes solutions) for problems of this world: sickness, untimely death, disappearance of people and animals, crop failure, house fires, building collapses, storms, and the like.

Fairy Lore and Medieval Christianity

The conversion of Europe from various pagan or heathen religions to Christianity—essentially complete by the year 1000—at first did little to change indigenous views about fairies. Instead of abandoning these primeval beliefs, early Christians typically incorporated them into their new religion.

Church rituals and religious amulets were added to traditional means of protection against fairies, and Bible passages and saints' legends were reinterpreted to explain and defend various pre-Christian beliefs.

The church, officially or otherwise, adjusted many of its rituals to appeal to pagan converts. Major Christian holidays were set to correspond to existing pagan festivals, most of which had connections to fairy lore: Christmas was placed at Yuletide, a time marking the winter solstice and the return of the sun. The summer solstice (Midsummer Day) and its accompanying celebrations were assimilated into the Feast of St. John the Baptist (June 24). All Saints' Day and its companion All Souls' Day (November 1 and 2) adopted some aspects of Samhain, the Celtic precursor to Halloween, a night when fairies, witches, and other demons were (and still are—if only playfully) particularly active. The church protested the celebration of other heathen holidays, notably January 1 and May 1 (Beltane), but with little success.

Special religious rituals and blessings evolved, designed at least in part to protect the faithful from fairies. In Scotland newly delivered mothers and newborn babies were "sained" in a special church service, and before this blessing both were deemed particularly vulnerable to fairy abduction (Gregor, p. 5). It is said that as late as the nineteenth century in Ireland, priests, if requested, would add to the normal baptism ritual a special prayer against the fairies, and "a priest can't refuse it when he's asked" (Yeats, p. 15).

Modifications moved in both directions. While the church adjusted some of its practices to accommodate heathen beliefs, fairy lore itself developed a new complexion when viewed through Christian eyes. W. R. Wilde observed: "It is … very difficult to find any genuine pagan Irish superstition without being more or less modified by the wonders of the Old or New Testament" (p. 126).

Jacob and Wilhelm Grimm, who knew as much about ancient beliefs as anyone of their generation, reached similar conclusions, adding that the early church's attempts to demonize heathen beliefs gave fairy lore a negative image that lasted for centuries. Quoting from their essay "On the Nature of the Elves," written as a supplement to Thomas Crofton Croker's *Fairy Legends and Traditions of the South of Ireland*:

The belief in fairies and spirits prevailed over all Europe long before the introduction of Christianity. The teachers of the new faith endeavored to abolish the deeply-rooted heathenish ideas and customs of the people by representing them as sinful and connected with the devil. Hence many originally pleasing fables and popular amusements gradually assumed a gloomy, mixed, and dubious character. … The dances on the Brocken [a mountain in central Germany famous as a gathering place for witches], those around the fire on Midsummer Eve, were nothing more than festivals of the elves of light. They have been transformed into hideous, devilish dances of witches. (vol. 3, pp. 140–42)

From the Renaissance onward fairy belief found itself further marginalized by the relentless advance of this-worldly rationalism. Lady Wilde, writing in the late nineteenth century, stated succinctly:

Amongst the educated classes in all nations, the belief in the supernatural, acting directly on life and constantly interfering with the natural course of human action, is soon dissipated and gradually disappears, for the knowledge of natural laws solves many mysteries that were once inexplicable; yet much remains unsolved, even to the philosopher, of the mystic relation between the material and the spiritual world. Whilst to the masses—the uneducated—who know nothing of the fixed eternal laws of nature, every phenomenon seems to result from the direct action of some nonhuman power, invisible though ever present; able to confer all benefits, yet implacable if offended, and therefore to be propitiated. (p. xii)

First demonized by organized religion and then explained away as fantasy and imagination by the Age of Reason, fairy legends adjusted themselves to new conditions, but they did so slowly and unevenly. As early as the fourteenth century, Chaucer's wife of Bath could claim, "no one sees elves any more" (*Canterbury Tales*, line 864), but fairy belief flourished in many remote regions—especially in Ireland and Iceland—well into the twentieth century. Even today there are many who profess belief in fairies. However, these are only rarely the malevolent fairies of antiquity, who seem to have been replaced by friendly and helpful earth spirits.

Continuing Belief

"The belief in fairies was all but universal," states Walter Gregor, (p. 59), referring to northern Scotland in the mid nineteenth century, a claim made repeatedly by writers of this era about other districts as well. But with the advance of secular education ordinary people became ever more reluctant to admit such belief, especially to outsiders.

Jeremiah Curtin, an American folklorist collecting material in Ireland in the 1890s, quotes his host, a man who retained a belief in fairies, as saying, "When I was a boy, nine men in ten believed in fairies, and said so; now only one man in ten will say that he believes in them. If one of the nine believes, he will not tell you; he will keep his mind to himself" (p. 2). But even self-proclaimed skeptics often exhibit behavior suggesting that they are not entirely secure in their disbelief. Thus Lady Gregory, writing in Ireland in 1916, quotes an informant: "Though my father ... didn't believe in such things [as fairies], to the day of his death he never dared to go up to bed without leaving a bit of food outside the door" (p. 175).

Not everyone is so reticent. The Irish poet William Butler Yeats famously believed in fairies, as did Sir Arthur Conan Doyle, ironically best known today for his fictional Sherlock Holmes, a paragon of dispassionate logic. Both men lived well into the twentieth century. More recently, the Icelandic Tourist Board reports: "Surveys show that despite their obsession with modern technology, as many as 80% of Icelanders believe in the existence of elves. Even today, roads have been rerouted and building plans redesigned or abandoned to avoid disturbing rocks where elves are said to live" (http://www.icetourist.is/).

PHYSICAL EVIDENCE

Geological Features

Traditional place names throughout Europe reveal a persistent reluctance to abandon old beliefs. From Odense, Denmark's second largest city, to Tórshavn, capital of the Faroe Islands—citing just two examples—pre-Christian deities such as Odin and Thor are remembered a full millennium after their worship was formally abandoned. Fairy names abound as well, but these typically refer to smaller local geographic features rather than to prominent sites. Thus names such as Troll Hill, Mermaid's Rock, Nix's Well, Fairy Oak, and Dwarf Cave are found in many locales.

Every region has legends giving supernatural explanations for the creation of unusual physical features, and these explanations often involve fairy folk. A giant created the Wrekin, a prominent peak in Shropshire, England (Hartland, pp. 85–86); and a troll was responsible for Tis Lake in Denmark (Thiele, vol. 2, pp. 7–8). In Ireland a cut in a hill is cited as proof of a fairy legend. It all started when the fairies carried off a woman to serve as bride to their king. The woman's human husband, knowledgeable about fairy matters, dug into their hill, strewing salt on the earth to prevent them from hindering his work, until he reached her place of captivity and succeeded in rescuing her. And, the storyteller assures us, "the deep cut in the hill remains to this day, and is called 'The Fairy's Glen.' So no one can doubt the truth of the story as here narrated" (Lady Wilde, pp. 42–45).

Ancient Monuments

Although they do not necessarily carry fairy-related names, prehistoric structures and artifacts throughout northern Europe have longstanding fairy connections. Stone-age arrowheads formerly were called fairy darts and were treasured as charm pieces against harmful supernatural powers (Lady Wilde, p. 203). Ancient gaming pieces and talismans, also deemed to have fairy origins, were collected and revered for similar purposes.

Prehistoric circular earthworks, known in Ireland as raths; and ancient grave mounds in many countries were believed by later generations to house underground people and were avoided whenever possible. Ancient stone monuments—dolmens, menhirs, and stone circles—were virtually always associated with fairy legends.

A famous instance is the workshop of Wayland the Smith, said to be located in a prehistoric stone tomb in Oxfordshire, England. Wayland's role as lord of the elves and as a master smith is treated in chapter two of this handbook. For additional examples of legends associating fairies with stone monuments see "The White Cow of Mitchell's Fold," "Legend of the Rollright Stones," and "The Gnoll Fairy Stone" in chapter three.

Legends about ancient monuments often warn against their destruction or desecration. Indeed, the continued existence and veneration of such artifices, after 5,000 or more years, may in part be due to these cautionary tales.

Artifacts

The Luck of Edenhall

Objects deemed to have been made or used by fairies play a substantial role in traditional stories and beliefs. Their tangible existence is offered as proof of the accounts that explain how they were acquired. Of special importance are the many legends that depict cups, dishes, and other household vessels abandoned by or stolen from fairies. In many instances these items function as good-luck pieces for their new owners.

The most famous such object is an ornate glass goblet known as *The Luck of Edenhall.* Edenhall (sometimes spelled Eden Hall) was a seat of the Musgrave family in northern England. According to legend, one day the butler surprised a band of fairies making merry near a well. Standing on the well's ledge was a beautifully decorated glass goblet, which the butler seized. A struggle ensued, but the butler managed to maintain possession of the glass. The fairies fled, warning as they departed:

> If that glass either break or fall,
> Farewell the luck of Edenhall (Keightley, p. 292).

The Musgraves preserved the glass for many centuries. In 1926 they placed it on loan at the Victoria and Albert Museum in London, and a short time afterward Edenhall Manor was demolished. The museum subsequently purchased the goblet, where it is on display to this day. Modern science places its date and place of origin in thirteenth-century Syria or Egypt. It was probably brought to England during the Crusades, but its claimed fairyland provenance is the story most responsible for its fame.

In 1834 the German poet Ludwig Uhland wrote a ballad titled "Das Glück von Edenhall" (The Luck of Edenhall) in which, taking full advantage of poetic license, he has a Lord of Edenhall challenge the fairies' prophecy by purposely breaking the glass. Immediately following this reckless act enemies storm the castle and kill the young lord. Henry Wadsworth Longfellow translated the ballad into English, making the story, as altered by Uhland, known throughout the English-speaking world.

The Oldenburg Horn and the Shetland Jug

Another fairy drinking vessel on public display is the Oldenburg horn, which can be seen at Rosenborg Castle in Copenhagen. As recorded in the Grimm brothers' *German Legends* (no. 547), Count Otto of Oldenburg, while hunting in the year 990, was offered a drink from an ornate silver and golden horn by a mysterious woman who suddenly appeared from within a cleft in the side of Mount Osenberg. The suspicious count poured the contents onto the ground and fled with the container, which remained in his family's possession until 1689 when it was acquired by the King of Denmark. One version of this legend includes an element of added mystery, stating that the tip of the horn was broken off, but that no goldsmith or silversmith was able to repair it, because it was made of a metal unknown to any human (Kuhn and Schwartz, pp. 280–81).

In other legends unusual containers abandoned by fairy folk are presented as evidence for a story's truth, although the artifacts themselves may no longer be available. For example, a Shetland legend tells how some trows abandoned an earthenware jug, which was recovered by a certain Laurence Farker, a sickly man. He drank from the bottle, and "all his ills departed." The jug's fame spread, and, as the legend asserts: "Its contents never grew less, and proved a never-failing cure for all disease" (Nicolson, p. 38). This story claims credibility by including the human owner's name. However, it does not reveal where the jug is today.

Personal Items

Clothing and personal items play similar roles in verifying fairy lore, and again the evidence will convince those who want to believe but may seem questionable to skeptics. A mermaid's comb plays a prominent role in the Cornish legend "The Old Man of Cury," and we are assured that the hero's family retains it to the present day, although—the collector slyly adds: "Some people are unbelieving enough to say the comb is only part of a shark's jaw" (Hunt, pp. 152–55).

Another account from Cornwall describes how a Mr. Trezillian of St. Levan was attacked by a number of little creatures but rescued himself by turning his glove inside out and throwing it among them. Returning the next day to the site of his adventure, he found a pair of very small knee buckles of ancient design. The family kept these buckles for some time, but there is no mention of their current location (Hunt, pp. 119–20).

Miniature shoes often feature in fairy legends. Thomas Crofton Croker's "The Little Shoe" offers a prominent example. Following a well-established tradition, the story is told by a named informant, Molly Cogan, whose grandfather once captured a leprechaun who was busying himself making a shoe. The captor allowed himself to be distracted, and the fairy cobbler escaped, leaving behind only the tiny shoe, which the family kept for many years. However, when asked if she herself had seen the shoe, Molly answered, "Oh! no, my dear, it was lost long afore I was born, but my mother told me about it often and often enough" (vol. 1, pp. 188–90).

The Fairy Flag at Dunvegan Castle

No discussion of fairy relics would be complete without mentioning the fairy flag at Dunvegan Castle on the Scottish Isle of Skye. Visitors to this famous historic house are shown a faded scrap of yellow-brown cloth carefully preserved behind glass. It is said to have the supernatural power to rescue its holders, the MacLeod Clan, from imminent danger three times, and twice already this protection has been evoked by waving the flag.

Castle guides give competing accounts as to how the cloth came into human possession. Some say that it is a remnant of a cover that fairies once laid over a MacLeod infant to protect him from evil. Others tell of a union between a MacLeod chieftain and a fairy maiden. After some years together, the fairy escaped back into a hill. The desperate husband tried to restrain her but succeeded only in tearing off a piece of her gown—now known as the fairy flag. The stone bridge where they parted still stands and is named Fairy Bridge.

Crop Circles

Much of the support for fairy belief in our own time comes from the advance, especially since the 1960s, of Neo-Paganism, with its emphasis on paranormal phenomena. Including groups known as Asatru, Wicca, Celtic Druidism, and Heithni, this loosely-knit movement attempts to restore beliefs and rituals practiced in pre-Christian Europe. These beliefs typically incorporate the honoring of fairy-like land spirits, often referred to by the Old Norse term *Landvættir.*

Neo-Pagans pay particular reverence to crop circles, patterns that from time to time mysteriously appear in grain fields, especially in Great Britain. Explanations for these often complex designs include fairy dances, earth energy (ostensibly intensified along so-called Ley lines), symbols created by extraterrestrials, and pranks perpetrated by ordinary humans.

In defense of the non-supernatural view, Sam Taylor, writing for London's *Daily Mail* on August 7, 1999, reports how he accompanied a team of tricksters, who, during the night leading to July 29, 1999, tramped out an elaborate pattern in a wheat field near the Avebury stone circle in Wiltshire. News of the phenomenon traveled quickly, and early the next morning television crews and enthusiasts gathered to observe and to benefit from the mysterious powers that had laid down the grain overnight. As reported by Taylor, Susan and Peter Chittenden, a middle-aged, middle-class couple from Devon, had no doubt as to who was responsible: "If you go into the circles you can feel the presence of fairies. They are trying to reach out to us. It's just a matter of looking for them. They dance around, lightly, spreading good, and they are making the circles to send us messages that we need more goodness in the world.... If the fairies don't make the circles, then show us who does." In his newspaper article a few days later, Taylor gave them an explanation devoid of fairy involvement. Predictably, true believers in fairies and extraterrestrials countered his exposé with scorn and derision.

Photographing Fairies

The development of photography during the late nineteenth and early twentieth centuries brought hope to many that at long last the existence of spirits, fairies, extraterrestrial visitors, fabulous beasts, and other paranormal phenomena could be verified (or disproved) with certainty. Perhaps the most dramatic chapter thus far in this never-ending saga is "The Curious Case of the Cottingley Fairies." I choose this title advisedly because of the involvement of Sir Arthur Conan Doyle, creator of the famous consulting detective Sherlock Holmes. The facts surrounding the case have been widely published, including in a book by Conan Doyle himself, *The Coming of the Fairies* (1922). My own summary relies heavily on the well-documented treatment by Paul Smith (1991).

In 1917 two cousins, Frances Griffiths and Elsie Wright, then respectively ten and fifteen years of age, startled the world with two photographs clearly depicting fairies. The pictures were taken in a meadow behind the Wright household in the Yorkshire village of Cottingley with a camera borrowed from Elsie's father. They had borrowed the camera to verify their excuse for going to the meadow so often. "I go to see the fairies," explained Elsie.

To Mr. Wright's surprise, when he developed the photographic plate it revealed Frances with four winged fairies—each about one foot tall—dancing in mid air before her. He immediately suspected that the fairies had been cut from paper and pinned onto the bushes, a logical conclusion given the fact that a waterfall in the background was blurred due to a slow shutter speed, while the flying fairies and their wings were perfectly sharp. Furthermore, Elsie was a gifted artist who easily could have drawn such figures. However,

Frances and the fairies, the first of the Cottingley fairy photographs. From Arthur Conan Doyle, *The Coming of the Fairies* (1922).

a search of the premises revealed no evidence of any cutouts. A few months later the girls borrowed the camera again and produced a second photograph, this one revealing Elsie with a gnome-like male figure.

What almost certainly began as a well-executed children's prank developed a life of its own when the girls' mothers announced at a meeting of a local chapter of the Theosophical Society that their daughters had photographed fairies. Edward L. Gardner, one of the society's leaders, and one with a strong interest in spirit photography, took up the cause and organized an examination of the photographs to ascertain their authenticity. Showing no signs of double exposure or blatant retouching, the photographs were pronounced genuine by experts.

Conan Doyle, through his connections with Gardner, became involved, and in 1920 he published the two photographs in the *Strand Magazine* under the title "Fairies Photographed: An Epoch-Making Event Described by A. Conan Doyle." An explosion of publicity followed, as did pressure on the girls to produce more photographs. In the summer of 1920 the cousins presented three additional fairy photographs. In spite of Gardner's best efforts, their photographic endeavors never succeeded in the presence of adults. Fairies, it seems, show themselves more readily to children than to grownups.

Like many a well-wrought mystery story, this case too ends with a confession. Elsie Wright, finally freed from the involvement of adult celebrities, publicly admitted what her father had suspected from the beginning and skeptics had surmised throughout. As reported in the *Yorkshire Evening Post* on March 19, 1983: "Residents of a Yorkshire village famous for fairies which two young cousins claimed to have photographed more than sixty years ago were today mourning the death of a legend.... Miss Wright, now Mrs. Hill, 82, and living in the village of Bunny, Nottinghamshire, said: 'The photographs were a fake—I admit it at last'" (as quoted by Smith, p. 371).

The *Yorkshire Evening Post* notwithstanding, the legend has not died out entirely. Two recent motion pictures, each featuring Conan Doyle, keep the hope alive of capturing fairies on film. The first, *Photographing Fairies* (1997), is based only loosely on the historic event, whereas *FairyTale: A True Story* (1997), presents itself as a reenactment of the affair at Cottingley. Here the famous illusionist Harry Houdini is added to the cast, although he was not involved in the historical events. Also unlike the original case, both films end with the fairies asserting themselves and verifying their existence.

Akin to the above discussion is the recent book by Suza Scalora, *The Fairies: Photographic Evidence of the Existence of Another World* (1999). The book presents itself as the log (with resulting photographs) of a fairy-hunting expedition. Unlike the usually fuzzy, ill-composed snapshots that one sees from time to time purporting to record sightings of the Loch Ness Monster, Bigfoot, or extraterrestrials, Scalora's photographs are technically perfect and esthetically very satisfying.

But are they what they claim to be—images of real fairies? Catalogers at the Library of Congress apparently did not think so. They list the book under the subject heading *Fairies—Fiction*. But the book is marketed, not as a fairy tale, but rather as an explorer's journal. The dust jacket announces: "Suza Scalora has been fascinated by fairy lore for as long as she can remember. She began her research while working in New York City as a commercial photographer.... When the opportunity presented itself, Suza Scalora set out to discover and capture images of the fairy world. In what became a yearlong expedition of epic—and at times perilous—proportions, she was finally able to prove something that she has known all along: fairies are real."

MANUSCRIPTS AND BOOKS

Writing about Fairies

Ironically the demise of fairy belief was accelerated in part by some of the very people who wished to preserve it by recording and publishing some of its legends. As W. R. Wilde astutely observed: "Nothing contributes more to uproot superstitious rites and forms than to print them; to make them known to the many instead of leaving them hidden among, and secretly practiced by the few" (p. vi).

Early written (in contrast to orally transmitted) information about fairies is sparse and scattered. Because literacy was first introduced to northern Europe by Christian missionaries and clerics, there are essentially no pre-Christian written accounts. Some references to fairies survive from the Middle Ages, although as a rule medieval scholars did not find fairy lore a topic worthy of serious study.

In the early 1500s the German-Swiss medical researcher Theophrastus von Hohenheim (Paracelsus) wrote *A Book on Nymphs, Sylphs, Pygmies, and Salamanders, and on the Other Spirits,* a metaphysical treatise on elemental spirits that belong to fairy lore. I discuss his views at length in chapters one and two of this handbook. In the mid 1600s the German writer Johannes Schultze, better known with his penname Praetorius, published a number of relevant legends, which—rewritten and often unattributed—were included in many later collections. In the mid 1700s Johann Karl August Musäus published legends about the shape-shifting Bohemian forest sprite named Rübezahl.

Travel accounts from the Renaissance through the eighteenth century often include sketches of local and regional fairy beliefs. Creative writers through-out the ages have included fairies in their epics, dramas, poetry, and fiction. Visual artists, frequently illustrating literary works, have contributed greatly to our conception of fairies, although rarely could one argue that their repre-sentations are based on anything other than imagination.

Robert Kirk

One of the earliest and most complete written surveys of traditional fairy belief is *The Secret Commonwealth of Elves, Fauns, and Fairies,* written in 1691 by Robert Kirk, a bilingual minister serving a Celtic parish in Aber-foyle, Scotland. It was not published until 1815 but was apparently known by his parishioners. In this treatise he theorizes about the origin and nature of fairies. He describes their subterranean realms, discusses their personal and social habits, their religion (actually their lack of religion), and their propensity to harm humans by stealing children, abducting midwives and nurses, and taking the essence from their crops. In short, he presents an extensive catalog of fairy lore, as believed in Celtic Scotland during the seventeenth century.

Kirk died under mysterious circumstances one year after writing this treatise. On May 14, 1692, the minister—only forty-eight years old—collapsed and died while taking his daily walk up Doon Hill, also known as Fairy Hill, near his church. Villagers rumored that the corpse was actually an image—a stock—created by the fairies, who had imprisoned him inside their hill as punishment for his exposé of their secrets. Tradition dictates that he communicated to a cousin that he would be present at the baptism of the child his wife had delivered shortly after his disappearance. Kirk's message continued, that the cousin could rescue him by throwing a knife over his head. Kirk did indeed appear at the baptism, but the cousin was too terrified to throw the knife, so the prisoner was forced to return to the hill, where presumably he still lives (Scott, 101–102).

Oral Tradition

Our richest source of information about fairy belief is an oral tradition that remained strong well into the nineteenth century. Comprising legends, ballads, customs, and superstitions, this material was passed—mostly by word of mouth—from one generation to the next for many centuries.

The word *legend,* as used by folklorists, denotes an account that claims to be true. Stories stemming from cultures that believe in magic may be seen as implausible fiction by later generations, but this does not change the fact that at one time they were accepted as truth. In the foreword to their collection *German Legends,* which contains many stories about elves and other underground people, Jacob and Wilhelm Grimm noted that, as of 1816, "the folk have not yet stopped believing in their legends" (p. 2). Collectors from other nations have made similar observations, especially with reference to legends about fairies.

Collectors and Editors

Jacob and Wilhelm Grimm

Famous around the world for their monumental and pioneering collection of fairy tales titled *Kinder- und Hausmärchen* (Children's and Household Tales, 1812–14), the brothers Grimm were also leading scholars and collectors in other folklore fields. Their *Deutsche Sagen* (German Legends, 1816–18), totaling 585 numbered accounts, presented Europe's first comprehensive and systematic collection of legends. Many of these (especially numbers 28–91) deal with elves, kobolds, nixes, and other such sprites. (Germans and Scandinavians seldom refer to their underground people as *fairies,* preferring instead Germanic-rooted words.)

Contrary to a popular notion, the Grimms themselves were not active field workers. Employed at the time as librarians in Kassel, Germany, they found their legend material in manuscripts, local and regional chronicles, and printed books, all of which they cited in an appendix to their collection.

Their two major folklore collections—the fairy tales and the legends— received great praise and were widely emulated, both by regional collectors within Germany and by others throughout Europe. In some instances the influence became circular. Thomas Crofton Croker, openly following the Grimms' example, published *Fairy Legends and Traditions of the South of Ireland* in 1825. The following year the Grimms published a faithful German translation of this collection titled *Irische Elfenmärchen* (Irish Elf Tales), adding to it their own substantive and insightful introductory essay. In 1828 Croker expanded his collection to three volumes (it was originally a single volume), and included the Grimms' lengthy essay in their third volume (pp. 1–154).

Another important contribution to European fairy lore is Jacob Grimm's *Deutsche Mythologie* (German Mythology, 1835), which brings together ancient northern European supernatural beliefs from a wide variety of linguistic, folkloric, literary, and historical sources. Written for specialists rather than the general public, this compendium is not easy to read. Grimm quotes most of his sources in the original language—be it Latin, Greek, Scandinavian, Anglo Saxon, Dutch, English, French, or German—obviously expecting his readers to have a foreign-language competence similar to his own, which will rarely be the case.

The Grimm brothers left a permanent mark on the collecting, editing, and publication of folklore worldwide. Many future collectors dedicated their works to them, or mentioned them prominently in their prefaces. Reviewers and publishers were quick to draw comparisons between new writers and the venerable brothers Grimm.

After the Grimm Brothers

In addition to Germany's many regional collectors who followed the Grimms, numerous individuals emerged from other countries emulating their example. These pioneering folklore collectors include:

- Brittany: Paul Sébillot, *Traditions et superstitions de la Haute-Bretagne* (Traditions and Superstitions of Upper Brittany, 1882).
- Cornwall: Robert Hunt, *Popular Romances of the West of England; or, The Drolls, Traditions, and Superstitions of Old Cornwall* (1871).

- Denmark: J. M. Thiele, *Danmarks Folkesagn* (Denmark's Folk Legends, 1843–60).
- England: William Henderson, *Notes on the Folk-Lore of the Northern Counties of England and the Borders* (1879).
- Iceland: Jón Árnason, *Íslenzkar þjóðsögur og æfintýri* (Icelandic Folk Legends and Fairy Tales, 1862–64).
- Ireland: Thomas Crofton Croker. *Fairy Legends and Traditions of the South of Ireland* (1825–28).
- Norway: Peter Christen Asbjørnsen and Jørgen Moe, *Norske Folkeeventyr* (Norwegian Folktales, 1841–44).
- Scotland: J. F. Campbell, *Popular Tales of the West Highlands: Orally Collected* (1890–93).
- Sweden: Arvid August Afzelius, *Svenska folkets sago-häfder* (Swedish Folk Legend Booklets, 1839–70).
- Wales and the Isle of Man: John Rhys. *Celtic Folklore: Welsh and Manx* (1901).

These were the pioneers, the first in their respective areas to record the legends and stories that constitute fairy lore as the nineteenth century inherited it, mostly by word of mouth, from the distant past. Others followed, often with distinction; but without the publications of these forerunners, we would know much less about the beliefs of our European ancestors.

Two additional names must be added to the above list of early contributors to published fairy lore. The first of these is Thomas Keightley, whose *Fairy Mythology* first appeared in 1834, followed by expanded editions in 1860 and 1878. This compendium brings together fairy accounts from around the world, but with a focus on the Germanic and Celtic cultures. Keightley demonstrates a remarkable skill with foreign languages, exceptional knowledge of history and literature, and the ability to piece together disparate elements into a meaningful whole.

The final name in this group is W. Y. Evans-Wentz. Born in New Jersey, Evans-Wentz was educated at Stanford, Oxford, and the University of Rennes in Brittany. In Europe he specialized in comparative religion and Celtic studies, counting as his teachers some of the most eminent scholars in the field, including John Rhys and Andrew Lang.

The unique feature of his fairy-lore research, which culminated in the book *The Fairy Faith in Celtic Countries* (1911), was that he approached it as a true believer, a person who offered no excuses for his acceptance of an unseen world. It may be argued that such a position is inherently unscientific. Did he know in advance what he was going to find before he started looking for it? Acting as an apologist for a "faith," did he skew his results in a prede-termined direction?

On the positive side, his personal and unashamed belief may have opened doors for him that would have remained closed for more skeptical field workers. Folklorists have long decried the fact that potential informants resist talking to them for fear of being ridiculed. Whatever influence his admitted bias had in his work, Evans-Wentz produced a substantial collection of anec-dotes and recollections from ordinary people throughout the Celtic countries, and no study of fairy lore would be complete without consulting it.

Ballads

Rhymed or rhythmic narratives are among the most durable folk-art forms in northern Europe. Since the Middle Ages these songs have been sung by ordinary people as well as professional entertainers. The texts are retained both in the folk's collective memory and in manuscripts and printed sheets called broadsides. Ballads, like migratory legends and other folklore genres, do not recognize national or language boundaries. Thus the repertoires of balladeers in different countries often show striking similarities. The interac-tion between humans and fairy folk—including abduction, seduction, and marriage—is a common theme in ballads.

Ballads were among the earliest folk literature genres to gain appre-ciation among educated Europeans. A pioneer in this regard was Thomas Percy, whose collection *Reliques of Ancient English Poetry* (1765), was praised and emulated throughout Europe, especially in Germany, where Johann Gottfried von Herder, Achim von Arnim, Clemens Brentano, and others created substantial collections of folk poetry, foremost ballads. Scandinavia too yielded a rich harvest of ballads, as exemplified in the col-lections of the Norwegian Svend Grundtvig and the Swede Gunnar Olof Hyltén-Cavallius. In Scotland the momentum for ballad collection and appreciation was accelerated by Sir Walter Scott with his *Minstrelsy of the Scottish Border* (1802–03).

The final name in ballad collecting is that of Frances J. Child, a Harvard scholar whose work culminated in *The English and Scottish Popular Ballads* (1882–98). More than a collection, this authoritative compendium brings together texts, analogues, historical data, and annotations for the major ballad types found in northern Europe. Of the 305 ballad families cataloged by Child, a substantial number include fairy motifs, such as the celebrated "Thomas Rymer" (no. 37), whose text is reproduced in chapter three of this handbook, and the equally famous "Tam Lin," also known as "Tamlane" (no. 39).

Common Weaknesses

Sources

If W. Y. Evans-Wentz's work is potentially marred by the author's prejudg-ment, other works display different weaknesses. The most common short-coming, from the perspective of modern folkloric expectations, is the failure to identify sources. The social setting where a story was told and recorded; the age, gender, and occupation of the informant; and the date and place of the recital are all important elements by today's standards, but more often than not these were omitted by nineteenth-century collectors.

John Rhys's criticism of Wirt Sikes's otherwise laudable book of Welsh folk-lore applies to many other collections of that era: "As frequently happens with him, he does not deign to tell us whence he got the legend" (p. 191). The Celtic scholar Douglas Hyde has essentially the same criticism of the folklore collections of Lady Wilde and others: "Like her predecessors, she disdains to quote an authority, and scorns to give us the least inkling as to where such-and-such a legend, or cure, or superstition comes from, from whom it was obtained, who were her informants, whether peasant or other, in what parishes or counties the superstition or legend obtains, and all the other collateral infor-mation which the modern folklorist is sure to expect" (p. xiii).

Literary Style

Another common shortcoming of collectors and editors is a desire to "improve" the informants' language. Some alteration of style is warranted. Many stories are told in dialects barely intelligible to most readers, and inevitably an oral pre-sentation includes false starts, unintended repetition, self corrections, and other problems that even purists of today would fix in the editing process.

Many—perhaps most—nineteenth-century collectors transformed the stories they heard from ordinary people by rewriting them in a stylized, liter-ary language. It seems that they were more often guided by potential book buyers' expectations than by a desire to accurately record what was actually spoken. Addressing this issue, Douglas Hyde claimed: "Crofton Croker is, alas! too often his own original. There lies his weak point, and there, too, is the defect of all who have followed him" (pp. x–xi).

Language Competence

Another obstacle faced by many field workers is the difficulty of commu-nicating with ordinary people in *their* language. The problem was especially acute in places like pre-industrial Germany where the differences were substantial between the language of commerce and education (High German) and any number of regional dialects spoken primarily by uneducated people (for example, Low German).

In Celtic regions the problem was even more extreme, with the ruling and educated classes speaking English, and the uneducated speaking Gaelic, two languages that bear little relationship to each other. Addressing this problem, Douglas Hyde praised the work of the American folklorist Jeremiah Curtin but found his Irish lacking: "Mr. Curtin tells us that he has taken his tales from the old Gaelic-speaking men; but he must have done so through the awkward medium of an interpreter, for his ignorance of the commonest Irish words is as startling as Lady Wilde's" (p. xv).

Lady Wilde, in the preface to her *Ancient Legends, Mystic Charms, and Superstitions of Ireland,* defends herself on the language front by claiming that her principal sources were "oral communications made by the peasantry . . . , taken down by competent persons skilled in both languages, and as far as possible in the very words of the narrator" (p. xii). However, she identifies neither her scribes nor their informants.

Self Censorship

A final problem faced by scholars collecting stories from ordinary people is that some of the material will be ordinary, or to use a synonym, vulgar. When Victorian-age collectors were confronted with "unprintable" material, they most often followed one of two paths: They omitted it altogether, with or without informing the reader; or they bowdlerized it.

J. F. Campbell's Scottish collection offers an example of the first route. After summarizing a particular fairy legend, he then noted that one version from the Isle of Lewis contained "curious variations unfit for printing" (vol. 2, p. 52); but he does not give his readers the slightest hint as to what he found objectionable about the stories.

A second approach called for the replacement of objectionable features with euphemisms. Joseph Jacobs, a prolific and popular editor working in the 1890s, took substantial liberties with his texts, especially when he thought that certain passages were inappropriate for younger readers, but to his credit he regularly appended to his collections scholarly notes in which he identified his sources and explained any changes that he had made. His Victorian sensitivity is illustrated in his editing of "The Fairy's Midwife," re-titling it "Fairy Ointment" and changing the title heroine's profession from midwife to "a nurse that looked after sick people and minded babies" (p. 210).

RECENT SCHOLARSHIP

Scholarly interest in fairy lore is not waning, as a search through the offerings of any major bookseller or a perusal of periodicals such as *Folk-Lore* or the *Journal of American Folklore* will ascertain. Modern scholarly studies typically place fairy accounts within the larger context of legend research. This broader field thus includes figures of mythical proportion, such as King Arthur or Friedrich Barbarossa; local and regional creation stories, for example, how a particular lake was formed; contemporary, or so-called urban legends, such as stories about extraterrestrials or vanishing hitchhikers; and personal accounts of premonition, visits from the dead, and other paranormal events.

Contemporary legend research is active in all the geographic areas covered in this handbook. Due to strong local interest, it is typically published first—and often only—in the language of its homeland. A few names of scholars of permanence whose work appears mostly in English stand out. These include the Scandinavian specialist Jacqueline Simpson, the German specialist Donald Ward, the central European specialist Linda Dégh, and above all the English specialist Katharine M. Briggs, the undisputed dean of fairy lore studies.

Born in 1898, Katharine M. Briggs distinguished herself at Oxford University, where she earned a doctorate, writing her dissertation on folklore in seventeenth-century literature. A long teaching and publishing career followed. Her work is always marked by thoroughness and academic integrity. Never pretentious, her books are accessible to the general reader, but her erudition and insight are always impressive, even to seasoned scholars. Her principal book publications are listed in the bibliography of this handbook. Katharine M. Briggs died in 1980.

WORKS CITED

Árnason, Jón. *Icelandic Legends.* Trans. George E. J. Powell and Eiríkur Magnússon. London: Bentley, 1864.

Beowulf. Trans. Howell D. Chickering. New York: Doubleday, 1977.

Bord, Janet. *Fairies: Real Encounters with Little People.* New York: Dell, 1997.

Campbell, Archibald. *Waifs and Strays of Celtic Tradition: Argyllshire Series.* London: Nutt, 1889.

Campbell, J. F. *Popular Tales of the West Highlands.* 4 vols. Paisley and London: Gardner, 1890.

Conan Doyle, Sir Arthur. *The Coming of the Fairies.* London: Hodder and Stoughton, 1922.

Croker, Thomas Crofton. *Fairy Legends and Traditions of the South of Ireland.* 3 vols. London: Murray, 1825–28.

Curtin, Jeremiah. *Tales of the Fairies and the Ghost World.* London: Nutt, 1895.

Evans-Wentz, W. Y. *The Fairy-Faith in Celtic Countries.* London: Frowde, 1911.

Gander, Karl. *Niederlausitzer Volkssagen.* Berlin: Deutsche Schriftsteller-Genossenschaft, 1894.

Gregor, Walter. *Notes on the Folk-Lore of the North-East of Scotland.* London: Folk-Lore Society, 1881.

Gregory, Lady Isabelle Augusta. *Visions and Beliefs in the West of Ireland.* New York and London: Putnam, 1920.

Grimm, Jacob and Wilhelm. *The German Legends of the Brothers Grimm.* Trans. Donald Ward. 2 vols. Philadelphia: Institute for the Study of Human Issues, 1981.

Grimm, Jacob. *Deutsche Mythologie.* 3 vols. Frankfurt am Main: Ullstein, 1981. Reprint of the 4th edition of 1876. First published 1835.

Grohmann, Josef Virgil. *Sagen-Buch von Böhmen und Mähren.* Prague: Calve, 1863.

Hartland, Edwin Sidney. *English Fairy and Folk Tales.* London: Scott, 1890.

Haupt, Karl. *Sagenbuch der Lausitz.* 2 vols. Leipzig: Engelmann, 1862–63.

Hofberg, Herman. *Swedish Fairy Tales.* Chicago: Conkey, 1893.

Hreinsson, Vidar, ed. *The Complete Sagas of Icelanders.* 5 vols. Reykjavik: Leifur Eiriksson, 1997.

Hunt, Robert. *Popular Romances of the West of England.* London: Hotten, 1871.

Hyde, Douglas. *Beside the Fire: A Collection of Irish Gaelic Folk Stories.* London: Nutt, 1910.

Jacobs, Joseph. *English Fairy Tales.* London: Nutt, 1898. First published 1890.

James I, King of England. *Daemonology.* San Diego: Book Tree, 2002. First published 1597.

Keightley, Thomas. *The Fairy Mythology.* London: Bohn, 1850.

Kennedy, Patrick. *Legendary Fictions of the Irish Celts.* London: Macmillan, 1891. First published 1866.

Kirk, Robert. *The Secret Commonwealth of Elves, Fauns, and Fairies.* London: David Nutt, 1893. Based on a manuscript of 1691.

Knoop, Otto. *Volkssagen, Erzählungen, Aberglauben, Gebräuche und Märchen aus dem östlichen Hinterpommern.* Poznan, Poland: Jolowicz, 1885.

Kuhn, Adalbert, and Wilhelm Schwartz. *Norddeutsche Sagen, Märchen und Gebräuche.* Leipzig: Brockhaus, 1848.

Kuhn, Adalbert. *Sagen, Gebräuche und Märchen aus Westfalen.* 2 vols. Leipzig: Brockhaus, 1859.

Lang, Andrew. Introduction to Robert Kirk. *The Secret Commonwealth of Elves, Fauns, and Fairies.* London: Nutt, 1893.

Luther, Martin. *Werke, kritische Gesamtausgabe: Tischreden.* Weimar: Böhlau, 1912–21.

Nicholson, John. *Some Folk-Tales and Legends of Shetland.* Edinburgh: Allan, 1920.

Rhys, John. *Celtic Folklore: Welsh and Manx.* Oxford: Oxford UP, 1901.

Saxo Grammaticus. *The First Nine Books of the Danish History [Gesta Danorum] of Saxo Grammaticus.* Trans. Oliver Elton. London: Nutt, 1894.

Scalora, Suza. *The Fairies: Photographic Evidence of the Existence of Another World.* New York : Cotler, 1999.

Scot, Reginald. *The Discoverie of Witchcraft.* New York: Dover, 1972.

Scott, Sir Walter. *Letters on Demonology and Witchcraft.* Ware, Hertfordshire: Wordsworth Editions, 2001. First published 1830.

Sikes, Wirt. *British Goblins: Welsh Folk-Lore, Fairy Mythology, Legends, and Traditions.* Boston: Osgood, 1881.

Smith, Paul. "The Cottingley Fairies: The End of a Legend." In *The Good People: New Fairylore Essays,* ed. Peter Narváez, pp. 371–405. New York: Garland, 1991.

Snorri Sturluson. *The Prose Edda.* Trans. Jean I. Young. Berkeley: U of California P, 1954.

Spence, Lewis. *Legends and Romances of Brittany.* New York: Stokes, [1917].

Taylor, Sam. "The Night Those UFOs Didn't Land," *Daily Mail.* London, August 7, 1999.

Temme, J.D.H. *Die Volkssagen der Altmark.* Berlin: Nicolai, 1839.

Thiele, J.M. *Danmarks Folkesagn.* 3 vols. Copenhagen: Rosenkilde og Bagger, 1968.

Wilde, Lady Francesca. *Ancient Legends, Mystic Charms, and Superstitions of Ireland.* London: Chatto and Windus, 1919.

Wilde, W.R. *Irish Popular Superstitions.* Dublin: McGlashan, 1852.

Yeats, William Butler, ed. *Fairy and Folk Tales of Ireland.* New York: Macmillan, 1983. Contains *Fairy and Folk Tales of the Irish Peasantry,* first published 1888, and *Irish Fairy Tales,* first published 1892.

Five
Contexts

FAIRIES ARE EVERYWHERE

By all accounts fairies are very long-lived. Throughout recorded history they have been a part of human life—sometimes helping, sometimes hindering; sometimes visible, but most often unseen. Anciently they filled various niches in a nature-based religion. Medieval Christianity demoted them to demon status. Subsequently the Age of Reason further marginalized them, if it did not explain them away altogether. Through all this, fairies have proven to be very durable. The psychological, social, and esthetic needs that they filled centuries ago are still with us. If fairies do not fill these wants, then some other supernatural or emotional agent will take their places. Paraphrasing Voltaire's famous remark concerning God, "If fairies did not exist, it would be necessary to invent them."

Fairies are with us in many contexts, whether they are real and independent entities or only figments of imagination. They are known by many different names, but as Shakespeare's Juliet observed: "What's in a name? That which we call a rose, by any other name would smell as sweet" (*Romeo and Juliet,* act 2, scene 2). Fairies' exploits were once celebrated at a workday's end around the fire. Even then they went by many names, depending on the local dialect and the fairies' own environment: brownie, pixie, elf, mermaid, gnome, and too many more to repeat here.

Today, again under varying names, they make appearances as advertising mascots, characters in fantasy literature, dancers on a ballet stage, decorative motifs on porcelain dinnerware, imaginative paintings, Santa Claus's helpers, the sleep-inducing sandman, a sprite who pays children for discarded baby teeth, humorous garden statues, visitors from outer space, and strange little humanoid creatures in video games and science-fiction motion pictures. Even the name *Sith,* the clan of evildoers in the *Star Wars* films, is a long-accepted alternate spelling of *sidhe,* a Gaelic word for *fairy family.* Who would deny that Yoda, one of *Star Wars'* most unforgettable characters, is a quintessential elf? Does not E.T., the extraterrestrial, owe much of his appearance and behavior to Frodo, the hobbit? Are not the hobgoblins that dominate fantasy role-playing games such as *Dungeons and Dragons* space-age clones of creatures described in *Beowulf* and the *Eddas?*

Fairies continue to haunt burial sites, ancient monuments, secluded coves, and primeval forests, but they have also moved, quite readily, into the popular culture of the twentieth and twenty-first centuries. For some, these appearances are pure fantasy, to be treated much the same as other emotional or esthetic experiences; for others, they are part of a real—if mostly unseen—world, with many characteristics of religion.

The contexts in which the legacy of ancient fairy belief manifests itself are numerous and varied, each one complex enough to warrant a book-length study by itself. Many such books have already been written, including recent monographs by Nicola Bown and Carole G. Silver, to name but two eminent examples. The following pages are not designed to supplant any of these already existing studies, but rather to outline the most important situations where fairies traditionally have played a role and in some instances continue to make their presence known. Supplementing this outline, I elaborate more fully on a handful of topics, selected to show the wide variety of contexts where fairies appear.

LITERATURE

From the Middle Ages to the Enlightenment

In a sense most fairy lore derives from the spoken word—histories communicated by word of mouth for the enlightenment and entertainment of all who would listen. The ancient epics of northern Europe had roots in oral stories before they were committed to paper or vellum in the Middle Ages. And virtually all of these feature dwarfs, elves, fairies, nixies, and such—if not as leading characters then at least in supporting roles. Legendary heroes such as Arthur, Beowulf, Holger Danske, Merlin, Oisin, Siegfried, and Tristan all had dealings with fairy folk.

Fairies did not die with the Middle Ages but continued to make appearances in imaginative literature. Geoffrey Chaucer's "The Merchant's Tale" (ca. 1390) features Pluto and Prosperina, the king and queen of Faerie.

The Elizabethan Age produced numerous literary works with fairies as leading characters, including Edmund Spenser's *The Faerie Queene* (1590), Ben Jonson's *Oberon, the Fairy Prince* (1616), and Michael Drayton's *Nymphidia: The Court of Fairy* (1627).

Foremost in this group, of course, is William Shakespeare, whose *A Midsummer Night's Dream* (ca. 1595) is possibly the greatest fairy tale ever written. Not only is it a dramatic and literary masterpiece, but it also reveals a substantial body of sixteenth-century fairy belief. Fairies engaged Shakespeare throughout his career, with the sprites earning roles (or being mentioned) in *The Comedy of Errors, Romeo and Juliet, The Merry Wives of Windsor, Hamlet, King Lear, Cymbaline, The Winter's Tale,* and *The Tempest.*

The cultural epoch known as the Enlightenment or Age of Reason dominated northern Europe from the late 1600s through most of the 1700s, during which time supernatural phenomena of all kinds were essentially banned from so-called high literature.

Romanticism

Toward the end of the eighteenth century the esthetic pendulum changed directions, ushering in a new cultural epoch: Romanticism. This movement legitimized the emotional and irrational aspects of art and literature. A leading genre in this new era was the literary fairy tale. These stories were based in part on traditional folklore but gained most of their momentum through their creators' inventiveness, no longer tied to this-worldly reality.

Another genre favored by the Romantics was the ballad, an art form inherited from the distant past, and one with a tradition of supernatural plots. It was rejuvenated as a literary genre in Europe with the publication of Thomas Percy's *Reliques of Ancient English Poetry* in 1765. Johann Wolfgang von Goethe was among the many noteworthy poets who, influenced by Percy's collection, turned to that art form. One feature of this genre that appealed to Goethe was its fusion of the three forms of classical literature: narrative, lyric, and dramatic. Goethe's best known ballad, and probably the most famous ballad in German literature, is "Erlkönig," written in 1782. This famous piece is an exemplary representative of fairy lore in the literature of Romanticism.

Erlkönig / Erl-King / Elf King

One of Germany's most famous fairy figures is the *Erlkönig*, whose name can be translated as *Erl-King*, or *Elf King*, but is usually left in the original

German because of two untranslatable masterpieces: Johann Wolfgang von Goethe's ballad and Franz Schubert's art song.

Goethe's text is a mini-drama with four characters: a narrator who sets the stage in the first strophe then reveals the tragic ending in the last strophe. The internal strophes present a dialogue between a father and his son, who are riding furiously through the night for some undisclosed reason. Their dialogue is interrupted repeatedly by the tempting calls of the sinister *Erlkönig*, but true to fairy tradition, only the child can hear his voice. In the end, as the narrator informs us, the father reaches his destination but the child is dead.

The piece lends itself to different interpretations. Rationalists will claim that the boy was sick from the beginning (hence the nighttime race through the woods), and that his visions were nothing more than hallucinations brought on by fever. Fairy believers, on the other hand, will see in this piece a child-abduction legend, not unlike countless others in folklore. The boy was taken by the *Erlkönig* and his sensuous daughters. The corpse in the father's arms is nothing but an image.

An oil painting by Moritz von Schwind leaves no doubt as to his interpretation. The artist depicts a fleeing father and son pursued by a ghostly airborne man in a white robe, while four seductive young women eagerly look on from a grove of trees. This painting is on display in Munich's Schack Gallery.

Goethe's mini-drama also makes a powerful mini-opera. A number of composers have set the ballad to music, usually for piano and solo voice. Carl Loewe's setting (1818) is worthy of performance, but the undisputed masterpiece was created by Franz Schubert in 1815. The song makes substantial demands on a singer, presenting—as it does—four different speakers, each with a different voice quality.

Like all great poetry, Goethe's "Erlkönig" is untranslatable. Knowing this, in 1799 Scotland's great ballad connoisseur and folklore collector, Sir Walter Scott, nevertheless made a noble attempt. Goethe's original poem and Scott's translation are printed side by side in the following lines. Note that Goethe marks a change of speaker only with punctuation (or, in the case of an oral performance, with different voice inflections), Scott is less subtle, explicitly telling his readers which lines belong to the Erl-King.

Erlkönig	The Erl-King
Johann Wolfgang von Goethe	Translated by Sir Walter Scott
Wer reitet so spät durch Nacht und Wind?	O who rides by night thro' the woodland so wild?
Es ist der Vater mit seinem Kind;	It is the fond father embracing his child;

Er hat den Knaben wohl in dem Arm,

Er fasst ihn sicher, er hält ihn warm. —

Mein Sohn, was birgst du so bang
dein Gesicht? —
Siehst Vater, du den Erlkönig nicht?

Den Erlenkönig mit Kron
und Schweif? —
Mein Sohn, es ist ein Nebelstreif. —

»Du liebes Kind, komm, geh mit mir!
Gar schöne Spiele spiel ich mit dir;

Manch bunte Blumen sind an
dem Strand,
Meine Mutter hat manch gülden
Gewand.«

Mein Vater, mein Vater, und hörest
du nicht,
Was Erlenkönig mir leise verspricht? —
Sei ruhig, bleibe ruhig, mein Kind;

In dürren Blättern säuselt der Wind. —

»Willst, feiner Knabe, du mit mir gehn?
Meine Töchter sollen dich warten schön;

Meine Töchter führen den nächtlichen
Reihn
Und wiegen und tanzen und singen
dich ein.«

Mein Vater, mein Vater, und siehst
du nicht dort

And close the boy nestles within his
loved arm,
To hold himself fast, and to keep
himself warm.
"O father, see yonder! see yonder!"
he says;
"My boy, upon what dost thou fearfully
gaze?"
"O, 'tis the Erl-King with his crown and
his shroud."
"No, my son, it is but a dark wreath of
the cloud."
The Erl-King Speaks:
"O come and go with me, thou loveliest
child;
By many a gay sport shall thy time be
beguiled;
My mother keeps for thee many a fair
toy,
And many a fine flower shall she pluck
for my boy."
"O father, my father, and did you not
hear
The Erl-King whisper so low in my ear?"
"Be still, my heart's darling—my child,
be at ease;
It was but the wild blast as it sung thro'
the trees."
Erl-King:
"O wilt thou go with me, thou
loveliest boy?
My daughter shall tend thee with care
and with joy;
She shall bear three so lightly thro' wet
and thro' wild,
And press thee, and kiss thee, and sing
to my child."
"O father, my father, and saw you not
plain

Erlkönigs Töchter am düstern Ort? —

Mein Sohn, mein Sohn, ich seh es genau:
Es scheinen die alten Weiden so grau. —

»Ich liebe dich, mich reizt deine schöne Gestalt;
Und bist du nicht willig, so brauch ich Gewalt.« —
Mein Vater, mein Vater, jetzt fasst er mich an!
Erlkönig hat mir ein Leids getan! —

Dem Vater grauset's, er reitet geschwind,

Er hält in den Armen das ächzende Kind,
Erreicht den Hof mit Mühe und Not;

In seinen Armen das Kind war tot.

The Erl-King's pale daughter glide past thro' the rain?"
"Oh yes, my loved treasure, I knew it full soon;
It was the grey willow that danced to the moon."
Erl-King:

"O come and go with me, no longer delay,
Or else, silly child, I will drag thee away."
"O father! O father! now, now, keep your hold,
The Erl-King has seized me—his grasp is so cold!"
Sore trembled the father; he spurr'd thro' the wild,
Clasping close to his bosom his shuddering child;
He reaches his dwelling in doubt and in dread,
But, clasp'd to his bosom, the infant was dead.

Although the subject of Goethe's text clearly belongs to traditional folklore, the name *Erlkönig* does not. This word was first used by Goethe's contemporary Johann Gottfried von Herder in a ballad loosely translated from the Danish and titled "Erlkönigs Tochter" (Erl-King's Daughter, 1779). The term *Erlkönig* is most likely Herder's mistranslation of the Danish *ellerkonge*—elf king, which would best be translated into German as *Elfenkönig*. It is also possible that Herder, taking full advantage of poetic license, avoided a traditional word and coined instead an expression clouded in mystery. Whether stemming from a faulty translation or a literary innovation, the name *Erlkönig* is firmly rooted in German culture and—primarily through Schubert's art song—around the world as well.

Herder's ballad, which served as the impetus for Goethe's masterpiece, deserves a short discussion. Like its Danish forebear, it fits into the tradition of the English ballads "Tam Lin" and "Thomas Rymer," both of which depict the seduction of a human male by a fairy queen. In Herder's ballad, Herr Oluf (spelled *Olof* in some versions) comes upon a company of elves dancing in a circle. One of them, the elf king's daughter, extends her hand to him and invites him to join their circle. He declines, explaining that tomorrow is his wedding day. She grows ever more insistent, promising him great riches if he will dance with her. He refuses repeatedly. Finally, with a curse, she strikes him "on his heart," then scornfully tells him to ride home to his bride. The next morning he does not appear at his wedding ceremony. The bride finds him lying on the forest floor, dead (vol. 2, book 2, no. 27).

CHILDREN'S LITERATURE

Fairy Tales

The words *fairy* and *tale* occur together so often that they seem almost inseparable, especially in the context of children's literature in its many forms, including bedtime stories, picture books, novels for young adults, and—thanks to modern technology—motion pictures and television programs. However, as I explain in the companion to this handbook, *Folk and Fairy Tales* (pp. 31–32), the English term *fairy tale* is somewhat of a misnomer. Most stories so designated—say those by the Grimm brothers and Hans Christian Andersen—may involve the supernatural, but fairies per se are not normally its agents. *Magic tale,* the term favored by specialists, would be a more precise designation.

Charles Perrault and the Brothers Grimm

The word *fairy tale* comes to English from the French *conte de fées.* The most influential collection of such stories created in that language is Charles Perrault's *Histoires, ou contes du temps passé* (Stories, or Tales of Times Past, 1697). It contains a dozen familiar stories, about half of which involve fairies. Note that the word *fairy* does not occur in Perrault's title.

Similarly, the world's most famous collection of so-called fairy tales, the Grimm brothers' *Kinder- und Hausmärchen* (Children's and Household Tales, 1812–14), does not use the word *fairy* in its title. The Grimms' collection contains over 200 stories, with only a handful employing elves or fairies. German folklore prefers to label its underground people with words of Germanic origin, such as *elf,* rather than with those stemming from Latin, such as *fairy,* even though their functions may be quite similar.

A brief discussion of the fairy involvement in a few well-known German and French tales of the same type is in order. In Perrault's "Sleeping Beauty"

(Aarne-Thompson type 410) seven fairies are invited to be godmothers at a princess's christening. An eighth fairy, uninvited, shows up and curses the princess, ultimately causing her to fall asleep for 100 years. The Grimms' version, which they titled "Little Brier-Rose," develops similarly, except the magic guests are wise women, not fairies; and they number twelve, not seven. A thirteenth wise woman shows up and curses the infant princess.

"Cinderella" (Aarne-Thompson type 510A) is another well-known story told by both Perrault and the Grimms. In Perrault's version—celebrated through Walt Disney's 1950 animated film—the persecuted heroine receives magic aid from her godmother, a fairy. In the Grimms' version the supernatural help comes from a little white bird sitting in a tree above the grave of Cinderella's mother. Here the magic helper, instead of being a fairy, is a representative of the girl's deceased parent, if not the mother's actual spirit or ghost, embodied as a bird. The relationship between fairies and ghosts was explained in chapter four of this handbook, and this pair of Cinderella stories makes the association all the clearer. A fairy godmother helps the French heroine, whereas a bird from her mother's grave helps her German counterpart. The agents differ in appearance and name, but their function is identical in each of the tales.

Literary Fairy Tales since Perrault and Grimm

Whatever the source of magic aid, stories of this kind are generally known in English as fairy tales, and these have become the preeminent form of children's literature. However, this development came slowly. Citing Michael Patrick Hearn: "John Locke, in *Some Thoughts Concerning Education* (1693), cautioned against fairy tales, chapbooks, and old wives' tales, which with all their wild bugaboos might damage impressionable infant minds" (p. xvii).

Ironically, this message dates from the same decade as the publication of Charles Perrault's famous fairy-tale collection in France, a country much influenced by Locke's Enlightenment philosophy, but one that also became a great producer and exporter of literary fairy tales. Throughout the eighteenth century opinions similar to Locke's were expressed elsewhere in Europe by leading educators and philosophers. Fairy tales for children were criticized, not because of the violence that they often portrayed, but rather because they ostensibly promoted superstition and irrational belief.

As noted above, the Age of Romanticism, with its emphasis on emotion, spontaneity, and the mysterious, brought many changes in Europe's cultural attitudes. These changes stimulated a wave of juvenile fairy literature that continues into the twenty-first century. New acceptance of fairy lore by the intelligentsia, at least for entertainment purposes, corresponded with a rise in general literacy and new paper-making processes (using wood pulp) that made inexpensive books possible.

A new market was created: mass-produced story and picture books for children. A great many writers and publishers—unfortunately not always of high quality—moved into the niche. The anonymous *Fairy Grove* (ca. 1840), admittedly a work of only mediocre quality, is a good example of the type of material being produced for children in the mid nineteenth century. Its text is reproduced in chapter three.

The Little Mermaid

The 1800s did produce children's fairy literature of permanent value. Hans Christiansen Andersen's magic stories, originally published between 1835 and 1872, are still read worldwide, and a number of them grew out of authentic fairy traditions. For example, his "Little Mermaid" has as a central theme a mermaid's concerns about having no eternal soul. She hears from her grandmother: "We can live until we are three hundred years old; but when we die, we become the foam on the ocean. We cannot even bury our loved ones. We do not have immortal souls" (p. 66). This topic is featured in numerous folk legends, for example those reproduced under the heading "Prospects for Salvation" in chapter three. Andersen's mermaid heroine, through great personal sacrifice, gains the possibility of salvation.

However, in another of the story's intertwining plots, she fails to gain the love of a mortal prince, who passes her by in favor of a beautiful but less-deserving woman. The mermaid's disappointment in love reflects not only a series of unfulfilled romances in her creator's lifetime, but also the difficulties of maintaining a marriage between a human and a fairy, the theme of innumerable folk legends. For examples see the texts reproduced under the heading "Fairy Brides" in chapter three.

A Modern Changeling Story

Another Scandinavian who artfully turned fairy motifs into children's stories is Selma Lagerlöf, who in 1909 won the Nobel Prize for literature, the first woman and the first Swede to be so honored. Her children's story "Bortbytingen" (The Changeling, 1915) deserves special discussion because it treats a subject central to traditional fairy lore, but one that is today largely forgotten: the abusive treatment of children deemed to be changelings.

True to folklore tradition, Lagerlöf describes the kidnapping of a mortal child by an old troll woman, who leaves her own misshapen baby in its place.

Following the pattern of countless legends, the parents are told to beat the changeling if they want to recover their own baby. The father is only too willing to abuse the ugly troll child, but the mother's maternal instincts cause her to intercede on the changeling's behalf. Several episodes are described in which the father attempts to follow the community's expectations by cruelly punishing or even killing the unwanted child, but each time the mother self-lessly protects the troll baby.

Her kindness and perseverance are rewarded in the end, and the two children are restored to their original parents. Only then do we learn that during his absence, the human child had lived in an unseen parallel world. Every act of cruelty or of kindness visited upon the troll child by his human guardians had been duplicated upon him by his troll stepmother. It is a mother's kindness and humanity rather than the prescribed abuse and neglect that rescues her child. Lagerlöf thus cloaks an ancient and cruel superstition in a modern and humane dress.

Lagerlöf's story, first published in her collection of short prose *Troll och människor* (Trolls and Humans), remains popular in Sweden. It has been dramatized for performance on stage, and the composer Staffan Mossenmark turned the story into an opera, also titled *Bortbytingen,* first performed in 1998.

Gremlins

In 1943 Roald Dahl, then a flight lieutenant in the Royal Air Force, wrote a book commissioned by Walt Disney titled *The Gremlins.* Since ancient times fairies have provided explanations for misfortunes ranging from the failure of milk to produce butter to the premature death of an apparently healthy person. Dahl, a pilot who himself had been seriously injured in a crash landing, turned to British fairy lore to explain to young readers why the RAF aircraft developed so many mechanical problems as World War Two intensified. The failures, according to his book, were caused by little malicious imps called gremlins. This word is of recent coinage, whether by Dahl himself—as he claimed—or by unnamed contemporaries who were also serving in the RAF.

In Dahl's book the gremlins tell their own story: Long ago Britain was covered with forests and swamps that were inhabited by goblins, trolls, hob-goblins, and pixies. They were everywhere except in one northern forest, which was inhabited by gremlins, described as funny little people with funny little horns growing out of their funny little heads, and wearing funny little boots on their funny little feet. The gremlins lived in peace until one day their forest was invaded by men who cut down their trees and built a factory where big tin birds were manufactured.

To avenge the destruction of their homeland, the gremlins turned to sabotage, wreaking havoc with airplane machinery at every opportunity. But the story has a happy ending. The fliers befriend the gremlins, especially one old fellow nicknamed Jamface, whom they then train as airplane mechanics, and the imps thus turn their talents to aid the British war effort.

Walt Disney, the sponsor and copyright owner of Dahl's book, intended to turn it into a full-length animated film, but this did not materialize. Gremlins appeared in a number of his short pieces, although they were never featured in the titles. The Disney corporation attempted to gain copyright and trademark protection for the *gremlin* name and concept, but these efforts were frustrated by the ever-increasing references to the little troublemakers in the press and in ordinary conversation as the 1940s advanced. The word *gremlin* quickly entrenched itself in the English language as a designation for the cause of otherwise unexplainable failures in mechanical and electronic equipment. A generation later their sinister reputation expanded with the comedy-horror motion picture *Gremlins* (1984)—not a Disney offering—in which little green monsters overrun an idyllic small town. In its sequel, *Gremlins 2* (1990), the infestation occurs in a high-tech building in New York City.

Other Fairy-Tale Authors

The above discussion, ranging from Cinderella's magic helpers to World War Two mischief-makers, illustrates the diversity of roles played by fairies in children's fiction. Although space does not allow a full discussion of other fairy-tale types and their creators, a list of prominent names is in order.

The Italian author Carlo Lorenzini, writing under the penname C. Collodi, created one of the most enduring fantasy characters in Pinocchio, whose adventures first appeared serially in 1881, then in book form. Pinocchio, himself a magic figure, endears himself to young readers by displaying both the positive aspirations and the weaknesses of children everywhere. Guided by a good fairy, Pinocchio ultimately achieves his goal: human boyhood, a symbolic event that readers can interpret individually to satisfy their own personal desires. Collodi's book has achieved world-wide success.

The English-speaking world, too, has produced its share of word-famous fairy figures. Apart from Shakespeare's marvelous creations Puck and Ariel, the best known of these is J. M. Barrie's boy-turned-fairy, Peter Pan. First conceived in a book titled *The Little White Bird* (1902), Peter Pan premiered as an independent dramatic figure in the play *Peter Pan; or, The Boy Who Wouldn't Grow Up* (1904). The play met with immediate success and has been performed regularly—especially as a Christmastime event—for more than a century. In 1906 the Peter Pan episodes of *The Little White Bird* were published under the title *Peter Pan in Kensington Gardens,* with illustrations by Arthur Rackham. In 1911 Barrie adapted his popular play as a novel titled *Peter and Wendy.* This book is most often published under the title *Peter Pan.*

Other English-language authors of fairy tales for children include Oscar Wilde, George MacDonald, Frank Stockton, and L. Frank Baum. Also deserving mention is Andrew Lang, whose "colored fairy books," beginning with *The Blue Fairy Book* in 1889 and ultimately comprising twelve volumes, met with great popular success. These collections brought together fairy tales from around the world, all cautiously rewritten to meet Victorian expectations.

VISUAL ARTISTS

Book Illustrators

Much of the success of Lang's fairy-tale collections can be attributed to the handsome illustrations created by H. J. Ford, both line drawings and full-page colored plates. Fairies, mermaids, elves, and trolls make excellent artists' models, allowing for a full range of imagination and creativity.

From the mid nineteenth century onward, drawings have been an integral part of children's fairy books, with visual images created by illustrators becoming inseparably attached to the stories themselves. The honor roll for fairy-book artists is both long a varied. Included are John Baur, Walter Crane, George Cruikshank, Gustave Doré, Edmund Dulac, H. J. Ford, Wanda Gág, Kate Greenaway, Theodor Kittelsen, Lois Lenski, Arthur Rackham, Ludwig Richter, Maurice Sendak, Moritz von Schwind, Margaret Winifred Tarrant, and Erik Werenskiold. Many of the members of this list illustrated other types of books as well.

Some illustrated fairy books are nearly devoid of text, existing primarily for their pictorial content. Suza Scalora's *The Fairies: Photographic Evidence of the Existence of Another World* (1999), discussed in chapter four, fits into this category. With sales exceeding 1,000,000 copies, the most popular such book is *Faeries* (1978) by Brian Froud and Alan Lee. Although the authors do comment on the folklore behind their illustrations, it is the fanciful drawings and paintings that attract their almost cult-like followers, sometimes playfully dubbed *Froudians.*

The Bogles in the Courtyard

A typical illustration by Arthur Rackham, from Flora Annie Steel, *English Fairy Tales* (1918).

The Fine Arts

Fantasy pictorial treatments of beings from fairy lore have a very old heritage in Europe, possibly dating back to prehistoric stone art. For example, the Lagnö rune stone from Södermanland in Sweden depicts an elf-like figure entwined by two snakes, and several of the famous Gotland picture stones depict airborne females usually interpreted as valkyries, who have a traditional association with the swan-maiden fairies (Davidson, pp. 40–46, 116).

Some of European art's most fanciful figures are demons cast from heaven as depicted by the late medieval Dutch painter Hieronymus Bosch, especially in *The Hay Wain, The Last Judgment,* and *The Garden of Earthly Delights,* all painted between about 1490 and 1505. His demons—at home in air, earth, and water—are grotesque figures, some with wings, many half human and half animal.

Their connection with fairy lore is obvious when one recalls the popular theological position (treated in chapter four) that fairies are fallen angels cast out of heaven. Furthermore, descriptions of fairy folk in traditional legends often correspond to Bosch's surrealistic beings—for example, humans with duck feet or creatures that have a human-like appearance from the front, but are hollow from the rear. A number of Bosch's successors, notably Pieter Bruegel the Elder and Pieter van der Heyden, continued with this tradition of creating fanciful images of grotesque demons with ties to fairy lore through the fallen-angel belief.

Many other pictorial depictions exist as well, often emphasizing grace, beauty, and pleasure. From the Renaissance onward fairy motifs—including

Gargoyles often have the appearance of elves and dwarfs, as illustrated by these figures surrounding the columns of the St. Klemens Church in Schwarzrheindorf, Germany. Photograph by the author.

mermaids, elves, pixies, and the like—have decorated objects ranging from maps to dinnerware. Mermaid-shaped pitchers, dinner plates adorned with dancing fairies, and the like, have been popular for centuries. Even religious art has succumbed, as illustrated by the famous mermaid carving on a bench end in the church at Zennor, Cornwall, or the Green Man carvings found in churches throughout Europe, especially in England. The ubiquitous cherubs and gargoyles are arguably borrowed from fairy belief as well.

Famous literary treatments of fairies—above all Shakespeare's *Midsummer Night's Dream* and *The Tempest*—have given rise to visual interpretations by innumerable painters. The list includes such distinguished names as William Blake, Joseph Noel Paton, and Joseph Severn. Two additional painters to make use of fairy motifs are Richard Dadd and Richard Doyle, both active in Victorian England.

The Night-Mare

One of Europe's most famous paintings based on fairy lore is Henry Fuseli's *The Nightmare* (1781). A native of Switzerland (his original name was Johann Heinrich Füssli), the artist settled in England in the 1760s. Long before the coinage of such words as *surrealistic* and *Kafkaesque,* he integrated these terms' basic concepts into paintings that distort reality and bring together seemingly unrelated images onto the same canvas. His work—with its delving into the human psyche—anticipates later artists, psychologists, and psychotherapists.

Fuseli's *Nightmare* depicts a negligee-clad woman reclining on a bed, apparently asleep. Her eyes are closed, but her head and arms droop uncomfortably and unsupported from the side of the bed. Squatting on her midsection is a hideous imp, naked, hairy, and with pointed elf-like ears. A seemingly detached horse's head, with bulging eyes and a demonic grin, leers from the dark background. Although criticized by critics for its overt eroticism, the painting was a commercial success. Fuseli created at least two versions, one is on display at the Detroit Institute of Art, the other in the Goethe Museum in Frankfurt-am-Main, Germany. Engravers were quick to make copies, one of which hung in Sigmund Freud's Vienna apartment.

For more than a century art critics and students of psychology have probed Fuseli's painting for its symbolic and esthetic values, but they do not often mention its debt to traditional fairy lore. Fuseli's title *Nightmare* is appropriately—and intentionally—ambiguous. His painting depicts a woman suffering from a terrifying dream, but it also shows the source of the dream: the imp perched on her abdomen. The imp is a night-mare, a mare of the night. Here *mare* is the now obsolete term designating a supernatural being that attacks sleeping victims by sitting or lying atop them, literally pressing the air from their lungs. Bad dreams follow, perhaps conception, perhaps even death, with the victim being suffocated from the mare's weight. Belief in this creature, a particularly malevolent member of the fairy family, once extended across all of northern Europe. In Germany, to this day, a bad dream is called an *Alpdruck* (elf-pressure) or *Alptraum* (elf-dream). Other languages reflect this belief as well. For example, the Danish word for nightmare is *mareridt* (mare-ride).

Night-mares (the spirits, not the dreams that they cause) have much in common with other fairies. Their attacks can be repelled with iron, signs of the cross, special prayers, or by calling out their name (Grimm, no. 81; Kuhn and Schwartz, pp. 418–420). They are gifted shape shifters, and like mermaids and swan maidens, they can be captured and wed, although they too will fly away home if given the opportunity, as evidenced in the German legend "The Alp," reproduced in chapter three. Also contained in that chapter are two "Charms to Control the Night-Mare," one from England and one from the Shetland Islands, addressed respectively to Saint George and King Arthur. Similar charms and prayers were also used in Germany (Kuhn, vol. 2, p. 191).

MOTION PICTURES

Fairy Tale Films

The transition from the graphic arts to motion pictures is as easy one. Each genre is dependent upon visual images, and neither art form is limited to the everyday realities of this world.

Fairy presentations in motion pictures have, for the most part, been adaptations of traditional children's fairy tales. *Peter Pan* leads the pack, with three films, each representing a different generation: 1924, 1953, and 2003, plus the sequels *Hook* (1991) and *Return to Never Land* (2002). Closely related is *Finding Neverland* (2004), a film celebrating the life of J. M. Barrie.

Fairy-tale films have been dominated by the animated work of Walt Disney and his successors. Their adaptations of traditional fairy tales, in addition to *Peter Pan* (1953), include *Snow White and the Seven Dwarfs* (1937), *Pinocchio* (1940), *Cinderella* (1950), and *Sleeping Beauty* (1959), all with important parts for fairies and dwarfs. *Shrek* and its sequel (2001, 2004)—not Disney productions—follow the Disney tradition of imaginative animation, but the content of these films is more a parody of traditional fairy material than an imitator. Shrek himself is an elf-like ogre, surrounded by a cast of familiar fairy tale characters, but playing unfamiliar roles.

The year 1997 saw the release of two worthwhile films about fairy lore, *Photographing Fairies* and *FairyTale: A True Story,* each discussed under the heading "Photographing Fairies" in chapter four of this handbook. Related, but in a category by itself, is the documentary film *The Fairy Faith* (2000), directed by John Walker and distributed by the National Film Board of Canada. This beautifully filmed travelog features traditional fairy sites in Ireland, Scotland, and Nova Scotia, plus interviews with people who believe in fairies, including a segment with Brian Froud, the famous illustrator. Important as a record of fairy belief in our own time, the presentation is, however, flawed in that it presents only one side. The director, apparently wanting to promote and defend the fairy faith, does not seek out interviewees who might challenge this position.

Water Fairies

Mermaids, the subject of innumerable legends, have found their way into relatively few films. The year 1948 saw two mermaid films produced, both focusing on the traditional topic of seduction and forbidden love: *Miranda* and *Mr. Peabody and the Mermaid.* Not until 1984 did another major mermaid film appear: *Splash,* directed by Ron Howard and starring Tom Hanks and Daryl Hannah. A pleasant romantic comedy, this film too probes the possibilities of romance between sea fairies and earth mortals, but without the sinister overtones that so often accompany legends about mermaids and mermen. Predictably, the Walt Disney company created animated versions of H. C. Andersen's "The Little Mermaid" (1989, 2000).

Of all mermaid films, the one that remains closest to its folklore roots is *The Secret of Roan Inish* (1994), directed by John Sayles. Unpretentious and devoid of special effects or high drama, the film unwinds like a the yarn of an unhurried Irish storyteller. Set in Ireland in the mid 1940s, this beautifully filmed story features Fiona, a ten-year old girl sent to live with her grandparents in a remote fishing village. There she hears the local legend that one of her ancestors had married a selkie under circumstances that exactly parallel traditional legends (for example, "The Lady of Gollerus," reproduced in chapter three).

Tightening her connection to the selkies, Fiona also learns that years earlier her baby brother had been washed out to sea in a cradle. Village rumors suggest that the selkies had rescued him and were raising him as one of their own. While exploring the abandoned nearby island of Roan Inish (Gaelic for Island of Seals), Fiona uncovers its secret and at the same time learns the truth of the selkie legends circulating in the village. Remaining faithful to both the letter and the spirit of the folklore that prompted his film, Sayles leaves his viewers believing that selkies do indeed exist, and not just in the imagination of children and old folks.

MARKETING

Tourism

The twentieth century inherited from the past a generally favorable image of fairies. Previous centuries' fears that they steal children, pilfer crops, cause ship-wrecking storms, and the like, were largely forgotten, leaving mostly positive memories. Additionally, many fairy types are identified with a particular region. The combination of a positive image and strong regional identification creates a successful formula for travel and tourism marketing.

Ireland, once belittled for its ostensible superstition, persevered long in its fairy belief, to the embarrassment of many of its higher educated citizens. But during the last half century this same fairy belief has become an asset—a tourist attraction. Today Irish gift shops feature fairy items of every description: picture books, fairy-decorated porcelain, and cute figurines. Similarly, dwarfs dominate the tourist scene in Germany's Black Forest region, as do trolls in

A troll welcomes customers at an ice cream parlor in Narvik, Norway. Photograph by the author.

Norway. Emigrants from such places continue to exploit the old traditions to promote tourism. For example, Mount Horeb, Wisconsin, the center of an area settled by Norwegians, presents itself as the troll capital of the world. The town is prominently decorated with a dozen or more life-sized wooden troll statues. It goes without saying that the images of fairies, dwarfs, and trolls used in tourist promotion display none of the sinister qualities found in many traditional legends, capitalizing instead on the whimsical and the loveable.

Advertising Mascots

Our pre-industrial European forebears cut crosses into unbaked bread to keep fairies from stealing it, hung amulets on cows' horns to keep the fairies from taking the butterfat out of the milk, and many performed innumerable similar rituals to protect their scarce food from fairy theft. We are no longer afraid of such pilferage. Instead, we now invite fairy folk into our homes, via the advertisements on cereal boxes and on television, to tell us which foods we should prefer.

An elf purchased in a souvenir shop in Trondheim, Norway. Photograph by the author.

Among the longest lived of such mascots are the three elves Snap, Crackle, and Pop, who promote the Kellogg breakfast cereal Rice Krispies. According to the Kellogg website, their names first appeared on cereal boxes in 1932, with the characters themselves following one year later to personify the sound of milk being poured over the cereal.

General Mills, a Kellogg competitor, also uses a fairy mascot to promote one of its popular breakfast cereals, Lucky Charms. A relative latecomer, L. C. Leprechaun, also known as Lucky Leprechaun has been pitching his favorite cereal since 1964, primarily on television commercials targeting children.

Another fairy type who promotes food on television is Ernie, who claims to be one of the elves who bake uncommonly good cookies in a hollow tree. He joined the venerable Keebler Company in the 1960s and soon became one of America's most easily recognized advertising icons. Ernie and friends announce to the world on the corporation website: "We're not leprechauns, gnomes or dryands, shoemakers, fairies, or sprites. We're Keebler Elves, and our job is to bake uncommonly good cookies and crackers." Not promoted as an elf, but still exhibiting elfin characteristics, is the Pillsbury Doughboy, who has served as a mascot since 1965.

Similarly, the Jolly Green Giant, introduced in 1928 and owned by Green Giant Vegetables, does not present a stereotypical fairy image. However, as explained in chapter one, traditional fairies come in different sizes, including the giant size. The Green Giant's color and garb are reminiscent of the Green Man figure in medieval English folklore. Furthermore, his familiar laugh "Ho, ho, ho" is also characteristic of Robin Goodfellow.

Mermaids, traditionally also called sea fairies, have lost their most sinister aspects. They no longer cause shipwrecks or tidal waves, although they have retained at least some of their seductive allure. They make good advertising mascots, especially for seafood. The Chicken of the Sea company introduced their mermaid logo in 1952, and she has been successfully promoting their canned tuna fish ever since. The company's slogan proclaims:

> Ask any mermaid you happen to see,
> What's the best tuna?
> Chicken of the Sea.

Another famous mermaid logo belongs to the Starbucks Coffee Company. Although today it is a rather demure and modest figure who greets visitors to the thousands of coffee shops around the world, the logo that marked the original store in Seattle was bold and audacious. Bare breasted and posing provocatively, she was as seductive as the coffee itself was intended to be.

Automobiles

In America two quite different motor cars have labels borrowed from fairy lore, the same number that are named after gods from classical mythology (Mercury and Saturn). The first fairy-named car was the Gremlin, introduced by American Motors on April 1, 1970. Reflecting the car's unusual design and size (it was the first American sub-compact), the marketing team took a measured risk with the vehicle's name and its launch date, both of which suggested some sort of joke. Gremlins, as any dictionary will attest, are gnome-like goblins that cause mechanical or electronic equipment to fail, hardly a propitious label for an automobile. The bad reputation of gnome-gremlins notwithstanding, the Gremlin automobile was a commercial success through most of the 1970s. Its last year of production was 1978.

Near the other end of the automobile spectrum is Toyota's Avalon, introduced in 1995 and named after the magical fairyland of Arthurian legend. Toyota calls this popular luxury automobile their "flagship sedan." Whether or not Avalon buyers know that their car was named after a mythical fairyland, it is a name with positive connotations.

Traveling Garden Gnomes

One of the best-known qualities of fairies is their great mobility. Often depicted with wings, they travel from place to place seemingly without effort. This ability was exploited in a recent advertising campaign by Travelocity, an Internet travel service. Launched in 2003 by the McKinney and Silver Advertising Agency, this mixed-media series featured the "Roaming Gnome," a two-foot tall garden statue, appropriately wearing the traditional red pointed cap expected of his type. He appeared in photographs and films in settings from around the world, thus promoting interest in travel.

With this campaign, McKinney and Silver cleverly exploited a popular-culture prank that has been active, especially in Australia and Europe, for twenty years or longer. The practical joke, in its simplest form, unwinds when a prankster "kidnaps" a garden gnome from someone's yard, then sends the owner a "ransom" note, accompanied by a photograph of the gnome in some distant place. Additional notes follow, each one with a photograph showing the traveling gnome in a new location. The prank ends with the return of the well-traveled gnome, his face possibly smeared with shoe polish to suggest a suntan.

Other forms of the prank exist as well, as an Internet search under the keywords *traveling gnome* or *roaming gnome* will quickly verify. Episodes based on the traveling-gnome prank have appeared in a number of films and television programs, including the British film *The Full Monty* (1997), the French motion picture *Le Fabuleux destin d'Amélie Poulain* (2001), and the British soap opera *Coronation Street.*

Garden gnomes, long ridiculed as tasteless kitsch by sophisticated art connoisseurs, have at last received their proverbial fifteen minutes of fame.

Cleaning Products

Household spirits, particularly brownies and pixies, have a traditional reputation of assisting in ordinary domestic chores. Furthermore, they punished with nighttime pinches—and worse—maids guilty of "sluttishness," a catch-all term describing any number of vices abhorrent to the fairies, but one that most decidedly included uncleanliness. However well this tradition has been remembered by housekeepers of the twentieth and twenty-first centuries, manufacturers of cleaning aids have made substantial use of fairy names and images in their marketing.

Two names stand out, both trade marks of Proctor and Gamble, and both used extensively in Europe, although not in America: Ariel laundry detergent and Fairy Liquid. Ariel, named after the "airy spirit" in Shakespeare's *The Tempest,* is marketed throughout Europe, even in those language areas where the name loses its airy implication, although not its connection with Shakespeare's sprite.

Fairy Liquid has been a favorite dishwashing product in the British Isles, including Ireland, for many decades, and is also marketed under the same name in Scandinavia. Exploiting the detergent's good reputation, Proctor and Gamble have also attached the name "Fairy" to an entire family of cleaning and skin-care products marketed in Britain and Ireland.

Neither Ariel nor Fairy products are available to Proctor and Gamble's North American customers. Instead they have Mr. Clean, introduced in 1958 and arguably a very masculine genie who comes out of a bottle to magically rid the house of dirt and grime.

Another cleaning product promoted by fairy lore is Ajax Cleanser, a product of the Colgate-Palmolive Company. Initiating a form of advertising that would find many followers in the following decades, in 1948 the Sherman and Marguette Advertising Agency introduced a series of television commercials featuring three tiny pixies who frolicked through bathrooms and kitchens merrily cleaning with Ajax. The Ajax pixies are credited with being the first animated mascots used in television commercials. They continued to promote their product throughout the 1950s.

Another company to exploit the pixies' reputation as house cleaners is Hoover. In Britain this name is synonymous with vacuum sweeping, such that *to hoover* has become a common verb. In at least one instance the Hoover Company enlisted the fairies to help maintain its reputation. Throughout the mid twentieth century Hoover marketed a line of vacuum sweepers named variously the "Pixie Cleaner" or the "Pixie Quick-Broom Handivac." Befitting their name, these were compact machines, with at least one of the models designed to be carried on the user's shoulder with a strap.

Another group to adopt a fairy name in recognition of housekeeping abilities are the Brownies, a division of the Girl Scouts (known in Great Britain as the Girl Guides). Originally known as Rosebuds, they changed their name to Brownies in 1968. As explained in their UK website: "A Brownie is a magical

A Brownie camera advertisement in the *Cosmopolitan Magazine* (July 1900).

creature who slips into the home very early before anyone is awake and tidies toys, irons clothes, washes dishes, and does all sorts of helpful things, in secret" (http://www.brownies.freeuk.com/how.htm). This explanation is accurate, as far as it goes. Left unmentioned are the brownies' famous mischievous—and sometimes malicious—pranks, and well as their legendary ragged and disheveled appearance.

Cameras

The Girl Scouts and Girl Guides, in choosing the label *Brownie* for one of their divisions, may have been mindful of that name's great success with a line of cameras marketed by the Eastman Kodak Company. Kodak's famous Brownie camera marks perhaps the most successful use of fairy lore in commercial marketing. Featuring an elf-like figure as a logo and designed for use by children, this camera was introduced in 1900 and sold for $1.00. Various successors were marketed under the Brownie name into the 1970s.

Following this tradition, in 1996 Canon introduced the ELPH line of compact, easy-to-use film cameras in the North American market. ELPH, usually written entirely with uppercase letters, is an obvious homophone for *elf.* In the early 2000s Canon transferred the name to a line of popular compact digital cameras. However, in most markets outside the United States the series is named IXUS, and thus loses its identity with elves.

WORKS CITED

Andersen, Hans Christian. *The Complete Fairy Tales and Stories*. Trans. Erik Christian Haugaard. Garden City, NY: Anchor/Doubleday, 1983.

Ashliman, D. L. *Folk and Fairy Tales: A Handbook*. Westport, CT: Greenwood, 2004.

Bown, Nicola. *Fairies in Nineteenth-Century Art and Literature*. Cambridge: Cambridge UP, 2001.

Dahl, Roald. *The Gremlins, from the Walt Disney Production. A Royal Air Force Story*. New York: Random House, 1943.

Davidson, H. R. Ellis. *Scandinavian Mythology*. Feltham, Middlesex: Newness, 1984.

Goethe, Johann Wolfgang von. *Werke*. 12 vols. Hamburg: Wegner, 1962–67.

Grimm, Jacob and Wilhelm. *The German Legends of the Brothers Grimm*. Trans. Donald Ward. 2 vols. Philadelphia: Institute for the Study of Human Issues, 1981.

Hearn, Michael Patrick. *The Victorian Fairy Tale Book*. New York: Pantheon, 1988.

Herder, Johann Gottfried. *Volkslieder*. 2 vols. Leipzig: Weygand, 1778–79.

Kuhn, Adalbert. *Sagen, Gebräuche und Märchen aus Westfalen*. 2 vols. Leipzig: Brockhaus, 1859.

Kuhn, Adalbert, and Wilhelm Schwartz. *Norddeutsche Sagen, Märchen und Gebräuche*. Leipzig: Brockhaus, 1848.

Lagerlöf, Selma. "Bortbytingen," http://runeberg.org/troll1/bortbyt.html.

Scott, Sir Walter. "The Erl-King," http://graham.main.nc.us/~bhammel/erlkng.html.

Silver, Carole, G. *Strange and Secret Peoples: Fairies and Victorian Consciousness*. Oxford: Oxford UP, 1999.

Steel, Flora Annie. *English Fairy Tales*. London: Macmillan, 1918.

Glossary

Alberich, Alberon. *See* OBERON.

Alfheim. In Norse mythology a division of heaven and the dwelling place of light elves.

Alp. Akin to ELF; a being that torments a sleeper by sitting on his chest, thus depriving him of sleep. A synonym is MARE, not the female horse, but rather a fairy or spirit that causes nightmares.

Astral. Derived from the Latin word *astrum,* for star, this term has come to designate a highly refined substance that somehow exists in a "fourth-dimensional" space overlying the plane occupied by humans but normally invisible and intangible. Fairies are often defined as astral beings.

Avalon. The island home of Morgan le Fay, sister of the legendary King Arthur. Because of its magical qualities, Avalon is often viewed as a quintessential FAIRYLAND.

Ballad. A narrative, often rhymed, and composed in a rhythmic form suitable for singing or chanting. Many fairy LEGENDS have been preserved as ballads.

Banshee. A female spirit in Irish folklore whose wailing foretells an imminent death.

Beltane, also spelled *Beltaine.* An ancient Celtic holiday falling on May 1 and celebrating the beginning of summer. Witches and fairies were thought to be particularly active on the eve of this day, when special ceremonies (often involving bonfires and the cutting of greenery) were practiced to evoke protection. *See also* MIDSUMMER DAY, SAMHAIN, YULE.

Blue-Cap. An English mine spirit.

Boggart. A mischievous HOUSEHOLD SPIRIT similar to the BROWNIE in the folklore of northern England.

Bogle. A term used, especially in northern England and Scotland, to designate a variety of GOBLINS, particularly those of a malicious nature.

Bogey. *See* BUGBEAR.

Bogeyman, Boogeyman. *See* BUGBEAR.

Breton. Of or relating to Brittany, a Celtic region in northwestern France that is rich in fairy lore.

Brownie. A Scottish HOUSEHOLD SPIRIT.

Bucca. A Cornish mine spirit, also known as a KNOCKER.

Bugbear. An imaginary GOBLIN, typically used by adults to frighten children into good behavior. Other words used to designate such beings include *bogey, bogeyman,* and *boogeyman.*

Burning Man. An apparition in German folklore, usually deemed to be a GHOST returning to make amends for sins committed while alive.

Changeling. The child of a fairy or demon left in exchange for an abducted human child, and traditionally distinguished by various physical and mental deficiencies.

Charm. *See* INCANTATION.

Child Ballad. One of the 305 basic types of traditional BALLADS compiled and catalogued by Francis James Child in his *English and Scottish Popular Ballads* (1882–98).

Clairvoyance. The ability to see things invisible to ordinary humans, for example, fairies, spirits, and future events. *See also* SEER.

Cluricaun. *See* LEPRECHAUN.

Coblynau. A Welsh fairy that haunts mines, quarries, and underground regions.

Cohuleen Druith, also spelled *cohuleen driuth.* A headpiece used by WATER FAIRIES to enable their passage between underwater kingdoms and earth.

Contamination. The introduction of an unrelated MOTIF or episode into a folk narrative, usually caused by a storyteller's faulty memory.

Conte de Fées. Literally, *tale of fairies,* the French term from which the English word *fairy tale* is derived.

Corrigan. A Breton WATER FAIRY.

Co-Walker. *See* DOPPELGÄNGER.

Crop Circle. *See* FAIRY RING.

Cunning Man, Cunning Woman. Synonyms for WISE MAN, WISE WOMAN.

Daemon, Demon. An evil spirit, typically one cast onto earth following the war in heaven described in the Book of Revalation, and as such closely associated with fairies.

Dolmen. A prehistoric monument consisting of two or more upright stones connected by a horizontal capstone and often thought to have fairy connections. *See also* MENHIR, MOUND, RATH, STONE CIRCLE.

Domestic Spirit. *See* HOUSEHOLD SPIRIT.

Doppelgänger. A fairy or spirit counterpart of a living person. Similar apparitions are known in different regions by such names as, *co-walker, fetch,* and *waff. See also* WRAITH.

Drake. A fiery German HOUSEHOLD SPIRIT, sharing many attributes with the KOBOLD. The name *drake* is problematic, as is its German cognate *Drache.* Both words designate a fire-breathing dragon as well as a fire-related domestic spirit, although the two beings have little in common apart from their association with fire. *See also* SALAMANDER.

Dryad. A forest NYMPH in Greek mythology.

Dwarf. A diminutive, human-like being, typically living underground. The term comes from the Old Norse *dvergr*, and dwarfs play an important role in Norse mythology. None of the early accounts of dwarfs mention their small size, although in recent centuries this quality has evolved into such an important characteristic that the word *dwarf* has come to be a synonym for *small*.

Earth People, Earth Man, Earth Woman. Common designations for DWARFS and other underground beings, especially in Germany.

Edda. Two works carry this name: the *Prose Edda,* written by the Icelander Snorri Sturlusson in the 1220s, and the *Poetic Edda,* a collection of Old Norse mythological and heroic epics and poems assembled in the late 1200s. Both books are based on much older oral traditions, and both contain frequent references to ELVES, DWARFS, and similar beings.

Elf. In many contexts *elf* is used as a synonym for *fairy,* especially when referring to small and mischievous ones. In English *elf* is the older term, with Germanic roots in Anglo-Saxon and Old Norse, whereas *fairy* is a more recent borrowing from the French *fée*.

Elf Bolt. *See* FAIRY DART.

Elf Locks. Hair knotted and tangled in the night by fairies, usually as punishment for SLUTTISHNESS.

Elf Shot. *See* FAIRY DART.

Ellylldan. A Welsh elf corresponding to the English WILL-O'-THE-WISP.

Erlking. Elf king, a corruption of the Danish *ellekonge* (elf king), from Goethe's German ballad "Der Erlkönig."

Euphemism. An expression or circumlocution with positive connotations used in place of one that might give offense. Traditional folklore dictates that to avoid insulting them, fairies should be referred to indirectly with such terms as "the good neighbors," "the gentry," "the fair family," "the little people," or "the quiet folk."

Faerie, also spelled *Faërie* or *Faery.* The realm of fairies, and by extension the quality or essence of being a fairy (in this latter sense *witchery* and *sorcery* are parallel constructions). The spellings *faerie, faërie,* and *faery* are also used as synonyms for the more usual FAIRY, presumably to elicit an archaic and hence mysterious tone. *See also* FAIRYLAND.

Fairy. A generic term for any of the numerous types of hidden beings. According to common belief, each elemental region—air, fire, earth, and water—has one or more species of these creatures. Although different kinds of fairies differ greatly from each other in size, habitat, and character, they share many qualities. They live close to humans, somehow in a parallel world, but they remain invisible except under special circumstances. When visible, they normally resemble humans, although their power of SHAPE CHANGING gives them the ability to assume many different forms. Fairies possess supernatural powers, which they can use either to help or to harm humans. Among the better-known fairy types are BANSHEES, BROWNIES, DWARFS, ELVES, GENIES, GNOMES, GOBLINS, GREMLINS, HOBBITS, IMPS, KELPIES, KOBOLDS, LEPRECHAUNS, MERMAIDS, NYMPHS, PIXIES, SELKIES, SPRITES, TROLLS, and WILL-O'-THE-WISPS. *See also* FAIRY TALE, FAIRYLAND.

Fairy Animals. Different contexts suggest at least three definitions for this phrase: Animals owned by fairies (most often cattle, horses, or dogs, appropriately scaled to the size of their masters); fairies disguised as animals through their power of SHAPE SHIFTING (for example, KELPIES, SELKIES, and WATER BULLS); and mysterious animals who themselves are fairies.

Fairy Circle. *See* FAIRY RING.

Fairy Dart. A small stone arrowhead, typically chipped from flint or obsidian, deemed to have been used by fairies to inflict injury on humans or cattle. Tradition dictated that such weapons inflict no visible wound but bring serious, even fatal, consequences. However, once recovered, these items were highly valued as amulets against further attack by fairies. Modern science interprets such artifacts as stone-age knife blades and projectile points.

Fairy Doctor. A person knowledgeable about charms for protection against fairies and with the means to counter the ill effects of fairy assaults. *See also* WISE MAN.

Fairy Fort. *See* RATH.

Fairy Gold, Fairy Money. Payment given by the fairies, normally with the expectation that the beneficiary not disclose its source. Alternatively, fairies often pay for goods or services with apparently worthless woodchips, sweepings, or other refuse, which later turns to gold, if the recipient has the foresight to keep it. In contrast, yet another kind of fairy money at first appears to be coin of the realm but later turns to dust or withered leaves.

Fairy Hill. A natural or artificial hill deemed to be inhabited by fairies. Ancient burial mounds in particular have long been associated with fairies. *See also* MOUND, RATH.

Fairy Ring. A circular mark, typically in grass, deemed to have been caused by dancing fairies. A scientific explanation is that such rings are caused by mushrooms, especially the *Marasmius oreades,* that naturally propagate outward from a central point, creating circular traces that can exceed 1,000 feet in diameter. Recently reported similar phenomena are large geometric patterns (crop circles) tramped in grain fields and deemed by some to have been caused by earth energy or extraterrestrial powers. A more cynical view is that they are created by pranksters.

Fairy Stones. Distinctively shaped or patterned stones deemed variously to be petrified tears of fairies or talismans made and used by them for magical purposes. Such items may be stones naturally marked by cross-like or other geometric crystalline structures, pebbles ground into unusual shapes by erosion, or amulets and gaming pieces carved from stone in ancient times. Fairy stones have long been collected and venerated as good-luck charms. *See also* HOLED STONE.

Fairy Stroke. Illness or death deemed to have been caused by fairies. Fairy strokes can afflict both humans and animals.

Fairy Tale, Fairy Story. Derived from the French *conte de fées,* this is the normal term in English for *magic tale* or *wonder tale,* designating even stories that do not feature fairies per se. Fairy tales, whether told orally or composed on paper, are characterized by FANTASY and MAGIC. *See also* FOLKTALE, LEGEND.

Fairy Track. A route said to be used by fairies. According to tradition, to obstruct a fairy track with a building or to damage one through plowing invites retribution by the fairies.

Fairyland. According to popular belief, a realm occupied by fairies or similar supernatural beings. Traditionally named *Faerie* (also spelled *Faërie* or *Faery*), this land is variously described as existing beneath the ground, under water, above the clouds, or on a distant island. A more mystical view sees fairyland as a realm parallel to or overlapping the human world but normally invisible and intangible to humans. Literary FAIRY TALES are often set in otherworldly realms reminiscent of fairyland, for example L. Frank Baum's Oz, James Barrie's Never Never Land, Lewis Carroll's Wonderland, C. S. Lewis's Narnia, Charles Kingsley's Underwater World, and J.R.R. Tolkien's Middle Earth. *See also* AVALON, FAERIE, TIR NA N'OG.

Fairyology. A recent coinage, not in general usage, designating the study of fairy lore.

Familiar. A spirit, usually embodied in an animal and in the service of a person with supernatural powers. Toads, hares, and cats are traditional familiars in witchcraft and are also forms favored by SHAPE-SHIFTING fairies.

Fantasy. Throughout the ages, storytellers have entertained by providing audiences with an escape from their own existence. Fairy belief, with its emphasis on worlds parallel to our own but subject to quite different natural laws, has provided a context for such fantasy escape, not only within the context of FOLKTALES, but also by creators of sophisticated literature, theater, ballet, and the visual arts. *See also* MAGIC, FAIRYLAND.

Fates. In Greek and Roman mythology, three goddesses who determined a person's destiny at the time of his or her birth. The English word *fairy* ultimately derives from this term, by way of the French *fée.*

Faulty. A retold narrative with obvious omissions (such that the story loses its continuity) or with CONTAMINATIONS from other stories is said to be faulty.

Fay. From the French *fée,* a synonym for FAIRY.

Faydom. *See* FAIRYLAND.

Fenodyree. A Manx BROWNIE.

Fetch. *See* DOPPELGÄNGER.

Fée. French for *fairy,* sometimes anglicized as *fay* or *fey.*

Fifinella. A female GREMLIN.

Fion. A race of dwarfs in Brittany.

Fire Rider. Different contexts present two definitions of this phrase, both from German folklore: An apparition who can extinguish a burning building by riding into or around it; or a mysterious rider wearing a red cap whose appearance foretells an imminent house fire. *See also* SALAMANDER.

FOAF. An acronym for *friend of a friend*, and used by folklorists to designate the reputed participant in an event reported by an informant who heard the story at second or third hand.

Fog Cap (from the German *Nebelkappe*). A headpiece worn by dwarfs that renders them invisible to ordinary mortals.

Folklore. Coined as a substitute for the awkward phrase *popular antiquities* in the mid 1800s, *folklore* is a collective noun encompassing all information that humans preserve and transmit by personal (as opposed to institutional) demonstration and oral communication. Subcategories of folklore include customs, folk art, folksongs, folktales, legends, proverbs, riddles, games, ceremonies, folk remedies, and superstitions.

Folktale, also spelled *folk tale* or *folk-tale*. Strictly speaking, a folktale is any narrative made up within the group that is using it, then preserved and passed on by word of mouth. More generally, the term *folktale* has come to designate a story, regardless of its origin or mode of transmission, that resembles a tale traditionally made up by an unlettered storyteller and then communicated orally to future generations. *See also* FAIRY TALE, LEGEND.

Garden Gnome. A small whimsical statue depicting an ELF, DWARF, or GNOME, and usually placed in a garden or at the entryway to a house.

Genie. *See* JINNI.

Ghost. The spirit of a deceased person or animal, especially one doomed to haunt a particular place. In many popular traditions such spirits are identified as or deemed to be related to fairies.

Giant. A large sized mythical being, usually—but not always—an enemy of humans. In Scandinavian folklore giants are often indistinguishable from TROLLS. *See also* OGRE.

Glaistig. In Scottish folklore, a mortal who takes on the nature of a fairy.

Glamour. A magic spell, typically cast by fairies and giving objects an appearance quite different from normal reality.

Glashtyn. A Manx KELPIE.

Gnome. According to Paracelsus, a soulless, elemental being inhabiting the underground and said to be able to pass through solid rock and earth much as birds and fish travel through air and water. In folklore gnomes are often associated with mines and buried treasure. See also SALAMANDER, SYLPH, UNDINE.

Goblin. Derived ultimately from the Greek *kobalos* (rogue), *goblin* is a generic term designating a variety of mischievous sprites, typically perceived to be ugly and malicious.

Green Man. An enigmatic figure typically depicting a man peering out of a mask of leaves. Often found in medieval churches, especially in England, the green man is deemed by many to be a survival of a heathen forest or fertility god.

Gremlin. An elf-like sprite that causes malfunctions in technical equipment and machinery, especially aircraft. The term apparently was coined by British children's author Roald Dahl in his book *The Gremlins* (1943). A female gremlin is called a *fifinella*.

Hedley Kow. A shape-shifting trickster from northern England. Not to be confused with a common cow, this creature assumes external forms ranging from a wisp of straw to a large horse-like animal. His exploits resemble those of ROBIN GOODFELLOW.

Heinzelmann, Heinzelmännchen. A mischievous, but normally helpful German HOUSEHOLD SPIRIT.

Hidden People. A common EUPHEMISM in Scandinavia for elves, trolls, and other such folk.

Hob. A name applied to various mischievous, but friendly sprites, especially in northern England.

Hobbit. In the fantasy fiction of J.R.R. Tolkien, a small, peace-loving, human-like creature that lives underground. The term itself, a variant of HOB and HOBGOBLIN, stems from traditional English folklore.

Hobgoblin. Originally a mischievous, and usually harmless sprite related to the BROWNIE, but the term has also come to designate demons and other evil spirits.

Hoblin. A recent coinage in the United Kingdom combining *hobbit* with *goblin* and used to describe certain hybrid garden statues. *See also* GARDEN GNOME.

Hob-Thrush, Hob-Thrust. *See* HOB.

Holed Stone. A perforated stone said to be the work of fairies. These may be a part of a larger stone monument, such as the prehistoric Men-an-Tol group in Cornwall, which includes a holed stone large enough for a person to crawl through, or they may be small pendants, designed to be worn as amulets, and often hung on cattle for protection. *See also* FAIRY STONES.

Household Spirit. A usually solitary supernatural being attached to a household or farm. In most traditions they serve their hosts well, although they do punish laziness, slovenliness, ingratitude, and other vices. Examples include the Scottish brownie, the Cornish pixie, the Irish pooka, the German kobold, and the Scandinavian nisse.

Ignis Fatuus, plural *ignes fatui*. From a Latin term meaning *foolish fire,* and commonly called jack-o'-lantern or will-o'-the-wisp, the ignis fatuus appeared as a light that led travelers astray. Traditionally thought to be malicious fairies or the spirits of children who died unbaptized, such lights are now attributed to the spontaneous combustion of marsh gasses. *See also* SALAMANDER.

Illusion. *See* GLAMOUR.

Imp. Originally a shoot or graft on a plant, this word's meaning then shifted toward the supernatural, taking on the meaning of *little demon,* i.e., an offshoot of the devil. With time its definition broadened to include fairies of different types, but usually those with an evil disposition. Finally the word moved away from the supernatural, coming to designate an unruly child.

Incantation. A magic phrase chanted to achieve a specific supernatural effect. A number of incantations for protection against fairies and other supernatural threats have been recorded.

Incubus (masculine), **Succubus** (feminine). A spirit, sometimes said to be the devil himself, that plagues a human in bed, thus showing a kinship to the MARE.

Jack-o'-Lantern. *See* IGNIS FATUUS.

Jenny Green-Teeth. An English WATER FAIRY whose primary function is to frighten children away from places where they might drown. *See also* BUGBEAR, PEG-O'-THE-WELL.

Jinni, plural *jinn*. An Arabic or Muslim demon that like European fairies can assume different forms. Also called *genie,* plural *genies* or *genii.*

Joan the Wad. A Cornish name for IGNIS FATUUS.

Julenisse (Denmark), **Juletomte** (Sweden). A Scandinavian Christmas ELF.

Kelpie. In Scottish folklore, a supernatural horse-shaped creature that lures humans into riding it, then carries them into a river or lake where they perish. *See also* WATER FAIRY, WATER HORSE.

Kobold. A German HOUSEHOLD SPIRIT, but one that also frequents mines.

Knocker. A Cornish mine spirit known for the knocking signals it gives to show tin miners the location of rich ore. Also known as a *bucca.*

Korrigan. *See* CORRIGAN.

Legend. As folklorists use the term, a legend is an account that claims to be true, in contrast to FAIRY TALES and ordinary FOLKTALES, which are transparently fictitious. However, many traditional legends depict events such as encounters with fairies, sorcerers, witches, and such—all within the realm of belief for past generations but now normally relegated to the world of SUPERSTITION and FANTASY. The otherworldly nature of many legends and most fairy tales blurs the distinction between the two genres. Thus many tales are classified both as magic folktales and as legends by specialists. For example, "A Midwife for the Elves," one of the most widespread stories about the underground people, is classified both as a type 476* folktale and as a type 5070 migratory legend. *See also* MIGRATORY LEGEND.

Leprechaun. An Irish fairy type, also known as the *cluricaun* or *lurikeen.* Leprechauns reputedly are skilled shoemakers and very wealthy. If captured they can be forced to disclose the hiding place of their treasure, but only if the captor does not take his or her eye off the prisoner, which virtually never happens.

Localization. The process of altering a MIGRATORY LEGEND to make it fit in a new environment. For example, the story telling how a mortal steals a drinking vessel from the fairies (type 6045) often incorporates into its plot authentic geographic features, buildings, and artifacts specific to a particular locale. Thus "The Luck of Edenhall" and "The Oldenburg Horn," describe how a chalice and a drinking horn—now on display in museums in London and Copenhagen respectively—came into human hands from the fairies.

Logan Stone. A balanced stone that vibrates or moves to the touch, and—especially in Cornwall and Wales—said to be frequented by witches and fairies.

Lurikeen. *See* LEPRECHAUN.

Mab. In English folklore a mischievous but basically kind-hearted fairy queen. She is mentioned by name in the writings of William Shakespeare, Michael Drayton, Ben Jonson, John Milton, and Robert Herrick. *See also* OBERON, TITANIA.

Magic. Supernatural force, usually interpreted as being separate from the powers ascribed to standard religions. Magic pervades FAERIE. However, this world is not without its own logic, order, and restrictions, and popular lore is replete with specific rules granting humans at least a measure of control over fairies and other supernatural creatures. *See also* FANTASY, FAIRYLAND, SUPERSTITION, SURVIVAL.

Manikin. Literally a "little man," often used as a synonym for elf or dwarf.

Manx. Of or relating to the Isle of Man, a British island in the Irish Sea with mixed Celtic and Norse heritage and rich in fairy lore.

Mare, also spelled *mara*. A supernatural being that deprives its victims of sleep by sitting or lying on them. The mare also causes the terrifying dreams known as nightmares. See also ALP, INCUBUS.

Melusina, also spelled *Melusine*. A legendary water sprite who marries a human but who then abandons him because of his lack of trust.

Memorate. A term coined by the Swedish folklorist Carl Wilhelm von Sydow designating an account of personal experience. Memorates claiming first-hand encounters with fairies abound in communities where such beliefs actively exist.

Menhir. A prehistoric monument consisting of a single upright stone, and often thought to have fairy connections. *See also* DOLMEN, MOUND, RATH, STONE CIRCLE.

Mermaid, Merman, Merwoman. Sometimes called WATER FAIRIES, these aquatic beings are most often depicted as having human upper bodies with fish-like tails instead of legs. However in some accounts they have normal human appearance.

Merrow. An Irish designation for MERMAID.

Middle Earth, also spelled *Middle-earth*. A fantasy alternative world created by J.R.R. Tolkien as a habitation for hobbits, elves, dwarfs, and such in his trilogy *The Lord of the Rings*. He seems to have based the name on the *Midgard* (middle enclosure) of Norse mythology.

Midsummer Day. An ancient holiday marking the summer solstice, a period when fairies were thought to be especially active, as reflected, for example, in Shakespeare's *A Midsummer Night's Dream*. With the Christianization of Europe, many of the customs associated with Midsummer Eve (especially the lighting of bonfires) merged with Saint John the Baptist's Day (June 24). *See also* BELTANE, SAMHAIN, YULE.

Migratory Legend. A LEGEND, told in more than one place, with each version sharing a common plot but distinguished by place names and other details unique to its own location. Good examples are the CHANGELING legends found throughout Europe, often with striking similarities, but each one normally set in a specific place. *See also* LOCALIZATION.

Mine Monk. A German GNOME inhabiting or working in an underground mine and distinguished by his monk-like cowl, a hood formerly worn by human miners as well.

Morgan. A Breton WATER FAIRY, known as a dangerous seductress.

Morgan le Fay. A fairy enchantress and the sister of legendary King Arthur.

Motif. A basic narrative element used in constructing a story. Motifs used in folk narratives have been catalogued by Stith Thompson in his *Motif-Index of Folk-Literature* (1955). Fairy legends typically include a number of motifs, and they can be used in more than one account. For example, the concept of years spent in FAIRYLAND that are thought only to be days (motif 2011) is found in numerous legends about fairy enticement and abduction.

Mound. An artificial hill built in prehistoric times as a grave site or other monument and often deemed by later generations to be inhabited by fairies. *See also* DOLMEN, MENHIR, RATH, STONE CIRCLE.

Myth, Mythology. Myths are traditional narratives depicting and explaining universal concerns. Although fairy LEGENDS usually deal with local events and ordinary individuals—not the global issues and major deities or super heroes typical of traditional myths—they are still often classified as myths because they explain fundamental problems, such as why a child fails to develop properly or why an apparently healthy person dies in the prime of life. The term *mythology* refers both to an entire body of myths within a given tradition, as well as to the study of myths.

Naiad. A NYMPH presiding over springs, rivers, and lakes in Greek mythology.

Nereid. A NYMPH presiding over both saltwater and freshwater in Greek mythology.

Never Never Land. Specifically, a place inhabited by fairies, mermaids, lost boys, and pirates in J. M. Barrie's *Peter Pan* (1904), but in general a designation for a world that exists only in one's fantasy. *See also* FAIRYLAND, FANTASY.

Nicneven. A Scottish goddess, described by Sir Walter Scott in his *Letters on Demonology and Witchcraft* (letter 4), who rides at the head of a cavalcade of witches and fairies at Halloween.

Nightmare. *See* MARE.

Nisse. Derived from the name *Nicholas,* a Scandinavian HOUSEHOLD SPIRIT.

Nix, Nixie. Masculine and feminine forms of a word designating a diverse class of German WATER FAIRIES.

Nøkk. A Scandinavian shape-shifting WATER SPIRIT, similar to the Scottish KELPIE.

Norns. In Norse mythology, female beings that shape human destiny, similar to the FATES of classical mythology.

Nymph. A minor Greek female deity presiding over one of the natural realms of earth, for example oceans, forests, or mountains.

Oaf. Akin to ELF; in its original meaning, a CHANGELING; now any clumsy or slow-witted person.

Oberon. King of the fairies, elves, or dwarfs. Known also by the French name Alberon and the German name Alberich, Oberon is mentioned in numerous literary works from the Middle Ages onward. *See also* MAB, TITANIA.

Oceanid. An ocean NYMPH in Greek mythology.

Ogre. Often depicted as man-eating GIANTS, ogres are in many ways personifications of the devil in FOLKTALES, where typically their maliciousness is exceeded only by their stupidity. *See also* TROLL.

Ondine. *See* UNDINE.

Oread. A mountain NYMPH in Greek mythology.

Ouph. Akin to OAF; an archaic form of ELF mentioned in Shakespeare's *The Merry Wives of Windsor* (act 4, scene 4).

Pecht. A spelling variant of PICT.

Peerie Folk. A Scottish name for fairies.

Peg-o'-the-Well. An English WATER FAIRY whose primary function is to frighten children away from places where they might drown. *See also* BUGBEAR, JENNY GREEN-TEETH.

Pict. An ancient tribe in Scotland deemed by some to have been the forebears of Scottish fairies.

Pishogue. An Irish fairy spell causing a person to perceive things differently than they actually are. *See also* GLAMOUR.

Piskey, Piskie, Pisky. Cornish variants of PIXIE.

Pixie, Pixy. An English HOUSEHOLD SPIRIT known especially for its good-humored mischief.

Poltergeist. A German HOUSEHOLD SPIRIT known especially for its noisy pranks.

Pooka, Phooka. A usually horse-shaped spirit in Irish folklore. Although typically mischievous, even malicious, the pooka could also function as a helpful household spirit, similar to the Scottish BROWNIE.

Portune. A diminutive English HOUSEHOLD SPIRIT described by Gervase of Tilbury in his *Otia Imperialia* (1211).

Puck. Also named ROBIN GOODFELLOW, Puck is a fairy trickster made famous by his characterization in Shakespeare's *A Midsummer Night's Dream*.

Pwca. The Welsh form of PUCK.

Rath. Also called a *fairy fort,* a usually circular earthwork that served as an enclosure or a stronghold in ancient Ireland and deemed by later generations to be inhabited by fairies. *See also* DOLMEN, MENHIR, MOUND, STONE CIRCLE.

Red-Cap. A vicious goblin in the folklore of northern England.

Revenant. The GHOST of a dead person or the image of an individual spirited away to an otherworldly place that returns, usually temporarily, to its former abode.

Robin Goodfellow. Also known by the name PUCK, the most famous HOBGOBLIN in Great Britain of the sixteenth and seventeenth centuries.

Rowan. A tree (*Sorbus aucuparia*), also called *European mountain ash,* traditionally considered to have magical properties, especially for protection against otherworldly creatures, including fairies.

Saining Ceremony. A church-sponsored purification ritual, especially for mothers of newborn children. In Scottish folklore, women were particularly vulnerable to fairy abduction after delivering a baby and before being sained.

Salamander. According to Paracelsus, a soulless, elemental being inhabiting fire. Spirits and fairies associated with fire include the DRAKE, KOBOLD, FIRE RIDER, and IGNIS FATUUS. *See also* GNOME, SYLPH, UNDINE.

Samhain, also spelled *Samain*. An ancient Celtic holiday falling on November 1 and marking the end of summer. Witches, fairies, and other demons were thought to roam freely during the night preceding this day, making it the most dangerous period of the year. Many of the beliefs and customs of this day survive—albeit in a playful, non-threatening fashion—in the modern holiday Halloween. *See also* BELTANE. MIDSUMMER DAY, YULE.

Satyr. An ancient Greek forest deity, often depicted as half horse and half human, or half goat and half human, and given to licentious behavior.

Second Sight. A synonym for CLAIRVOYANCE.

Seelie Court, Unseelie Court. From a Scottish word for *blessed,* a division of fairies into two groups, one helpful toward humans, the other malicious.

Seer, Seeress. A person who can see things invisible to ordinary humans, for example, fairies, spirits, and future events. *See also* CLAIRVOYANCE.

Selkie, also spelled *silkie*. A large seal, deemed in the fairy lore of Orkney and Shetland to be an undersea fairy who assumes this shape while passing through the water from one realm to another. *See also* WATER FAIRIES.

Shape Changing, Shape Shifting. The ability to change one's size or form, either through a physical transformation or by deceiving viewers into believing they see something different from what is actually there. In most traditions, fairies are masters at shape shifting. *See also* GLAMOUR.

Sidhe. Pronounced *shee* and with numerous English spellings, one of the most common Gaelic names for fairies, both in Ireland and in Scotland. The word originally designated the mounds thought to be inhabited by fairies.

Siren. In Greek mythology a half-bird, half-woman sea sprite who lured sailors to destruction with her irresistible singing, behavior also attributed to MERMAIDS and other WATER FAIRIES.

Sluttishness. Here a synonym for *slovenliness*. This is the shortcoming for which maidservants were most often punished by HOUSEHOLD SPIRITS.

Social Fairies. *See* TROOPING FAIRIES.

Solitary Fairies. A designation advanced by W. B. Yeats and others for fairies—mostly of a malicious nature—who live detached from social groups. *See also* TROOPING FAIRIES.

Spriggan. A race of Cornish warrior fairies. They frequent ancient burial sites, often serve as guardians of buried treasure, are hideously ugly, and can change their size at will.

Sprite. Akin to the word *spirit,* the term *sprite* is often used as a synonym for ELF, FAIRY, elf-like person, or for essentially any disembodied apparition.

Stock. A piece of wood fashioned by fairies to take on the appearance of a person to be abducted. The victim's survivors, left with this inanimate image of their loved one, will assume that he or she has died. *See also* CHANGELING, GLAMOUR.

Stone Circle. A prehistoric monument consisting of upright stones set in a circle, and often thought to have fairy connections. *See also* DOLMEN, MENHIR, MOUND, RATH.

Succubus. *See* INCUBUS

Superstition. An irrational belief, often based on fear of the unknown. The fairy lore of previous centuries is dismissed as fantasy or superstition by most educated observers of today, but one should not forget that many of our forebears firmly believed in such beings.

Survival. As used by anthropologists and folklorists, a *survival* is an aspect of ancient culture that continues to exist as a motif in a folktale or an element within a traditional game or ceremony. An example is the hanging of a horseshoe above a door, now a mostly playful good-luck custom, but formerly a seriously believed method of protecting a household against fairies.

Swan Maiden. An airborne being reliant on a feathery robe for flight and the subject of a very large number of traditional fairy tales. *See also* VALKYRIE.

Sylph. According to Paracelsus, a soulless, elemental being inhabiting the air. In folk tradition sylphs sometimes appear in the form of butterflies. *See also* GNOME, SALAMANDER, UNDINE.

Sylvan. A forest SPRITE or deity.

Taboo, also spelled *tabu*. The prohibition of an action, often for religious or supernatural reasons. Taboos exist in all cultures and regulate many aspects of life. Fairy lore defines numerous taboos, some with indisputably practical consequences, for example: Do not leave newborn infants unattended, thus exposing them to the risk of abduction by the fairies. Other taboos are more theoretical and fantastic, for example: If taken to fairyland, refuse all food and drink offered there to avoid coming under permanent control of the fairies.

Tir na n'Og (Land of Youth). The most important otherworldly land in early Irish traditions, described variously as a FAIRYLAND or a Celtic paradise and usually perceived as an island west of Ireland. Variant spellings include *Tir nan Og, Tir na N-og,* and *Tír na nÓg.*

Titania. The queen of the fairies and OBERON's wife in Shakespeare's *A Midsummer Night's Dream. See also* MAB.

Tomte. A Swedish HOUSEHOLD SPIRIT, often associated with an entire farm.

Troll. A designation used throughout Scandinavia for numerous types of supernatural beings, ranging in size from tiny DWARFS to monstrous GIANTS and most often marked by maliciousness toward humans, stupidity, and grotesque ugliness. *See also* OGRE.

Trooping Fairies. A designation advanced by W. B. Yeats and others for fairies who live, work, and play in social groups. *See also* SOLITAIRY FAIRIES.

Trow. The name (akin to *troll*) given to "the little people" in Scotland's Orkney and Shetland Islands.

Tumulus, plural *tumuli*. An artificial MOUND, especially over a grave, and often considered to house fairies.

Tylweth Teg. Welsh for *fair family,* and in Wales a general designation for fairies.

Type. FOLKTALES within the Indo-European tradition are classified according to a system initiated by the Finnish folklorist Antti Aarne and continued by his American colleague Stith Thompson. This system identifies some 2,500 basic plots, assigning to each a type number. It was expanded by Reidar Christiansen to include MIGRATORY LEGENDS (type numbers 3000–8025), especially those found in his native Norway.

Underground People. A common designation for DWARFS and GNOMES, especially in Germany.

Undine, also spelled *ondine*. According to Paracelsus, a soulless, elemental being inhabiting water. Other water spirits include MERMAIDS, NIXES, NYMPHS, and NEREIDS. *See also* GNOME, SALAMANDER, SYLPH, GNOME.

Urchin. Originally a shape-shifting fairy who often assumed the form of a hedgehog, but now a mischievous human child.

Urisk. A Scottish BROWNIE whose usual form was half man and half goat, similar in appearance to the SATYRS of ancient Greece.

Utröst. A legendary island beyond Röst, the outmost of Norway's Lofoten Islands, and said to be a FAIRYLAND.

Valkyrie. In Norse mythology a supernatural woman charged by Odin to select warriors in battle who are worthy for a place in Valhalla. In some works, notably the "Lay of Völund" from *The Poetic Edda,* Valkyries are associated with fairy brides or SWAN MAIDENS.

Waff. *See* DOPPELGÄNGER.

Water Bull. A dangerous fairy animal that lives mostly in an underwater realm but that does come ashore to mate with domestic cows or to plague humans. Water bulls are notorious SHAPE CHANGERS.

Water Fairy, Water Spirit. Generic terms applied to various supernatural beings inhabiting or associated with water, including the CORRIGAN, KELPIE, MERMAID, MORGAN, MELUSINA, MERROW, NAIAD, NEREID, NIX, NJUGL, OCEANID, SELKIE, UNDINE, WATER BULL, AND WATER HORSE.

Water Horse. A fairy animal that lives mostly in an underwater realm but that does come ashore to mate with domestic mares. If captured, a water horse can outperform domestic horses in all contests, but it is very difficult to control and often proves fatally dangerous for its human rider. *See also* KELPIE.

Werewolf. A human who can turn himself or herself into a wolf, typically by putting on a magic belt or collar. Werewolves' connection to fairy lore is that both types of beings could be controlled with Christian piety, iron, or calling out the apparition's personal name. *See also* SHAPE CHANGING.

White Woman. In German folklore any of several spectral beings, always dressed in white and variously defined as the ghost of a wronged woman, a pre-Christian goddess, or a fairy.

Wicca. A Neo-Pagan religion that claims to follow pre-Christian beliefs and practices, including the positive aspects of witchcraft. Sensitive to various forms of "earth energy," many Wiccans affirm certain features of traditional fairy lore.

Wight. Although in modern English this term has come to designate any living creature, especially a human, in Middle English it was used for *elf* or *dwarf.* The German *Wicht,* a common word for *elf,* is a cognate.

Wild Hunt. A noisy nighttime cavalcade of riders, usually airborne, reported throughout northern Europe from ancient times to as recently as 1940. The band often includes supernatural beings of different types: witches, ghosts, and fairy folk. The leader, known by many regional names, is thought by many to be a SURVIVAL of the Norse god Odin (Wodan).

Willi, also spelled *wili.* In Austrian and Slavic folklore, the spirit of an engaged woman who died before her wedding and then dances, elf-like, before mortal men to torment them. Described in Heinrich Heine's *Elementargeister* (Elemental Spirits), the willis play a central role in Adolphe Charles Adam's ballet *Giselle* (1841).

Will-o'-the-Wisp. *See* IGNIS FATUUS.

Wise Man, Wise Woman. A person knowledgeable about supernatural phenomena in general and fairies in particular. *See also* SEER and SEERESS.

Wraith. The ghostly likeness of a living person, seen usually just before the individual's death. *See also* BANSHEE, DOPPELGÄNGER.

Yule, Yuletide. A pagan festival season marking the winter solstice, an important time in fairy lore, particularly in Scandinavia, where elves and trolls were thought to hold elaborate Yule celebrations. With the Christianization of Europe, many of the customs associated with Yuletide merged with Christmas. *See also* BELTANE, MIDSUMMER DAY, SAMHAIN.

Bibliography

COLLECTIONS

Arnason, Jón. *Icelandic Legends.* Trans. George E. J. Powell and Eiríkur Magnússon. London: Bentley, 1864.

Blecher, Lone Thygesen, and George. *Swedish Folktales and Legends.* New York: Pantheon, 1994.

Briggs, Katharine M. *A Dictionary of British Folk-Tales in the English Language.* Pt. A, 2 vols. Pt. B, 2 vols. London: Routledge and Kegan Paul, 1970–71.

Burne, Charlotte Sophia. *Shropshire Folk-Lore.* London: Trübner, 1883.

Campbell, J. F. *Popular Tales of the West Highlands: Orally Collected.* 4 vols. London: Gardner, 1890–93. First published 1860.

Child, Francis James. *The English and Scottish Popular Ballads.* 5 vols. Boston: Houghton, Mifflin, 1882–98.

Croker, Thomas Crofton. *Fairy Legends and Traditions of the South of Ireland.* 3 vols. London: Murray, 1825–28. A facsimile reproduction of the 1870 edition has been printed at Ann Arbor: Scholars' Facsimiles and Reprints, 2001.

Curtin, Jeremiah. *Tales of the Fairies and the Ghost-World, collected from Oral Tradition in South-West Munster.* London: Nutt, 1895.

Douglas, George. *Scottish Fairy and Folk Tales.* London: Scott, 1901.

Evans-Wentz, W. Y. *The Fairy-Faith in Celtic Countries.* London: Frowde, 1911.

Gregor, Walter. *Notes on the Folk-Lore of the North-East of Scotland.* London: Folk-Lore Society, 1881.

Gregory, Lady Isabelle Augusta. *Visions and Beliefs in the West of Ireland.* New York and London: Putnam, 1920.

Grimm, Jacob and Wilhelm. *The German Legends of the Brothers Grimm.* Trans. Donald Ward. 2 vols. Philadelphia: Institute for the Study of Human Issues, 1981. A translation of *Deutsche Sagen,* first published 1816–18.

Halliwell-Phillips, James. *Popular Rhymes and Nursery Tales.* London: Smith, 1849.

Henderson, William. *Notes on the Folk-Lore of the Northern Counties of England and the Borders.* London: Longmans, Green, 1866.

Hunt, Robert. *Popular Romances of the West of England; or, The Drolls, Traditions, and Superstitions of Old Cornwall.* London: Hotten, 1871.

Hyde, Douglas. *Beside The Fire: A Collection of Irish Gaelic Folk Stories.* 2nd ed. London: Nutt, 1910.

Jacobs, Joseph. *Celtic Fairy Tales.* London: Nutt, 1892.

———. *English Fairy Tales.* London: Nutt, 1898. First published 1890.

———. *More Celtic Fairy Tales.* London: Nutt, 1894.

———. *More English Fairy Tales.* New York and London: Putnam, n.d. First published 1894.

Jones, T. Gwynn. *Welsh Folklore and Folk-Custom.* London: Methuen, 1930.

Keightley, Thomas. *The Fairy Mythology, Illustrative of the Romance and Superstition of Various Countries.* London: Bohn, 1850. Reprinted as *The World Guide to Gnomes, Fairies, Elves, and Other Little People.* New York: Gramercy Books, 2000.

Kennedy, Patrick. *Legendary Fictions of the Irish Celts.* London: Macmillan, 1866. 2nd ed., 1891.

Kvideland, Reimund, and Henning K. Sehmsdorf. *Scandinavian Folk Belief and Legend.* Minneapolis, U of Minnesota P, 1988.

Lindow, John. *Swedish Legends and Folktales.* Berkeley: U of California P, 1978.

MacDougall, James. *Folk Tales and Fairy Lore in Gaelic and English, Collected from Oral Tradition.* Ed. George Calder. Edinburgh: Grant, 1910.

Morrison, Sophia. *Manx Fairy Tales.* London: Nutt, 1911.

Nicolson, John. *Some Folk-Tales and Legends of Shetland.* Edinburgh: Allan, 1920.

Poetic Edda, The. Transl. Lee M. Hollander. Austin: U of Texas P, 1988.

Rhys, John. *Celtic Folklore: Welsh and Manx.* Oxford: Oxford UP, 1901.

Scott, Sir Walter. *Minstrelsy of the Scottish Border.* 4 vols. Edinburgh: Blackwood, 1902. First published 1802–03.

Sikes, Wirt. *British Goblins: Welsh Folk-Lore, Fairy Mythology, Legends and Traditions.* Boston: Osgood, 1881. First published in London, 1880.

Simpson, Eve Blantyre. *Folk Lore in Lowland Scotland.* London: Dent, 1908.

Simpson, Jacqueline. *Icelandic Folktales and Legends.* Berkeley: U of California P, 1979.

———. *Scandinavian Folktales.* London: Penguin, 1988.

Snorri Sturluson. *The Prose Edda.* Berkeley: U of California P, 1954.

Spence, Lewis. *Legends and Romances of Brittany.* New York: Stokes, n.d.

Thomas, W. Jenkyn. *The Welsh Fairy Book.* London: Unwin, 1907.

Thorpe, Benjamin. *Yule-Tide Stories: A Collection of Scandinavian and North German Popular Tales and Traditions.* London: Bohn, 1853.

Waldron, George. *A Description of the Isle of Man.* Douglas, Isle of Man: Manx Society, 1865. Based on the edition of 1731. First published 1726.

Wilde, Lady Francesca. *Ancient Legends, Mystic Charms, and Superstitions of Ireland.* London: Chatto and Windus, 1919. First published 1887.

Wilde, W. R. *Irish Popular Superstitions*. Dublin: McGlashan, 1852.

Yeats, William Butler. *Fairy and Folk Tales of Ireland*. New York: Macmillan, 1983. Contains *Fairy and Folk Tales of the Irish Peasantry,* first published 1888; and *Irish Fairy Tales,* first published 1892.

———. *The Celtic Twilight: Myth, Fantasy, and Folklore*. Bridport, Dorset: Prism, 1990. First published 1893.

ENCYCLOPEDIAS AND HANDBOOKS

Aarne, Antti, and Stith Thompson. *The Types of the Folktale: A Classification and Bibliography*. Helsinki: Suomalainen Tiedeakatemia, 1961.

Ashliman, D. L. *Folk and Fairy Tales: A Handbook*. Westport, CT: Greenwood, 2004.

Briggs, Katharine M. *Abbey Lubbers, Banshees, and Boggarts: An Illustrated Encyclopedia of Fairies*. New York: Pantheon Books, 1979. An abridged version of the author's *An Encyclopedia of Fairies, Hobgoblins, Brownies, Bogies, and other Supernatural Creatures.*

———. *An Encyclopedia of Fairies, Hobgoblins, Brownies, Bogies, and other Supernatural Creatures*. New York: Pantheon, 1976. Published in England under the title *A Dictionary of Fairies, Hobgoblins, Brownies, Bogies, and other Supernatural Creatures*. London: Lane, 1976.

Christiansen, Reidar T. *The Migratory Legends*. Helsinki: Suomalainen Tiedeakatemia, 1958.

Davidson, H. R. Ellis. *Scandinavian Mythology*. Feltham, Middlesex: Newness, 1984.

Dubois, Pierre. *The Great Encyclopedia of Faeries*. Ill. Claudine and Roland Sabatier. London: Pavilion, 1999. Translation of *Grande encyclopédie des fées*, 1996.

MacKillop, James. *Dictionary of Celtic Mythology*. Oxford: Oxford UP, 1998.

Orchard, Andy. *Dictionary of Norse Myth and Legend*. London: Cassell, 1997.

Rose, Carol. *Giants, Monsters, and Dragons: An Encyclopedia of Folklore, Legend, and Myth*. New York: Norton, 2000.

———. *Spirits, Fairies, Gnomes, and Goblins: An Encyclopedia*. New York: Norton, 1998.

Simpson, Jacqueline. *European Mythology*. New York: Bedrick, 1987.

Thompson, Stith. *Motif-Index of Folk-Literature*. 6 vols. Bloomington: Indiana UP, 1955.

Zipes, Jack, ed. *The Oxford Companion to Fairy Tales*. Oxford: Oxford UP, 2000.

SECONDARY LITERATURE

Bown, Nicola. *Fairies in Nineteenth-Century Art and Literature*. Cambridge: Cambridge UP, 2001.

Briggs, Katharine M. *The Anatomy of Puck: An Examination of Fairy Beliefs among Shakespeare's Contemporaries and Successors*. London: Routledge and Paul, 1959.

————. *The Fairies in Tradition and Literature*. London: Routledge and Paul, 1967.

————. *The Personnel of Fairyland: A Short Account of the Fairy People of Great Britain for Those Who Tell Stories to Children*. Ill. Jane Moore. Oxford: Alden, 1953.

————. *The Vanishing People: A Study of Traditional Fairy Beliefs*. London: Batsford, 1978.

Clodd, Edward. *Tom Tit Tot: An Essay on Savage Philosophy in Folk-Tale*. London: Duckworth, 1898.

Dégh, Linda. *Legend and Belief: Dialectics of a Folklore Genre*. Bloomington: Indiana UP, 2001.

Dorson, Richard M. *Peasant Customs and Savage Myths: Selections from the British Folklorists*. 2 vols. Chicago: U of Chicago P, 1968.

Faulding, Gertrude M. *Fairies*. London: Batsford, 1913.

Grimm, Jacob. *Teutonic Mythology*. 4 vols. New York: Dover, 1966. A translation of *Deutsche Mythologie*, first published 1835.

Hartland, Edwin Sidney. *The Science of Fairy Tales: An Inquiry into Fairy Mythology*. London: Scott, 1891.

Latham, Minor White. *The Elizabethan Fairies: The Fairies of Folklore and the Fairies of Shakespeare*. New York: Columbia UP, 1930.

Lecouteuz, Claude. *Witches, Werewolves, and Fairies: Shapeshifters and Astral Doubles in the Middle Ages*. Trans. Clare Frock. Rochester, VT: Inner Traditions, 2001.

Maas, Jeremy, et al. *Victorian Fairy Painting*. London: Holberton, 1997.

Narváez, Peter, ed. *The Good People: New Fairylore Essays*. New York: Garland, 1991.

Scott, Sir Walter. *Letters on Demonology and Witchcraft*. Ware, Hertfordshire: Wordsworth, 2001. First published 1830.

Silver, Carole G. *Strange and Secret Peoples: Fairies and Victorian Consciousness*. Oxford: Oxford UP, 1999.

Thorpe, Benjamin. *Northern Mythology: From Pagan Faith to Local Legends*. Introduction by Jacqueline Simpson. Ware, Hertfordshire: Wordsworth, 2001. First published 1851.

Tolkien, J.R.R. "On Fairy Stories," in *Tree and Leaf*. London: Allen and Unwin, 1964.

Wood, Christopher. *Fairies in Victorian Art*. Woodbridge, Suffolk: Antique Collectors' Club, 2000.

POPULAR TREATMENTS

Curran, Bob. *A Field Guide to Irish Fairies*. Ill. Andrew Whitson. San Francisco: Chronicle Books, 1998.

Froud, Brian, and Alan Lee. *Faeries*. New York: Abrams, 2002. First published 1978.

Ratisseau, Elizabeth. *Meetings with the Fairies*. Seattle: Laughing Elephant, 2002.

Scalora, Suza. *The Fairies: Photographic Evidence of the Existence of Another World*. New York : Cotler, 1999.

TRUE BELIEVERS

Andrews, Ted. *Enchantment of the Faerie Realm: Communicate With Nature Spirits and Elementals.* St. Paul: Llewellen, 1993.

Bord, Janet. *Fairies: Real Encounters with Little People.* New York: Dell, 1997.

Bord, Janet and Colin. *The Secret Country: An Interpretation of the Folklore of Ancient Sites in the British Isles.* New York: Walker , 1976.

Conan Doyle, Sir Arthur. *The Coming of the Fairies.* London: Hodder and Stoughton, 1922.

Kirk, Robert. *The Secret Commonwealth of Elves, Fauns, and Fairies.* London: Nutt, 1893. Based on a manuscript of 1691.

McCoy, Edain. *A Witch's Guide to Faery Folk: Reclaiming Our Working Relationship With Invisible Helpers.* St. Paul: Llewellen, 1994.

Web Resources

INTRODUCTION

Scholarly research on the World Wide Web is both daunting and rewarding. At the time of this writing, a Google search on the keyword *fairy* yielded more than 9,000,000 citations. Obviously, no mortal could ever hope to sort through this mountain of material. The democracy of the Internet is both its greatest strength and a weakness. There are no gatekeepers to control the flow of images and words, neither in terms of quantity nor quality. Let the reader beware.

The following sites are starting places. Each location includes links for further study. Some represent the best work of careful researchers, others the fantasies of mystics and dreamers. The world needs both types, and the Internet provides the forum. The section featuring book-length texts is of special value, given the scarcity of many of the original texts of fairy lore.

GENERAL

British Myths and Legends (http://www.britannia.com/history/h100.html).
Celts, Encyclopedia of the (http://celt.net/Celtic/celtopedia/indices/encycintro. html).
Cornish Myths and Legends (http://www.connexions.co.uk/culture/html/folklore. htm).
Cottingley Fairies. Sponsored by the James Randi Educational Foundation (http://www.randi.org/library/cottingley/).
Elves: A Short History. Sponsored by *National Geographic Kids' News* (http://news. nationalgeographic.com/kids/2003/12/elves.html).

Elves in Modern Day Iceland (http://www.ismennt.is/vefir/ari/alfar/alandslag/aelvesmod.htm).

Encyclopedia Mythica. See especially the section on folklore (http://www.pantheon.org/).

Endicott Studio. A site dedicated to the mythic arts (http://www.endicott-studio.com/).

Fae Poetry (http://www.katyberry.com/Rosepetal/poetry.html#4).

Faerie Central (http://faerie.monstrous.com/index.htm).

Fairy Legends and Fairy Lore (http://www.efairies.com/fairy_lore.htm).

Folklinks. Links to sites about folklore and fairy tales (http://www.pitt.edu/~dash/folklinks.html).

Folktexts. A library of folktales, folklore, fairy tales, and mythology (http://www.pitt.edu/~dash/folktexts.html).

Green Children, The (http://www.woolpit.org/greenchildren/index.htm).

Green Man, The (http://www.mikeharding.co.uk/greenman/greenindex.html).

Legends (http://www.legends.dm.net/index.html).

Mermaid, The Historical (http://rubens.anu.edu.au/student.projects/mermaids/homepage.html).

Morgan le Fay (http://www.lib.rochester.edu/camelot/morgmenu.htm).

Puck (http://www.boldoutlaw.com/puckrobin/puck.html).

Scottish Belief in Fairies (http://www.fife.50megs.com/scots-folklore-fairies.htm).

Selkie Folk of the Orkney Islands (http://www.orkneyjar.com/folklore/selkiefolk/index.html).

Selkies (http://echoes.devin.com/selkie/selkie.html).

Tam Lin Balladry (http://tam-lin.org/).

Tolkien Society Home Page (http://www.tolkiensociety.org/).

True Thomas (http://www.legends.dm.net/ballads/thomas.html).

Wikipedia Free Encyclopedia. See articles on changelings, fairies, folklore, mermaids, trolls, and such (http://en.wikipedia.org/).

FANTASY AND TRUE BELIEF

Fairy Garden, The (http://jksalescompany.com/dw/fairies.html).

Froud, World of (http://www.worldoffroud.com/www/main.cfm).

Lavendise Fairy Books (http://www.lavendise.com/fairybooks/fairybooks.php).

Rosepetal's Path into Faerie (http://www.katyberry.com/Rosepetal/Rosepetal.html).

Very Faery Shoppe (http://www.veryfaery.com/).

BOOK-LENGTH TEXTS

Baring-Gould, Sabine. *A Book of Folk-Lore* (1913) (http://www.sacred-texts.com/neu/celt/bof/index.htm).

Bray, Anna Eliza. *A Peep at the Pixies; or, Legends of the West* (1854) (http://www.sacred-texts.com/neu/eng/ppx/index.htm).

Campbell, J. F. *Popular Tales of the West Highlands.* 4 vols. (1890) (http://www.sacred-texts.com/neu/celt/ptwh.htm).

Cashen, William. *Manx Folk-Lore* (1912) (http://www.isle-of-man.com/manxnotebook/fulltext/wc1912/index.htm).

Child, Francis James. *The English and Scottish Popular Ballads* (1882–98) (http://www.sacred-texts.com/neu/eng/child/index.htm).

Clodd, Edward. *Tom Tit Tot: An Essay on Savage Philosophy in Folk-Tale* (1898) (http://www.sacred-texts.com/neu/celt/ttt/index.htm).

Conan Doyle, Sir Arthur. *The Coming of the Fairies* (1922) (http://www.sacred-texts.com/neu/eng/cof/index.htm).

Cookson, Elizabeth. *Legends of Manxland* (1859) (http://www.isle-of-man.com/manxnotebook/fulltext/lm1859/index.htm).

Croker, Thomas Crofton. *Fairy Legends and Traditions* (1825) (http://www.sacred-texts.com/neu/celt/flat/index.htm).

Crossing, William. *Tales of the Dartmoor Pixies* (1890) (http://www.sacred-texts.com/neu/eng/tdp/index.htm).

Curtin, Jeremiah. *Myths and Folk-Lore of Ireland* (1890) (http://www.sacred-texts.com/neu/celt/mfli/index.htm).

———. *Tales of the Fairies and of the Ghost World* (1895) (http://www.sacred-texts.com/neu/celt/tfgw/index.htm).

Douglas, George. *Scottish Fairy and Folk Tales* (1901) (http://www.sacred-texts.com/neu/celt/sfft/index.htm).

Evans-Wentz, W. Y. *The Fairy-Faith in Celtic Countries* (1911) (http://www.sacred-texts.com/neu/celt/ffcc/index.htm).

Faulding, Gertrude M. *Fairies* (1913) (http://www.sacred-texts.com/neu/celt/fau/index.htm).

Gregor, Walter. *Notes on The Folk-Lore of the North-East of Scotland* (1881) (http://www.sacred-texts.com/neu/celt/nes/index.htm).

Gregory, Lady Augusta. *Visions and Beliefs in the West of Ireland* (1920) (http://www.sacred-texts.com/neu/celt/vbwi/index.htm).

Hartland, Edwin Sidney. *English Fairy and other Folk Tales* (1890) (http://www.sacred-texts.com/neu/eng/efft/index.htm).

———. *The Science of Fairy Tales: An Enquiry Into Fairy Mythology* (1891) (http://www.sacred-texts.com/neu/celt/sft/index.htm).

Hunt, Robert. *Popular Romances of the West of England* (1903) (http://www.sacred-texts.com/neu/eng/prwe/index.htm).

Hyde, Douglas. *Beside the Fire* (1910) (http://www.sacred-texts.com/neu/celt/btf/index.htm).

Kennedy, Patrick. *Legendary Fictions of the Irish Celts* (1891) (http://www.sacred-texts.com/neu/celt/lfic/index.htm).

Kirk, Robert. *The Secret Commonwealth of Elves, Fauns and Fairies* (1893) (http://www.sacred-texts.com/neu/celt/sce/index.htm).

Mackenzie, Donald Alexander. *Wonder Tales from Scottish Myth and Legend* (1917) (http://www.sacred-texts.com/neu/celt/tsm/index.htm).

Masson, Elsie. *Folk Tales of Brittany* (1929) (http://www.sacred-texts.com/neu/celt/ftb/index.htm).

Moore, A. W. *The Folk Lore Of The Isle Of Man* (1891) (http://www.isle-of-man.com/manxnotebook/fulltext/folklore/index.htm).

Morrison, Sophia. *Manx Fairy Tales* (1911) (http://www.ee.surrey.ac.uk/Contrib/manx/fulltext/sm1911/index.htm).

Rhys, John. *Celtic Folklore: Welsh And Manx* (1901) (http://www.sacred-texts.com/neu/cfwm/index.htm).

Scot, Reginald. *The Discoverie of Witchcraft* (1584) (http://historical.library.cornell.edu/cgi-bin/witch/docviewer?did=081&seq=1&frames=0&view=text).

Scott, Sir Walter. *Minstrelsy of the Scottish Border.* Excerpts (http://www.electricscotland.com/history/other/minstrelsy_ndx.htm).

———. *Letters on Demonology and Witchcraft* (http://etext.lib.virginia.edu/toc/modeng/public/ScoDemo.html).

Sikes, Wirt. "The Realm of Faerie" from *British Goblins: Welsh Folk-lore, Fairy Mythology, Legends and Traditions* (1880) (http://www.sacred-texts.com/neu/celt/wfl/index.htm).

Spence, Lewis. *Legends and Romances of Brittany* (1917) (http://www.sacred-texts.com/neu/celt/lrb/index.htm).

Spenser, Edmund. *The Faerie Queene* (1596) (http://www.sacred-texts.com/neu/eng/fq/index.htm).

Synge, J. M. *The Aran Islands* (1907) (http://www.sacred-texts.com/neu/celt/tai/index.htm).

Thomas, W. Jenkyn. *The Welsh Fairy Book* (1908) (http://www.sacred-texts.com/neu/celt/wfb/index.htm).

Waldron, George. *A Description of the Isle of Man* (1726) (http://www.isle-of-man.com/manxnotebook/manxsoc/msvol11/index.htm#index).

Wilde, Lady Francesca Speranza. *Ancient Legends, Mystic Charms, and Superstitions of Ireland* (1887) (http://www.sacred-texts.com/neu/celt/ali/index.htm).

Yeats, William Butler. *The Celtic Twilight* (1893, 1902) (http://www.sacred-texts.com/neu/yeats/twi/index.htm).

———. *Fairy and Folk Tales of the Irish Peasantry* (1888) (http://www.sacred-texts.com/neu/yeats/fip/index.htm).

Index

About the Author

D. L. ASHLIMAN is Professor Emeritus of German at the University of Pittsburgh and the author of *Folk and Fairy Tales: A Handbook* (Greenwood, 2004).